Lemuel Potter

Labors and Travels of Elder Lemuel Potter

Lemuel Potter

Labors and Travels of Elder Lemuel Potter

ISBN/EAN: 9783337211332

Printed in Europe, USA, Canada, Australia, Japan

Cover: Foto ©Andreas Hilbeck / pixelio.de

More available books at **www.hansebooks.com**

LABORS AND TRAVELS

OF

ELDER LEMUEL POTTER,

AS AN

Old School Baptist Minister,

FOR

THIRTY YEARS,

WITH A

Brief Sketch of his Earlier Life, Christian Experience, and Call to the Ministry,

TOGETHER WITH

HIS DOCTRINAL SENTIMENTS

ON SOME VITAL POINTS.

EVANSVILLE, IND.
KELLER PRINTING COMPANY
PRINTERS AND BINDERS.
1894.

Entered according to Act of Congress, in the year 1894, by
LEMUEL POTTER,
in the
office of the Librarian of Congress, at Washington, D. C.

PREFACE.

It may seem strange to many, that a man would offer to the public a book like this to read, and my reasons for doing so, are two: Several of my brethren have asked me to give a sketch of my life experience and labors, together with my call to the work of the ministry, and I have had some inclination to do so, thinking that my experience and labors given to others might be a comfort, at least to some.

The reader may find some things in the following pages which will be useful. At any rate, I hope there is nothing that will do the cause of the Divine Master an injury. The motive prompting me to write this work, and to place it before the public has been sincere, and with a view to the advancement of the Master's Kingdom. If, therefore, the reader should see any mistakes, of which, perhaps, there are many, I humbly hope that the mantle of charity may be thrown around and imperfections borne with, and hat it may not be forgotten that the author is noth. ing but an imperfect man, at best, and that to look for perfection in a human production is to find ourselves disappointed. It has been my object to relate facts precisely as they have occurred, and I can truly say it is my experience, without exaggerations or extravagancies in any of it.

Hoping that the reader may not become disgusted with it, I submit it to the perusal, criticisms and scrutiny of a reading world, with an humble hope that it may prove a blessing, at least to some of the Lord's little ones.

LEMUEL POTTER.

CHAPTER I.

It is said that "In the making of many books there is no end," and while the following may be put before the public as a candidate for patronage, and subject to the scrutiny of a reading public, its author only hopes that it may be interesting, and honorably fill its humble station among all the literary productions of the world. I have had, for some time, a sort of an aversion to a man, or his friends, undertaking to give a history of his life, because, if he writes it himself, as a rule, he leaves about half of it out; he is very particular to crowd into the work all his virtues, and leave out all his vices. This seems, at least, to be the rule as far as I have observed. The bias of a man in his own favor, is such as to disqualify him for giving a fair and impartial history of his own life deportment, in the world among men. Whenever there is a question to settle between himself and others, and he is to be the tribunal before which that question is tried, he is certain to gain the decision in his favor. If his children should undertake to write a history of his life, after he has left the world, the result would be about the same. While you read such a book, as a rule, you might just picture out to yourself a pure angel, and say to yourself, there is the life and character of the man of whom you are reading. But with all these objections, having been called upon many times, and by many brethren and friends, to write out and publish a history of my own life, experience and labors in the world, I have finally obtained the consent of my mind to do so. The reader need not expect anything very scholarly in this work, but just the plain, simple statement of facts, as my experience has taught me, during my lifetime in the world. If I do not give my own faults, many of them, I hope that I shall not appear egotistic in magnifying my virtues.

About one hundred and twenty-five years ago, more or less, Lewis Potter was born in the state of old Virginia, but I am not able to say what part of the state, nor to give the exact date of his birth. He lived and raised a family, of which Felix Potter was a member, born in the old state of Virginia. The latter moved to Kentucky in an early day and lived in Warren County in the vicinity of where Bowling Green is now located. When he was a man grown, he was married to a Miss Brown, and to them were born a number of children, among whom was Jesse Potter, born in Warren County, Kentucky, October 30th, 1821. When he was a boy they moved to southern Illinois, and at the age of nineteen Jesse was married to Miss Margaret Sams, and to them were born five children, of whom the author of this work is the oldest. I was born October 28th, 1841, in Edwards County, Illinois, within a half mile, perhaps, of where Samsville is now located. Samsville took its name from my grandfather Sams, on the corner of whose farm the little village was founded. I was born and raised in that part of the country, engaged in helping to clear out and cultivate a farm until I was a man grown.

CHAPTER II

During my boyhood days the country of southern Illinois was new. Perhaps there was not a mile of railroad in the state when I was born. It was quite a new country, and there were wolves, deer, turkey and other wild game in abundance. Land, a great deal of it was not taken up, and my father entered a considerable portion of the land where he now lives, at $1.25 per acre. It was then a wild bushy woods. The country was very sparsely settled, there being scarcely enough children in the whole township to justify a school teacher to teach them at the ordinary price. The advantages, generally, were very poor at that time in that part of the country. Men frequently cut their wheat, those who raised any, with a sickle, sometimes a cradle was used. A man on a farm who owned a wagon was considered a well-to-do farmer. There were no mills in the country of any consequence. Sometimes a man would take his wheat to mill, and while his own horses pulled the mill that ground it; if he got it bolted, he might have to turn the bolts with his own hands while it was being ground. Sometimes he would get it ground and take it home unbolted. Horse-mills and wind-mills were most common. Once in a while a water-mill, could be found on some creek or stream that would grind when the water was not too high nor too low. Very few people in that section of the country, at that time raised wheat, there being no mills and no market. There was one church in our neighborhood, and that was Long Prairie Church, of Old School Baptists, which is still in existence in the same neighborhood. The old house that we used to go to in my boyhood days, was a log house, and there were no other meeting-houses of any denomination, nearer than one within about seven miles. And as there were no places of pleasure or amusement, the people of that country in those days, almost, if not quite all, attended church at this place. The church was constituted in 1825, with nine members. The people in those days made their own living at home. They grew their own wool and flax, did their own spinning and weaving, and it did not take a great deal to live on then, as it does now. Clothes and provisions were hardly as fine as they are now. The fine May-meeting dress for the country woman was of home-made cotton, that she had made herself, with her own hands, taking everything from the stump, so to speak. Before the washboard came into use, the battling-stick was a very popular instrument in washing clothes, and it was about as common, while a woman was down at the creek, or branch, or spring, doing her week's washing, to hear the battling-stick, which sounded in the distance like heavy pounding, as it was to see the smoke from her fire. But amidst all these disadvantages, the people were happy, sociable and sober. All the people were neighborly, if not from good principles, they were from necessity, for a man could not afford to be selfish during such times, from the fact that many times he had work to do, such as raising houses and other heavy work that he could not do alone, and not being able to hire hands to do his work, he necessarily had to depend on what was then called "swapping" work with his neighbors.

CHAPTER II.

During my boyhood days I was taught that to be idle was disgraceful, and that nothing could be very respectable that did not have work attached to it. My father was a great worker, and those about him had to cultivate the spirit of industry. Hence, in my very early life, he was always able to find something that he thought would be profitable for me to engage in. I can hardly remember when I was not large enough to throw a limb or branch on a fire during the winter or spring, or to get up of mornings and make fires and go out and feed early, or to rake wheat up into bundles ready to be bound during harvest, or to hoe corn, or to follow the plow and remove the clods off the little corn while he plowed.

At the age of ten, my mother died of consumption. I was very small for my age, but the next spring after I was ten, I was put out in the field with a yoke of old gentle cattle, to harrow in some oats that father had sown broadcast, and from that time on I went to plowing with the same cattle, and from that on until I was grown I worked more with cattle than any other team, and worked them more or less every year. I helped plow, harrow, haul saw-logs, have gone to mill and market, gathered corn, hauled wheat and hay out of the field in harvest time, and plowed and harrowed in hot weather with cattle—in fact I have done almost everything with them that they are capable of doing on a farm. And so far as the ox being used in scripture, to illustrate the character and work of a minister as a servant, I have sometimes thought that I know something of the use of the ox, literally speaking, whether I know anything about the services of a minister, spiritually speaking, or not.

I never had very great advantages in obtaining an education. What little schooling I got was at home in our own district schools. I managed by the time I was a man grown, to procure what was called in Illinois, a second grade certificate, to teach school. The most of my education I have obtained since then. Examinations, however, were not so rigid as they are now, by any means. I do not think I ever got a first grade certificate. A teacher in those days was examined in the seven common branches, for teaching a country school. I taught my first school in 1862, a three months school in the summer. My salary was fifteen dollars per month, and I boarded myself. It was, however, not far from home, and I worked mornings, evenings and Saturdays for my board. So that I made in that three months, the sum of $45.00, cash. This is the first money I ever owned, more than a few pieces of small change, once in a while, less than a dollar at a time. I taught this school in the summer, and that fall I was twenty-one years of age. The next March I was married to Miss Lydia Jane Humphreys, who was my choice for a companion, of all women. We have now been married about thirty-one years, and to us have been born seven children, five of whom are now living, three of them married and two single. Three of them have possession of a hope in Christ, and two of them members of the Regular Baptist Church. The other two died in infancy.

CHAPTER IV.

As before stated I was married on the 22d day of March, 1863. During the preceding winter, I taught school three months, about a mile and a half southeast of West Salem, in my native county. I was fond of mirth and innocent pleasures, frequently attending the ball-room and enjoyed dancing. But I had always, from my earliest recollections, a great regard for good morals. I had a great desire, when I was a boy, to be recognized as a good boy. I wanted to be respected as a truthful boy. But, with all my desire to stand high, as I have before remarked, I was fond of mirth and innocent pleasures. Business, however, kept me engaged almost all the time, so that I did not spend as much time in going to shows, fairs, parties and other pleasure trips as my neighbor boys usually did. I thought at the time that it was a hardship that I was kept so close, and not allowed the privileges that other boys had, but I feel now that perhaps it was best for me. During my term of school, already mentioned, began my exercise of mind on the subject of religion. I think I had serious impressions occasionally, from my earliest recollection, and feel now that I have had promptings or cautions from the good Spirit, occasionally, all my life, if I ever had. I will now relate a reason for my hope in the Savior, that I experienced at the time already stated. About the beginning of the year 1863, I was permitted to have a full view of my own poor wicked heart, and O, how miserable! I need not look around now for a man with a heart full of evil and vain imaginations, for if there is not another heart in the world that answered the description given in the Bible, mine did. The very throbbings of my own heart seemed to speak the terror of the law to a poor sinner like I was. At first I tried to rid myself of the impression that I was the greatest sinner in the world, but all seemed in vain, I could not throw off the impression that I was the most miserable sinner in the world. I tried, under these impressions to ask the Lord for mercy, but it looked so much like solemn mockery for one so vile, who had nothing good to present to the Lord, that at times I was almost afraid to call on his name.

Often have I, in the great agony of my poor heart, taken a walk, more to be alone than anything else, and in those lonesome hours I would often find myself trying to ask the Lord for mercy as I walked along. Sometimes I was made to think that the Lord had shown me the wickedness of my poor, sinful self, that I might see His justice in my condemnation. It seemed that my time in the world was now going to close, and I must die and be lost. O, how wretched! It was not worth while to tell others of the trouble I was in, for they could not sympathize with me, I thought. Still I kept trying to do something good that the Lord would bless me with peace of mind, and it seemed that nothing would give that but mercy in the forgiveness of sins. If the Lord would forgive all my wrongs, and the innumerable sins I had committed, I thought I would be under greater obligations to Him than any poor sinner that ever lived in the world. In this way I went on for four or five weeks, and it seemed that I could see no peace at any time or place. Everything wore a gloomy, dismal appearance to me. Finally I came to the conclusion that there was something that I had not done that I must do before the Lord would have mercy.

In trying to call to mind what it might be that I had not done, it occured to me that I had never been humble enough to kneel down and pray to the Lord; and that was the reason I had received no evidence of the forgiveness of sins. Determined to do, what I thought I had committed sin in neglecting to do until now, I started to a place where I intended to get on my knees in prayer to the Lord for mercy to one of the vilest sinners of the race of Adam. I started with a full determination that when I got to that place I would kneel down without any hesitation, and try and pray to the Lord; but instead of doing so I walked past the place I had started to. I stopped, and the thought of my poor heart was, "you are too haughty, and your heart too obdurate, and the Lord will be just and send you to torment."

O, it is more than I can do to describe the anguish of soul just at this time. Lord, be merciful; if I am lost it is just, and if saved, it is a poor guilty sinner saved by Grace. It seems now that I stood in one place and was trembling like a leaf, trying to ask the Lord for mercy, and had almost given up in despair, when suddenly there was a change came over me that brought peace that I am not able to describe, and I felt like praising the Lord for his grace in the salvation of a lost and justly condemned sinner. My trouble was gone, and I thought I would not be troubled any more on account of sin, but, O, how mistaken! I have seen many troubles since then, and often think that my life is so imperfect, and bears so few marks of a Christian, that I often doubt the reality of my knowledge of the Lord.

In October, 1863, I united with the church, and have been trying to live in the service of the Lord. I have thought many times that my hope would not do, yet if I have to go into eternity in a moment, it is the very best I have. The fellowship of the brethren is worth more to me than all the friendship in the world.

I have now only given simply a relation of what took place with me some thirty-one years ago, and I leave my brethren and sisters to judge of the reality of its being the Lord's work. I thought when I first joined the church, that by the time I was thirty-five or forty years of age I would become more devoted in my feelings towards religious matters, and be more reconciled to the will of the Lord than I was then, but I see no difference in those particulars. I am still a poor sinner and do not deserve saving, yet God's mercy and grace is sufficient, so I still have hope.

CHAPTER V.

After school was out in the spring and I was married, I went to work to raise a crop, still under the impression that there was only one way to make a living, and that was by hard labor and constant employment. O, that all the boys could still be so impressed. The time I now refer to was right in the midst of the late war. Farm products were generally high. Tobacco, sometimes, brought as high as fifteen dollars per hundred, and a great many people in our part of the country raised cotton, as it was a very hard article to get at that time. While engaged in raising a crop, the subject of religion was on my mind every day of my life, and sometimes, perhaps, every hour in the day that I was awake. I was a constant reader and student of the Scriptures, and whenever I had a leisure hour I was perusing that sacred book. I was under the impression that as I had, I thought, obtained a hope in the Savior, there was a duty enjoined upon me, and frequently the importance of discharging my duty by submitting to the ordinances of God's house, bore upon my mind to such an extent, that it caused me a great deal of serious meditation. In fact, a great deal of the time I was in trouble, and felt sad and cast down, and it looked many times as if I was robbed of everything that was calculated to make me cheerful. Not because it was unpleasant to work and to make a living, and to enjoy the society of a young wife, the wife of my youth, but it seemed that my studies upon the subject of religion disqualified me for the earthly blessings and privileges that I had. The church that I have mentioned in a previous chapter, had gone down so that she had neither house to preach in, nor pastor to preach to her, and while there were, perhaps, thirty members belonging to that church, the only meetings they held were those held by transient ministers, who might pass through the neighborhood and preach at some private house, or school house, and it was frequently the case that I would not hear of such meetings 'till they were over. I felt a great desire frequently, to know if my wife was interested upon the subject of religion, as I was, but for a long time said nothing to her upon the subject. Two or three times during the summer, she and I got on our horses, and rode over to Mount Erie, in Wayne county, to Providence church. We thought it was a great treat to go to meeting where the brethren and sisters seemed to take an interest in church affairs, and we thought they did at that church. I studied a great deal about joining the church at that time, but there were several difficulties in the way. One was, that as far as I was acquainted with the Old School Baptists, they had no young members. All their members that I had ever seen were old men and women. Our neighbors had often predicted that they would soon all die out, and I could not see why they would not. The prospects looked very gloomy to me, especially when I would take Long Prairie church as an example; and I was better acquainted with that church than any other. I did not know whether they would want as young a person as I was in their church or not. I would often think when I would hear them talk on the subject, that a candidate for baptism among them must undergo a very rigid examination on the subject, of a reason for his hope. This, I was afraid that I could not give. My experience was very small if I had any, and I was not capable of telling it very well. I felt then, and do yet, that it would be a great sin to deceive the church, and be deceived myself, on the subject of religion. With all these difficulties before me, I went about a great portion of the time, with my head hung down, and often felt like I would love to talk on the subject of religion, if I had some person to talk to. to whom I thought such a conversation would be pleasant. I, however, finally resolved to go to Providence church, at the October meeting, and offer myself, and let the church be her own judge as to my fitness or unfitness to be baptized. Elders E. S. Madding and Isaiah Walker both preached on that day, and after preaching the opportunity was extended for members to come to the church, and I went up, and after I was through talking, before the brethren had time to say anything, it just seemed to me that they would not receive me, because I had told nothing, yet I had told all I had to tell. I will not say that I was surprised when they did receive me, neither will I say that I would not have thought hard of them if they had not received me. But after I was received and baptized, I felt like the change was a great one. I could be cheerful now. Instead of going about and feeling like I was forsaken, I might be heard whistling or singing, or giving some demonstration of peace of mind and joy of heart, while I was about my work every day. When I went to the house I was very fond of singing in the old hymnbook. It did then, and does yet, occur to me that it paid me, poor and unworthy as I felt, to join the church. By so doing, I cast my lot in among the best friends I had upon earth. No other people could have ever come so near being one with me as my brethren and sisters in the church have. It is, indeed a wonderful display of God's condescending love and mercy to His poor children, that He has established His church here as a home for His little ones, while they travel through this life, and battle with all its difficulties. I would say to all who have a hope in the Savior, and have never yet united with the church, you get the most pay for the least service rendered when you obey the Lord, more than anything else that I ever knew anything about. I felt like I was the least one of the whole family, when I joined the church. And I still feel that if there is any one place in the church more suitable for me than another, it must be at the feet of the brethren ; for I know that I am, at best, a poor, imperfect, needy and unworthy sinner. I am as dependent on God for His grace and mercy in my salvation, as the new-born child is on its mother for care, sustenance and protection. I feel like adopting the language of the great apostle to the Gentiles: "It is by the grace of God that I am what I am."

CHAPTER VI.

There has been quite a change in the country in southern Illinois since I first joined the church. There was the Ohio and Mississippi Railroad, then in operation from Cincinnati to St. Louis, running across the state of Illinois, running from Vincennes to St. Louis, and the Illinois Central was in operation, running from Chicago to Cairo, and the Evansville and Terre Haute was in operation, running from Evansville to Terre Haute, and was then called the Evansville and Crawfordsville Railroad. South of the O. & M., and east and west from the Illinois Central to the E. & T. H. was a country that had no railroads, most of it lying in southern Illinois. Under these circumstances, a man traveling through the country was necessarily compelled to furnish his own means of conveyance. Traveling on horseback was the most popular method at that time. Baptist ministers, as a rule, were farmers, living upon their own farms, making their own livings, and each one of them pastoring from one to four churches, and sometimes five. The idea of the brethren giving the preacher a living, or any part of a living, at that time, was entirely unknown among the Old School Baptists in southern Illinois. Some of the preachers were the most independent men in the church, so far as worldly possessions were concerned. This is still true in many cases. If a man had to go a certain number of miles to his church, it was understood that that amount of travel was required of him on horse-back, or in a buggy or some other conveyance of his own.

After I had joined the church, and felt that I had done my duty so far, it was not long till I began to be impressed with the thought of preaching the gospel. This was something very repugnant to my feelings and nature. I tried to fix the matter up satisfactorily with my own mind, for a long time. I tried to persuade myself that for me to entertain a thought that it was my duty to preach, must be a great delusion. There were many reasons I thought, why it could not be enjoined upon me to preach.

I was poor, and had all the responsibilities of a family as other men had. I was ignorant and inexperienced so far as the world was concerned. I do not think that I had ever been more than thirty or forty miles from home in my life, until I had joined the church and commenced trying to preach. My impressions to preach were all to myself. I kept them a profound secret as long as I could, but felt at times that I endured a great deal of trouble. I would sometimes fancy that I was in the presence of a congregation, preaching to them, or engaged in prayer publicly, or singing with a congregation, and shaking hands among them. Often in my meditatations, a text of scripture would crowd itself upon my mind, and I would frequently catch myself preaching to myself on that text, and when I would find myself thus engaged, I felt mean and ashamed, for I thought that it was wrong, and that some one might see me at such things, and if they should, I felt sure they would have no confidence in me. I tried to get rid of such impressions, that I might get rid of such a practice as that, but it increased, and I finally became so absorbed on the subject that I preferred to wander about, and rove the fields and woods alone, rather than the best company I had in the world. Sometimes I would go out for something, or to do something, and would wander about, I do not know how long. I would sometimes go to the barn to feed my horses, and when I had come back, I could not have told whether I had fed them or not. While in this great trouble and strain of mind, I was not unmindful of the responsibilities resting upon a minister of the gospel, although I did not know as fully what it all meant, as I hope I do now. My wife would sometimes tell me about the way I was doing, and would talk to me and try to get me to quit it, and sometimes she would laugh at me, and mimic me in order to break me of what she thought was a habit I had gotten into; but it all did no good. Badly as she might have hated it, she could not remedy the matter. Nothing that I could do, or that she could say, relieved my mind. The greatest privilege to me was frequently to get hold of the Bible, or hymn-book to read or sing.

During the winter of '64 and '65, I taught school, about three and a half miles from home, and as I walked across the fields to and from my school, mornings and evenings, scarcely did any other subject cross my mind. I finally concluded that to read a chapter and pray at night before going to bed, would be a great relief to my mind, and a portion of the time I thus engaged. It was a great pleasure to me to do so, and during the day I would frequently think what a pleasure it would be to me to-night to read a chapter, and get on my knees, and try to return to the Lord the gratitude of my heart for all His mercies and blessings to me and mine. I feel now that I lived nearer the Lord then, and realized more sensibly my need of His grace, and the fullness of that grace, than I am able to do since. In my great trouble of mind on the subject of preaching, I frequently thought that if I would go to the church and relate my feelings to the church, just once, that my work in that particular would be done, and that I would be relieved of all my trouble on that subject. At the same time, I felt that if it would, I would freely go the first opportunity, for I would be willing to do almost anything that was respectable and honorable, that would relieve my mind, and set me free from the burden that I was groaning under at the time. But I was afraid to venture, for fear it might be simply the beginning of my labors publicly, as a minister. I did not intend to preach as long as I could possibly keep from it. I said nothing to anyone about it as long as I could help it. I never did get relief of mind on this subject until I did engage in the public ministry of the Lord. The first effort I ever made was Saturday before the second Sunday in January, 1865. This was my birthday in the ministry, and I have been as constantly engaged in the work from then till now, as any man during that time.

CHAPTER VII.

While I am on the subject of my reasons for ever trying to preach, I wish to give a little narrative that occured just one month before my first effort. On Saturday of our December meeting, 1864, Elders Lewis Hunsinger, and Nathaniel Williams visited us. They lived about thirty miles away, and came on horseback to our meeting, and on that day our church called Elder Hunsinger to the pastoral care of the church, which he accepted. I was not acquainted with those two brethren, it was the second time in my life that I had ever seen Elder Hunsinger, and I had heard Elder Williams preach, in all, perhaps three or four times, and if I had ever spoken to him, or had an introduction to him, I had no recollection of it. I was quite young—only twenty-three years old past, and while I felt like it would be a pleasure to me to have some of the brethren go home with me, I had no thought of asking those preaching brethren to go. I felt that they would want to go among older people, where they could be better, and more agreeably entertained. So, rubbing right round them, I invited some of the brethren, with whom I was better acquainted, to go home with me, and said nothing to them. Finally, Elder Williams looked at me, and said, "Lewis and I are going home with you." That suited me very well, but I had entertained no thought that it would suit them. They went, and, it being cold weather, we had no meeting that night, and I built a large fire, and we had a very pleasant time, sitting by the fire and talking on the subject of religion. During our conversation, Elder Williams suggested that we all tell our experiences, beginning at the oldest and going down to the youngest. I thought that a good idea, for my wife was not a member of the church at that time, and I thought that those brethren had had some conversation with her during the afternoon, and feeling eager myself upon the subject, I was willing for us to tell our experiences, thinking that by the time she heard all of us talk, she would be willing and ready to talk, and I thought that was what the Elder made the suggestion for; so, agreeable to his own proposition, he, being the oldest person present, told his experience. And after relating a reason of his hope in Christ, and giving an account of his going to the church and being baptized, he went on to give an account of his impressions to preach. And while he was talking he pictured out my course to me as well as I could have done myself. I had never heard a man tell his call to preach before. I felt very badly to sit under his voice and hear him talk as he did. The thought occurred to me that some one had apprehended me and had told him all about what I had been doing, and that he had taken all the pains to come to my house and expose me; then again I would think that he was simply telling his own experience, and that he knew nothing about me, for he had never spoken to me in his life till to-day, but I was anxious for him to drop the subject. He went on, however, giving his own troubles, till he gave an account of his beginning to preach. When he got through he turned to me and said, "Do you know anything about that?" I was never more astonished, and I think I answered him about this way: "I have had some feelings that I do not understand." He then asked me, "Do you think you can answer me with a clear conscience that you will never try to speak in public?" My reply was, "The Lord only knows what I will do; I do not." The subject was dropped and I was glad. No one had ever hinted anything of the sort to me before, and why this strange man should come to my house and pick me out in any such a manner, was a mystery that I was not able to solve, neither am I yet. If any of the brethren had said anything to him, they never had to me. I have had thoughts about that occasionally, during my whole ministerial life, and I have thought in all probability that it might have been my duty to preach, and the Lord may have impressed that man, as his servant, with the fact, so that he might talk to me, and give me some encouragement to go immediately to the work.

Between that time and our next meeting, an old Brother Williams who lived in our little town, called, as he frequently did, to sit and talk till bedtime, and while he was there on this special occasion, I told him my secret. After giving him an account of some of the trouble and impressions that I had undergone, for it seemed that I must tell some one, I said to him, "Now, Uncle Jesse, if you can tell me what is the matter, I want you to do so, for I do not know." He rather laughed, saying, "I know what it is; you have to preach, that is what is the matter with you." I then felt like I had told a secret that I should have kept to myself, and I began to beg him to promise me upon the honor of a man, that he would never say a word about it to anyone. But he would not. He said, "I shall do nothing of the sort. If our pastor is with us next meeting, I will tell him about your case and have him invite you forward. If he should not be there, I shall preside over the meeting in the absence of the preacher, and

I shall invite you forward." That was all I could get out of him. He talked to me and so did my wife, on that occasion, giving me encouragement to obey the call, for the Lord had called me to the work of the ministry, and the sooner I obeyed the better it would be for me, and the more he would be honored. This gave me a great deal of trouble. I studied a great deal from that on till meeting time. I knew that Uncle Jesse would do what he said he would. I dreaded it from one standpoint, and I was perfectly willing from another. When meeting day rolled around, as I was sexton, I concluded to go early, and make fires and sweep out the house and leave before anyone came. That plan seemed all satisfactory till I got back home. But I was made to feel miserable and restless, to think of remaining at home and not going to meeting that day, so I picked up my hat and started. When I got to the meeting house I tried to be cheerful. I led in singing two or three songs, and finally, Uncle Jesse invited me, as the pastor did not come, to come forward and open meeting. I did so, by singing a song, and praying, the first time I had ever tried to pray in public. After prayer, I made the remark to the church that if no one had any objection, I would love to talk a little while. There was an old brother present whose name was Abner Cox, and whose memory I love to this day. He spoke out saying, "If you have anything to say, just say on." I talked awhile, and after meeting was dismissed, this old Brother Cox spoke about having services to-morrow,—Sunday,—saying that I could talk to the people,—and he and the brethren would not listen to anything else. Meeting was appointed. This was the first time I had ever tried to even sing and pray in public, and after I had gone home some of the brethren and sisters who went along with me for dinner, made some remarks about the meeting. One sister, in fun, spoke to me and called me her preacher. I cannot say that such a remark hurt my feelings for I knew that it was done in the greatest of kindness, and at the same time, was spoken more in the way of fun than anything else. But during the afternoon I heard of remarks that had been made, such as, "Who do you suppose preached at the Baptist church to-day?" "Potter preached, I am told," they would say, "and he is to preach again to-morrow, for they have no other preacher at their meeting this time," and some of them would say, "I intend to hear him to-morrow." All this kind of talk I heard during the afternoon, as it had been indulged in on the streets and in the stores of the little town where I lived. About four o'clock that afternoon, after the brethren had all gone away, I became deeply distressed about what I had done. It seemed to me that surely it was not my duty to preach, and that it was very much out of my place to undertake it. The very idea, that I should go into the stand and try to talk to the people concerning their spiritual interests and welfare was absurd in the extreme. I was poor, weak, ignorant, and in every way disqualified for such an important work.

Surely the Lord does not require such a work at my hands. And in this way I reasoned, and tried to beg the Lord to let me know what was right,—for about four hours. I felt as if I would give everything that I ever expected to have pertaining to this life if I could just call back a few hours. I did wish I had not gone to church that day, for by going I had exposed myself in a manner that I was fearful would result in great harm to myself and to the cause of the blessed Redeemer. I do not think I ever suffered more in mind, in four hours in my life, as to my impressions on the subject of the ministry. I felt that I wanted to do the will of the Lord, but can it be His will that I should ever try to preach? Does He require such a great and important work at my hands? I felt that if I were going to select some one among my acquaintances to preach the gospel, I could find hundreds of them who would be more likely to be useful and profitable preachers than it would be possible for me to ever be. I realized the responsibility resting upon me as a husband and father. I had poverty to contend with, as well as almost all other disadvantages that a poor fellow ever had. In this way I reasoned and agonized all the evening. My wife went to bed with her baby, at the usual hour for bedtime, and left me sitting up, perhaps totally ignorant of what was on my mind, and as I reasoned the matter over, it seemed to me that if I could only have a decision from the Lord, in some way or other, as to my duty in regard to the matter, that I would abide by it. About eight o'clock that night, as I was sitting all alone by the fire, my wife and baby both asleep, the thought presented itself to me like this: "If it is your duty to preach, you will have it to do, and the Lord will let you know by giving you the ability to preach, and if it is not your duty He will let you know by withholding that ability, and you will have to try it in order to find out. This has appeared to me ever since, as a sort of compact entered into between the Lord and myself. I felt perfectly resigned. I went to bed, slept and rested sweetly during the night, and arose the next morning with all the peace of mind and conscience that I desired, and felt as if the matter would soon be decided, for the Lord will let me know if it is my duty to preach by giving me the ability to do so, and if it is not my duty He will let me know by withholding that ability, and I will have to try in order to find out. I felt perfectly willing to test the matter that way, and if I should find out that it was not my duty to preach I should quit it at once. With this understanding I went in to the work, and I have been trying from then until now, and I have been undecided many times whether it was my duty to preach or not; for at times I have thought the Lord was with me, and that I was able to preach, and at other times I have felt confident that I was all alone, shut up in the dark and unable to say anything that would either encourage any of His people, or glorify His name. When I was younger I thought many times that I would quit preaching. I felt in earnest about that, but I suffered so much for such a resolution that I finally became afraid to say that I was not going to preach any more, and for many years it has been my determination to battle along with all the tempests of life incident to a minister of the gospel, the best I could, while the Lord seemed to have any use for me in the world. On Sunday morning I went to the meeting house with as great a desire and as great a delight in trying to preach as I have ever had in my life since then. That morning when I got to the meeting house I found this same Brother Cox and two or three other old brothers standing out waiting for me to come. When I stepped up to where they were and spoke to them, they told me they wanted to see me a few minutes, and took me around back of the house. They told me they did not want me to feel that I would be in the way when I arose to talk, or that they did not want to hear me, but that they wanted me to feel at liberty and that they were anxious to have me talk and had a great desire to hear me. They gave me every kind of encouragement that a set of good old brethren could, letting me know at the same time that they would pray the Lord to bless me in my efforts. Such kindness as this I have never forgotten. Those dear old fathers are all asleep, and I am still battling with life, and I love and cherish their memory to this day. When I arose before the people that day, it was not with the impression that those dear old brethren did not want to see me get up, for they had given me full assurance to the contrary. I would say now to brethren, when the Lord gives you a young gift in the ministry, treat him kindly. He is like a tender plant just springing up from the ground, and a very slight look of disapprobation, is calculated to discourage and kill him. If the Lord calls a man to preach among you, it is for your good, and not for his, and you should treat him as a gift from God.

CHAPTER VIII.

My object in trying to preach the gospel was to discharge a duty that I thought the Lord had enjoined upon me, and relieve my mind of the terrible burden and trouble that seemed to rest upon it. When I was under impressions to preach, before I ever began, certain localities of country would be on my mind, and especially was this true of the vicinity of Grayville, Illinois. And I thought more of preaching to the people there than in any other locality in the world. At the same time, I did not know a single person in that neighborhood. I was aware that there was a church in Grayville, but I did not know who its pastor was nor who the members of the church were. I never had been to that place, except to go to mill or market, and consequently knew nothing about the condition of affairs there religiously. However, after I began trying to preach, I still thought of trying to preach in that neighborhood, and finally made it a point to visit there a time or two, and sometimes met brethren of that church at the associations, and by that means got acquainted with two or three of them, and finally under very peculiar circumstances in January, 1868, I was called to the care of that church, and I had the name of pastoring the church for about twelve years. When I took the care of the church at Grayville, her membership was run down to about twenty, most of whom were old sisters, perhaps half a dozen male members, and they were poor. The old house that had been built there, I think, in 1835, was very much dilapidated, and was not fit to hold meeting in, in cold weather, or at any other time. However, after I commenced my labors there the church revived, and her membership ran up to upwards of ninety members, and she repaired her house, and seemed to wield a good influence over the community for a long while, and still so continues. Large congregations attended my ministry while I preached there. But amid all the trials in my efforts in trying to preach, and discharge my duty as a poor servant of the Lord, I found many embarrassments to encounter. I was poor, inexperienced in the world, and was raising a family, and I thought and felt that great responsibilities rested upon me as a husband and father as well as a minister. It was not long after I commenced preaching until I had four regular appointments. In trying to preach and to make my own living, too, by my own labor on rented ground, it began to look to me that, in spite of everything, I would be compelled to neglect my farm or my ministry one or the other, if not both. I noticed that my neighbors were busy all the time, and that they could not more than get along in the world, yet when I left my work on Friday afternoon, everything stood still till I would get back, sometimes on Monday evening. This caused me a great deal of serious thought. The brethren who wanted me to preach for them had never been accustomed to assist their preachers in any way, and from the best I could learn from their conversations, they had been educated to think that it was sinful to pay a preacher for preaching. If the text should be quoted that "The laborer is worthy of his hire," or that "The Lord had ordained that they who preach the gospel should live of the gospel," they would put some spiritual interpretation on the text, so that their obligations to their ministers were entirely obviated. I remember, on one occasion, when I was in company with two or three old brethren, who I thought, were as good friends as I had in the church, that I concluded I would mention this subject to them, and that perhaps they would give me some comfort. I very timidly, and with great diffidence broached the subject, when one of the old brethren made me this reply: "If you want money for preaching you had better go to the Missionaries, where they hire their preachers." Such an answer from one in whom I had great confidence was rather discouraging to me, and of course I naturally touched the subject very lightly in his presence at that time. There are, no doubt, a great many brethren among our churches who think that old brother was just right, and who, at the same time would insist on a man leaving his home and family and going a long distance at a great expense to preach, and would tell him that he had to preach because the Lord had made it his duty to do so, whether the people gave him anything to live on or not. As far as I am concerned, what I say now is not for my own benefit, but I am simply giving my own experience upon this subject, not to censure or reprove anyone. Another embarrassment which I met with that may be interesting to the reader, I will mention here.

Shortly after I had commenced exercising in public, through the solicitations of some of the brethren of my own church, who lived some ten miles away from the neighborhood, I made an appointment to preach at a school-house in their neighborhood. They were in the habit of having preaching at that place whenever they could get a preacher. In the meantime, an old brother in the ministry, had moved into my neighborhood, who was a stranger to all of us, and with whom I had become acquainted more than any of the rest of the brethren. After he had moved into the neighborhood, he seemed to have a perfect dislike to me. If I approached him with the most pertinent question, he was more likely to snub me than any other way. My recollection is that I did not fear him, and that his snubs did not make me more backward, but it made his company unpleasant to me and caused me to entertain a feeling which paralyzed every desire I might have had to hear him preach. On Sunday morning, I hitched up to my buggy, and took my wife and baby and started out to my appointment. I passed this old brother's house and saw his horse standing hitched at the gate with the saddle on, and when I saw that, I supposed that perhaps he might be going to my meeting. He came out, mounted his horse, and rode along behind my buggy all the way out there. Soon the people began to gather, and while they were singing, he took out his hymn-book and testament, selected his song and text, and without any invitation from myself or any one else, he arose, introduced services, took his text and preached, and when he got through, dismissed the audience without paying any more attention to me than if I had not been there. He was not mentioned in the appointment, and the people had no idea that he would be there, still they did not object to his preaching that I know of. I thought that was rather cool treatment, and I still think that it is very unbecoming in any old minister to treat a young minister in that manner. I did not feel very much discouraged at it, it does not seem to me, but it made an impression on my mind that I have not yet forgotten. It was simply embarrassing to me, as I think it certainly would be to any young man just starting out in the ministry. I give this incident in order to show that old ministers may make some very great mistakes. It is very unbecoming in an old minister, or an old man otherwise, to be overbearing with the young.

CHAPTER IX.

In the foregoing chapter I have given an account of the cold treatment of an old brother in the ministry, and will now say, that had I known that he was going to go there and preach that day, my feelings were such toward him that I should not have gone. I have heard remarks from old brethren before now, that made me think that they thought the more severe they could be on a young brother the more Godly they would be. However, I think that is a grand mistake, and that no man, because he is old, let him be minister or anything else, has a right to hide behind his old age to abuse younger people. While I would impress the minds of young people, everywhere, to respect old age and gray hairs, I would also give a hint to old ones to keep in their places. But amid all embarrassments, I had calls and invitations to visit churches and brethren, more than half a dozen men could fill. I had not been engaged long in the ministry until I had four regular appointments. My means of travel was on horseback, or in the buggy, but mostly on horse-back. I have started out to my appointments to be gone ten days or two weeks, on a tour, and my first appointment sixty miles from home, and I would go the whole trip on horse-back. I wish to give in this chapter, a narrative or two of some risks that I have run to get to my appointments. When I was young, I was very small, weighing at one time that I remember, since I was thirty years old, as low as one hundred and seventeen pounds. I was always blest with excellent health, and was used to hardship and very few men could stand cold better than I could, or do with less sleep, or go longer without food without suffering more than I did. I have got on my horse, and rode to the creek or river within two or three miles of my appointment, and being unable to get my horse across, would hitch him, coon a log, cross the creek and go on to my appointment on foot, and then come back, cross the creek and go home, and feel very good over the affair. But I will relate here, that at one time, on one Sunday morning, in June, the Little Wabash was between me and my appointment for that day. There were no bridges across that stream at that time except one, at Masilon, Wayne County, which was about seven miles from where I lived, and by going to this bridge to cross the river, it made the distance about fourteen miles to my appointment that day. The river was up, and I knew of no other way to get across, so I took my wife and child in the buggy and we started. We struck the river about two miles or such a matter above the bridge, and from there on to the bridge we were in the river-bottoms, sometimes immediately on the bank of the river, and sometimes a mile or such a matter from the river. The river was level bank full, and as a matter of course, running out into the sloughs and bayous. We had some of these to cross. When we came to the first one or two I did not know but that it might be swimming, so I would get out of the buggy, take my horse out, get on and ride across, and then come back and hitch to the buggy, and drive across. After I had done this two or three times, we came to one slough that I knew would swim our horse, and it would not do to drive into it, but there were the remains of an old bridge, and I arranged the planks on that bridge so as to have a walk for my horse which I led across. I then arranged the planks again for the wheels of my buggy, which I drew over by hand. I then hitched up, and perhaps got on my horse once or twice more and rode across some of those sloughs, and found none of them very deep. I was satisfied there were no more between me and the bridge that would swim my horse, so I said to my wife, "The next water that I come to I intend to drive in." About half a mile before we came to the bridge the road forked, the right hand going to the bridge and the left hand going to the old ford below the bridge some half a mile. I passed this fork of the road without noticing it, and the first thing I knew I saw water before me which I thought was a slough, and as my word was out to drive into the next water I came to, I drove right up to this with the intention of driving in. But when I got near I saw by the current of the stream that it was the river, and looking across I saw the bluffs on the other side, which reminded me that it was the old ford, and that I had gone wrong back at the forks of the road. A few rods farther, and I, with my wife and child, horse and buggy would have been into that river which, at that time was perhaps seventy-five or one hundred feet deep. Of course we never would have gotten out alive. I felt that it was the hand of a greater power that caused me to look forward and see the current of the water, and that it was the river, and thus save our lives. It was then about half a mile right up the river to the bridge, but no road. The woods were open, however, and rather than drive back to the forks of the road, I pulled off my boots and stockings, and went before the horse to clear the way of chunks and brush, my wife driving, until we got to the bridge. Sometimes I was in water above my knees. I then put on my boots, got into the buggy and drove on to my appointment, feeling all right. I have been able to say what some of our good brethren in the ministry could not, and that is, that my wife has never been opposed to me in my labors in the ministry. In fact, she encouraged me to go to preaching before I ever began. It seems to me that many times I would have become so discouraged that I might have given the matter up, had it not been for her advice, and sometimes persuasion, for me to go on, trusting in the Lord as my only support. Amid all the dangers and embarrassments, the brethren and sisters have always borne with my manner and imperfections, and have, taking all things together, been better to me, perhaps than they have to a great many better men and ministers. I feel that I ought to be very thankful and humble, as well as very pleasant to my brethren wherever I see them, for the kindness and brotherly affection that they have always shown me. I was first liberated by the church to exercise a public gift in the churches in the bounds of the Skillet Fork Association. I have had a great many invitations to come to different neighborhoods to preach, with the promise from the one who invited me that they would help me pay my expenses there and back if I would come. To help pay expenses is very good, but to pay all expenses and let the minister get home as well off as he left home is still better. In that respect, however, I have fared very well, and feel that I have no complaint to enter, and what I say upon the subject of assisting the ministry is not for my own sake, so much as for the sake of other men in the ministry, who try to serve the churches, while, perhaps, the churches neglect their duty toward them. I think very little of a man hiring himself out to preach the gospel, but I also think very little of the idea of a set of people, who are blessed with an abundance of this world's goods, expecting a poor minister to come and preach to them at his own expense. But these practices, in my judgment, the Bible plainly opposes.

CHAPTER X.

It was a long time after I began to exercise in public before I was willing to say before a stranger, that I was a minister of the gospel. It always seemed to me that it was too great a mouthful for me. I think, however, that there are extremes in that direction. A man may be too diffident about claiming to be a minister. I feel certain that the calling is one that a man should not be ashamed of, if he can satisfy himself that it is really his duty to preach. Paul said, "I preach," he also said, "For I am not ashamed of the gospel of Christ for it is the power of God unto salvation to every one that believeth." But I am told that it is not because they are ashamed of the gospel that they are backward about claiming to be ministers; in fact, it does not occur to me that I was ashamed of the gospel, but I was young, and as I have already remarked, I was small. I had never had a great deal of experience in the world, and when I came to a strange place, I hardly knew how to observe good manners for I hardly knew what they were. If there is such a thing as a real native country rustic, I was certainly one when I started out in the ministry. I was more familiar with the road to the mill or to the blacksmith shop than anywhere else, during my life before I joined the church. I was raised, as already observed, in a new country, and can now remember the first frame or brick house that I ever saw. The people all lived in little log houses, and were all poor alike, and all ignorant about alike. To take a boy from this sort of life, and put him in the pulpit is a change, which, if he has good common sense, will make him feel many times, that he is badly out of place. When I went into a strange neighborhood, and had introductions to the brethren, I was aware that it called forth remarks from the people who were present concerning "That boy," because they had no thought from my appearance, that I was a minister. They thought that even if I claimed to be one, it was unreasonable to think that I could preach. To all such remarks, when I heard of them, I was very sensitive.

But I now wish to give a narrative, that I experienced when I was traveling. I had been preaching about three years. I had moved to Grayville, or near there, and in June, 1868, I sent some appointments out into Clay and Marion counties, Illinois. I rode on horse-back from Grayville to Olney, left my horse with one of the brethren, boarded the train and went from there to Iuka. My first appointment was at Summit Prairie Church, about five miles from Iuka. I had a brother-in-law living at Iuka, so I intended to stop off there and visit him and his family, and then go on to my appointments. After I boarded the train at Olney, I noticed one gentleman who seemed to be rather conspicuous, walking through the car and talking loudly, with his hat off, as if he were polite, and I thought in all probability, he might be a clergyman of some sort. He finally sat down in the seat with me and began conversation. I was very timid, and let him do the most of the talking. He finally asked me where I was going. I said, "I am going to Iuka." "What are you going there for?" he inquired. "I am going to see my brother-in-law and his family." "Does he live in Iuka?" "Yes, sir." "Is that the only place you are going to?" And I did not want to tell him that I was a preacher, and that I was going out on a preaching tour, but he pressed the matter, till I told him finally that I was going to fill some appointments that I had, at two or three different churches in that county. Said he, "You are a minister, then?" I told him I was a sort of a one. "What church do you preach for?" he inquired. I told him I preached for the Baptist church. "The Missionary Baptist church?" said he. I told him, "No, sir. The Old School Baptist church." He stormed out, "Haven't you any more sense than to preach such doctrine as that?" I told him, "No, sir, I did not have a bit more sense than to preach that doctrine; the Bible taught it and I felt confident that when I was preaching it I was preaching the truth, and that the Lord would approbate my course." He had considerable more to say but I do not remember any more of the conversation, but I do know that it was very impressive to me, and I was glad when I got rid of him as a companion.

CHAPTER XI.

I was first liberated by the church to exercise a gift in the bounds of the Skillet Fork Association. Whether the church has a right to limit a gift that is recognized as being of the Lord, to any locality of the world, is a matter that I now seriously doubt. However, I was submissive to the action of the church at the time, and would also advise young gifts to be submissive to their churches now, even if the church should make a mistake, the young minister is safer while living in humble submission to his church than he is under any other circumstances. In the course of a year, or such a matter, I was again liberated to exercise a gift wherever the Lord, in his providence might cast my lot. I will now state that I have my doubts as to the propriety of a church liberating a man to preach, or giving him license, as it is sometimes called. We find no account of anything of that kind in the Scriptures, and I am of the opinion, that if the church has a gift it is her duty to encourage him, and let him make full proof of his ministry, and if she becomes satisfied in her wisdom, that he should be set forward as a minister of the gospel, she should call for a presbytery and have him ordained to the full functions of the gospel ministry. While I am on the duty of the churches toward their young gifts, I will mention one evil that I think I have seen among a great many of our people, and that is a disposition to want to hear men who are able, instead of young men who have just started out in the ministry. I visited a church once, that had several young brethren, whom she had liberated to speak in public, and I invited one of them, on Saturday night, to preach, which he did very satisfactorily. I went home with a family that night, and was rather severely reprimanded for inviting the young man up, the good people informing me that if I wanted to hear him preach, I might invite him to my own home church, but they did not want to hear him, and they did not want me to invite him up any more. I thought they were very obliging to take the pains to give license to a man to preach to other people, whom they did not wish to hear themselves. The oldest and ablest minister in the church was the youngest minister at one time, and as we have no training schools in which to teach men how to preach, we should endure with great patience our young gifts whom the Lord calls and gives to us, knowing, that before they can be men, they must first be boys in the ministry. We should never erect a standard of perfection, and expect them to come up to it. A young minister is like the most tender plant when it first springs up out of the earth. He will wilt at the least unkindness, or token of disapprobation from his brethren. Sometimes old ministers think they have a right to speak short to or snub a young minister. I think I have seen some things of that kind that were taken by the old minister and his brethren as indications of smartness. But I think they were sadly mistaken, and that the cause of God is wounded whenever an old minister takes the iberty to domineer over a young gift in such a manner as to wound his feelings, and make him dread to go into the presence of his senior minister. The Lord calls men to preach, not for the accommodation of the preacher, but for the comfort, consolation and upbuilding of his church, and the preacher should be considered properly and in his place. He should never be looked on as a master by the church, neither should the church ever come to the conclusion that it is a great favor to the preacher to let him preach. If he is a servant of God he will get all the preaching to do that he can do, and the better he is treated, the more profitable his labors are likely to be. Sometimes the people get very uneasy for fear the preacher will be spoiled, and get above his brethren, and it becomes necessary for the brethren to watch that point very closely. At least, they seem to think so, from remarks they are in the habit of making many times. I have heard men say in regard to their treatment of a minister, something like this: "I go to hear you preach almost every time you preach in my neighborhood." Surely the man who treats a preacher that well must be a warm personal friend to the preacher, and the preacher ought to consider himself highly complimented if a good brother even goes to hear him preach.

CHAPTER XII.

When I had been exercising in public about two years, I was teaching our winter school, in the winter of '65 and '66 and there were no Baptist meetings for me to go to, except to go to my own church once a month, which was about twelve miles from where I lived, and I had to cross the river, which a portion of the time was disagreeable, and perhaps I had more zeal at that time than ability, and desired to be at meeting oftener than once a month. The church in the neighborhood where I lived, known as Long Prairie church, at that time was not holding meetings regularly. She had neither house nor pastor, and a membership of about thirty or forty members, as well as I remember. So, in order to have more meetings to go to, and hoping to bring the church together, I concluded to have meetings once a month, at the school-house where I was teaching. So I announced to my school-children that I would have meeting at that school-house on Sunday, which was the first Sunday in the month. That had always been the regular time of the meeting of Long Prairie church. When the time came there were a few people out to hear me, and I talked to them as well as I could and I felt that I had some evidence, at least, of divine approbation. At the close of my services, I announced that I would have meeting there again, on the first Sunday in next month. When the time rolled around, my congregation had increased considerably, and that encouraged me to think, that in all probability, my labors were not in vain. I again announced that on the first Sunday of the next month there would be meeting there again, when one brother spoke out saying, "Have meeting on Saturday the next time." I readily consented to that, and the church came together that time on Saturday, and reorganized. From that on we had meetings during that spring, summer and fall, part of the time at the school-house and part of the time in an arbor in the grove near by. During the summer there were two or three accessions to the church by experience and baptism. I, not being ordained, of course could not baptize them. My wife and I moved our membership to that church, and during the next winter I kept the meetings up there every month; and at the March meeting a brother rose and told the church that he had been studying about my case for some time, and he made a motion that the church send to sister churches for ordained authorities, to form a presbytery for the purpose of examining, and, if thought proper by the presbytery, to ordain me to the full work of the gospel ministry. When he sat down, and his motion was seconded, I arose to speak, and the Moderator ordered me to sit down, which I did, feeling somewhat hurt that he would not allow me to say anything. The motion carried, and the church agreed to send to certain sister churches, and requested me to go and bear a letter to one of them, and if I could not go alone, to go with some brother, which I utterly refused to do. I sincerely felt that I did not want to be at any sister church when such a letter was read. The brother appointed to go to one of the churches seemed determined to have me go with him and came past my house for that purpose, but I refused to go.

The day of my ordination was one of the most solemn days to me that I ever witnessed. While, from all that I could see, the old brethren, sisters and friends seemed cheerful, yet I felt very sad. When I looked up and down the road and saw the good people coming together, and especially the visiting ministry, I was glad to see them, but I was sorry they were there on the mission they were. I hope the reader will not understand me that I did not wish to be ordained, if the church thought I was a proper candidate for ordination, but I feared my own weakness and many imperfections. I was under the impression that an ordained minister was placed under a great many obligations and responsibilities that I was afraid I could never live up to. It seemed to me that I did not have enough confidence in myself to think that I was certain to live right, or even live in such a manner that the brethren might never regret having me ordained. I felt that a minister was responsible for all the false doctrines and heresies, both in doctrine and practice that ever came into the church. I was impressed, when quite young, with the thought that a good sound, orderly church was dependent on a sound, faithful, orderly ministry. That I believe yet, and for me to feel that I was a proper subject for ordination was something that I could not do. When the brethren came together and the sermon had been preached by Elder David Stewart, the church sat for business, and asked for the responses from the sister churches that had been called on. The brethren to compose the presbytery were received, and when they had organized for business they called for the candidate. I was sitting rather back of some of the brethren, next to the wall, and I just thought that I could not respond when they called for me. A brother came and took me by the hand and led me out, in front of the presbytery, where there was a chair for me to occupy during the examination. As I was being thus led by this good brother, I felt more like a prisoner than a minister of the gospel. I thought that I could not talk. My recollection is that from the time they called for me until I was ordained I was crying almost all the time, and what little I did say, was said amid sobs and tears. I never will forget that day. I believed that the brethren were composed of good, godly and devout men, faithful ministers of the gospel. But I was afraid they were mistaken in my case. It might have been that if they had not ordained me, I would have thought hard of them, but at the same time it seems to me that I would have thought it was all right. I still feel poor, weak and unworthy, and perhaps a majority of the times that I have had to try to preach from that day to this, I have dreaded the time to come when I should arise to talk. Very few of my efforts have been perfectly satisfactory. I sometimes think that I can make the most complete failures of any man that ever stood in the pulpit, and opened his mouth to preach the gospel. I seldom ever have been able to make any calculations beforehand, as to how, or what I should preach, and then afterwards work up to such calculations. It may seem strange to the reader, but it is nevertheless true, that, perhaps a majority of the times that I go into the pulpit, I do so, not knowing what will be my subject on that occasion, till I take my Bible down, and my eye strikes some text, that I conclude to talk about.

CHAPTER XIII.

After I commenced taking the care of churches, and baptizing and administering The Supper, it seemed like things were going along very smoothly except once in a while a brother would seem to criticise the doctrine of the resurrection. There was an old minister living in the country whose name was William Trainer, and who had been preaching in that country for many years before I was grown. He used to preach at my father's house when I was a boy. I held him in very high esteem as a man and a minister for some years after I commenced trying to preach. When I began to go out among the brethren, I would sometimes hear remarks made concerning him, that he did not believe in the doctrine of the resurrection of the body. He was occasionally accused of saying that he did not believe that anything would ever go to heaven that did not first come down from heaven. It was hard for me to believe but that he was all right, and I thought that some of the other ministers were jealous of him, and that that was the reason they found fault with his preaching. I was very fond of him, and I watched very closely after I had heard him accused, and I finally became satisfied that he did not believe in the salvation of the Adam man. He believed that the body—the earthly body—was no part of a child of God. After I became convinced that this was his faith I said nothing, for awhile, because I was young, and felt that I might be mistaken about the matter, until one time he preached at a school house a few miles from where I lived and I went to hear him. His appointment had been published the Sunday before, and on that Sunday I went to my father's in company with some others for dinner, and as we were about separating, I overheard my father and another brother, in conversation, speak of Elder Trainer's appointment. They both expressed a desire to go and hear him, saying that if he had ever denied the resurrection of the body, they had never heard him. I said nothing, but thought that I had heard him. I went to hear him on this occasion, and when I got there these brethren were there, and when he arose to preach, he stated that some people were mistaken as to who the child of God is, or else he was. He said some thought that the lady and gentleman were the children of God, but that he did not believe that. When he made use of that expression I thought, "they hear it now." I know now, and did then, that if the lady or gentleman is not the child of God, the doctrine of the resurrection of the body is not a true doctrine. Elder Trainer, at that time was on his way to Little Wabash Church, in White county, and I concluded to make the trip with him, which I did. I rode with him all day, during which time he talked a great deal, for he was a great talker. He satisfied me that he did not believe in the resurrection of the body, for he said it in so many words. His preaching among the churches in that part of the country caused a great deal of wrangling and considerable hardness among the brethren, and the exclusion of some good men from the church. This was rather embarrassing for me, to go among brethren who differed, and yet seemed to be good brethren. Matters went on in this way for some two or three years, before a final separation came on account of the non-resurrection doctrine.

In the winter of 1868, I was called to the care of Grayville church, and moved down into the neighborhood of that church. After I had been there about a year, it seemed that the non-resurrection doctrine advocated by Elder Trainer and others was causing more and more trouble all the time, and the feeling was getting very high, until finally the church at Little Wabash called a council from several of the churches around, to advise them what to do, which council advised all our churches to shut the anti-resurrection doctrine out of their houses. This most of the churches did throughout the Skillet Fork Association.

CHAPTER XIV.

While I am on the subject of the trouble concerning the non-resurrection doctrine, I will state that in the year 1869, the church at Little Wabash, White county, Illinois, at the request of her pastor. Elder David Stuart, called for the council mentioned in the preceding chapter. The council was to meet in February. Some of Elder Trainer's friends notified him of the meeting, and he and another preacher by the name of Enoch Tabor attended the meeting. On their way to that meeting, they had an appointment at my church at Grayville, for Tabor to preach on Friday night. I had never seen Elder Tabor, but he was said to be a very able man. Being in company with Elder Trainer, it was natural to suppose that he would be in sympathy with him on that doctrine. I went out to hear him preach, and he took for his text, "It is a faithful saying, and worthy of all acceptation that Christ Jesus came into the world to save sinners, of whom I am chief." For about an hour and a half, I thought he made as able a defense of the doctrine of salvation by grace, without creature conditions or merits, and against the charges on the part of conditionalists, as I ever heard a man make. I could not help but be pleased with his ability and the masterly and powerful manner in which he defended the doctrine of salvation as being by grace alone, through the Lord Jesus Christ. At the end of that time he began to inquire, "But who is it that is saved? Is it the Adam man, or any of his posterity?" and for another hour and a half, I do not think I have ever heard a man give his own people, claiming the Baptists as his people, more abuse for believing the doctrine of the resurrection, and the salvation of the Adamic sinner than he did. He said he had been in good standing with the Baptist people ever since the year 1827, and that he had opportunities to know what the Baptist doctrine was, and he wanted no better evidence that a man was a Pharisee, than for him to believe in the doctrine of the resurrection of the just and the unjust. He said that if a man had his name written in letters of gold upon his forehead, whose brilliancy would outshine the sun, "Pharisee," it would be no better evidence to him that he was a Pharisee than for him to say he believed in the resurrection of the just and the unjust. While he was preaching, I looked over my congregation and saw that the house was full of people, and that the majority of them were unacquainted with what the Baptists really did believe upon the question of the resurrection. All my responsibilities began to bear heavily upon my mind. Should I, young, weak and timid as I was, presume so much as to tell this intelligent and thinking audience that I did not believe or endorse this man's preaching on the question of the resurrection? If I undertake to argue against him the people will think I am foolish. If I let matters go and say nothing about it, I do injustice to my own cause. I am the pastor of this church, and have read in scripture the obligations resting upon a watchman who sees the foe coming and does not give the alarm, I made up my mind, however, that I would not say a word until after Elder Trainer had said what he had to say. So, at the close of Elder Tabor's remarks, Elder Trainer arose, and in a short speech, said he heartily endorsed the entire discourse, and seemed to be very enthusiastic in saying so. At the close of his remarks, he was about to dismiss the congregation, when I ventured to give his coat a pull, and told him I would love to speak. I arose, and, as near as I remember, made the following speech. I told my people that we would always do well to watch strangers. If the brother we had heard preach to-night was an honest man it would not hurt him to watch him, and if he was not an honest man, we should watch him, even if it did hurt him. I told them that he was one of those men, that the apostle frequently speaks of, who go about causing divisions and trouble in the churches. It was not my intention to say so positively that he was one of these men, but I intended to say he might be one of them, but in my embarrassment, and perhaps excitement, I said it the other way, and just let it go, believing that it was the truth anyway. I told the people that I believed in the doctrine of the resurrection, that I could not understand Elder Tabor's position, that it was the sinner who was saved, and at the same time that the sinner saved was not Adam, nor any of his posterity. It seemed to present to my mind a contradiction and an inconsistency. I remarked that I believed in the doctrine of the resurrection of the just and of the unjust, even if I must be called a Pharisee for saying it. For me to arise in the face of a large audience, and in the presence of two men who were as able as they were, and having so much the advantage of me in age, was one of the hardest trials of my life, as a minister. After I was through, and the meeting was dismissed, quite a number of my brethren and friends came to me and gave me their hand, and congratulated me on my faithfulness. And I felt that I had done no more than was my duty to do, although I was thought by those men to be egotistical. This meeting occurred on Friday night, and on Saturday morning I went down to the Little Wabash church, where those two brethren were going, and when I arrived there and met them on the ground, neither of them would speak to me. By some means the brethren had been informed of the meeting we had held at Grayville, the night before, and a number of them spoke to me about it before meeting time. There were brethren in the ministry, as well as other brethren from almost all our churches at the meeting on Saturday, and when it came time for preaching, the first thing I knew Elders Tabor and Trainer were invited into the stand, and I was called on to preach. That surprised me to some extent, but I could not prevail on the brethren to excuse me, so I took a seat in the stand between those two men and neither of them looked at me. I do not think I was ever acquainted with a preacher that I loved more dearly than I had loved Elder Trainer, having known him from my boyhood days. During the sermon, the night before at Grayville, he would speak out in approbation of Elder Tabor, during his discourse, and when I went into the stand, I felt determined in my own mind, that he should "grunt" for me a few times that day if the Lord would bless me with the ability to preach to him as I wished. He was very tender on the question of an experience, and I got him to sanction some of the internal evidences of grace, even to the extent that his tears flowed freely, and I asked him the question, "If this is not the sinner who feels and realizes those evidences, who is it?"

They had an appointment at Grayville, on their way home, for the Tuesday night following, and I went again, thinking, "I will make Elder Trainer speak to me now." We had always been good friends. So I went early to the church, and found only a few there, and I went and sat down by him and spoke to him, and in conversation, I asked him if he endorsed what that man had been preaching all the time. He said he did, and that if the Baptists did not believe it that Elder Tabor would debate the question with any of them. I told him we wanted no debate, but that I would love for him to state to me as nearly as he could, and in as few words as possible, what he believed. He said he believed that there were three generations of people. The generation of Adam, the generation of Jesus Christ, and the generation of vipers. The generation of Adam were made of the dust of the ground, and would go back to the dust where they came from, and remain there forever. The generation of Jesus

Christ came down from heaven, took up their abode in the Adam man, and they would finally go back to heaven where they came from. The generation of vipers came from hell, and they also took up their abode in the Adam man, and would go back to hell where they came from. I heard Elder Tabor preach that night, and during his trip, and he would frequently say that there were some old Baptists in this country, who were so large that Jesus Christ's overcoat would not make them a sleeve jacket. Of course he regarded me as one of those. But that is all right. I felt then, and do now, that I was willing to thus suffer for the sake of truth.

CHAPTER XV.

I hope the reader will not become impatient while I continue the history of this non-resurrection trouble. As the council which was called at Little Wabash Church, advised the churches of our faith and order, to close their doors against the anti-resurrection doctrine, our church at Grayville passed an act at their following meeting, closing her doors against the non-resurrectionists and the Universalists. Several other churches in the country did the same, relative to the non-resurrection doctrine. The church at Long Prairie, however, was not in a condition to agree on an action of that kind. If that church at that time had been forced to take action in the matter, I think perhaps three-fourths of her members would have voted in favor of allowing that doctrine preached in her pulpit. There was some little hardness on the part of some of her members toward our ministers who advocated the doctrine of the resurrection, and opposed that of non-resurrection.

One little circumstance occurred that I will here relate. Their pastor was a man by the name of Ford, and from all we can learn concerning him, he believed in the doctrine of no resurrection. My grandfather, who was also a minister, was a member of that church, and on one occasion undertook to preach on the question of the resurrection, when Elder Ford arose to follow him, and began to criticise his sermon. His course was such as to make the matter unpleasant, and he made a special appointment to preach on the subject of the resurrection, at which appointment he said he would give his views on that subject. I heard about the matter and concluded I would go and hear him, and as he was to preach on Sunday, I sent an appointment to the church that I would preach on the preceding Saturday night. When I arrived at the church that night, some of the brethren who had been my warmest and most intimate personal friends in that church, seemed very distant, especially, one brother who was a deacon. He came into the house and barely spoke to me, and then, after a few moments, went out again. I followed him out, and mentioned the condition of the church on the subject of the resurrection, and found that he was as I thought, rather out of humor. I asked him what he thought the church would do. He said he did not know, and, not giving me a short answer, he did not care much what they did. I asked him if he knew what they did at Little Wabash church, and he said he did. I asked him, "How did it suit you?" He replied to me in these words, "Lemuel, it did not suit me." He stated that the Little Wabash Church had Elder Trainer charged with saying that the tares were the children of the wicked one, and that it was one of the complaints against him. I told him I knew that was not the case. He disputed with me and said that he knew that it was the case; they had it in the neighborhood in black and white. I told him finally, it mattered not to me what they had in black and white, I knew that the church had no such complaint against Elder Trainer, for I was there and heard everything that was said. He told me that the word had gone out all over this country, that I was coming here to reply to brother Ford and I thought he seemed to talk short about it. I told him that such a report was entirely without any foundation whatever. I had never thought of such a thing. I asked him "Is Brother Ford a non-resurrectionist?" He replied to me, "They say he is." "Well," said I, "What do you say? You have heard him." "Well," said he, "I say he is not. If Elder Trainer is, he is." "Well," said I, "That settles it. For I know that Elder Trainer is." We went back into the house, and I filled my appointment the best I could, but felt no little embarrassment at the sad state of things in this dear old church, where I have been in the habit of hearing the gospel preached ever since I was old enough to listen to a sermon. The people were my brethren, neighbors, and friends, and for hard feelings to exist among them, and especially for them to think hard of me, was very discouraging, to say the least of it. I was quite young, and had only been in the ministry about four years, and if I was ever to know much, I had it almost all to learn. I believed in the doctrine of the resurrection of the body, both of the just and the unjust. I was satisfied it had always been the doctrine of the church, and that the apostles taught it, and for the brethren to be turned against the doctrine now, was sad to me, indeed.

On Sunday I went to hear Elder Ford's views on the resurrection, but he failed, from some cause, to put in an appearance, and the brethren invited me to preach, which I, at first, was very loth to undertake. But I finally went into the stand with a determination to say nothing whatever about the resurrection. But when I commenced preaching, I could talk about nothing else, and so I gave way to my own feelings, and the leadings of my mind on that subject, and perhaps I never said more on that subject in an hour than I did then. I felt when I was through, that I had simply discharged my duty in trying to defend the truth, and that the Lord had been with me, for I thought I could see some good indications beaming from the countenances of some of the brethren present who had been vascillating, at least upon that subject. An old brother came to me after dismission, and invited me to preach at his house that night, stating that he wanted to hear some more of it. I agreed to do so, and went directly home with him for dinner, and from that on, the feeling of that church seemed to turn in a different direction, and perdaps to-day it is as firm in the belief of the doctrine of the resurrection of the body as any church in the country. I do not claim any credit for being the salvation of that church. Whether I had any thing to do in the affair or not, the Lord only knows. But if I did—if my little efforts to preach were instrumental in restoring peace, and establishing the brethren in the doctrine of the gospel, the Lord be praised for it all.

CHAPTER XVI.

As I have stated in a preceding chapter, in 1868 I was called to the pastoral care of the church at Grayville. During the summer I lived in that vicinity, and when I was at home, we had meetings at a school house known as the Cole School House, every Wednesday night. We had very pleasant meetings at this little school house, and there grew to be a wonderful interest among the people of that neighborhood on the subject of religion. Our Church received and baptized quite a number during the spring, summer, and fall, at that place, and the revival spirit of the church seemed to be very attractive to other churches and ministers. Our congregations were large and enthusiastic, and it seemed as if I had as much evidence of divine approbation, in my feeble efforts to preach to the people in that community, as I have ever had in my ministry. I have felt many times in my life that in some respects my best days were the days spent in that community, for I was young and active both in body and mind, and thought nothing of doing a hard day's work on a farm during the long days of summer, and then going to meeting and preaching at night.

During the summer I was challenged by a young Campbellite preacher, who was familiarly known as Dick Flower, to engage with him in a joint discussion on some of the points of difference between the Campbellite doctrine and that of our people, which resulted in a three days' debate at the Baptist Church in Grayville, and by the old people of that country, that debate has been more clearly and distinctly remembered, perhaps, than any other debate that was ever held in that part of the country by me. I thought then and do now, that so far as arguments are concerned, neither of us did anything very great in that debate, however, the people seemed to concede the victory to me. I have thought many times that it was not so much because of my skill in arguing my points, and defending them, as the manner of my opponent's treatment of me. However, I have studied the doctrine of the Campbellite people a great deal since then, and have had a great many debates with them, and I think I know as well what they teach as they do themselves, so far as their fundamental principles are concerned. I have had opportunities of learning their doctrine having had about nineteen public discussions with them.

I remember on one occasion of going to hear one of their men preach, at the solicitation of a cousin of mine, who was a member of that church. When we came to the place my cousin introduced me to his preacher, Brother Williams, stating to him that I was a Baptist preacher. During the discourse, the preacher referred to that religion which has doubts and fears, in a manner that is very common to all the preachers of that sect; stating that he had no use for that religion, and illustrating it by saying that he knew that there was such a place as the city of Carmi, Illinois, because he lived there—it was his home; and that he had heard that there was such a city as New Orleans; but that he had never seen the city of New Orleans, but he said he doubted the existence of the city of Carmi as much as he did the city of New Orleans, and by the same course of reasoning he doubted the existence of God, the death, burial and resurrection of Jesus Christ, as much as he did the pardon of his own sins. He went on to state, during his discourse, that the sinner must take four steps in order to get into Christ, and that he had scripture for each one. He must believe—that is the first step the sinner must take, as the Apostle says, "With the heart man believeth unto righteousness," not *into it*, but *unto it*. That is the first step. The second step is that he must repent. The Apostle says, "Godly sorrow worketh repentance *unto*,"—not *into*,—"salvation." The third step is confession. The Apostle says, "With the mouth confession is made *unto*,"—not *into*,— "salvation." So that a man may take all three of these steps and not be in Christ unless he goes on and takes the fourth step. The fourth one is baptism. The apostle says, "As many of us as have been baptized into Christ have put on Christ." These are the four steps necessary to get into Christ, and no man gets there unless he takes them. This was the position of the preacher. He further stated that when we come to talk about what was enjoined upon us in the New Testament, we should never distinguish between essentials and non-essentials. He said that there were no non-essentials in the New Testament. Everything that we were required to do was essential. After he got through, an old gentlemen by the name of Smith, with whom I was acquainted, and who thought his preacher was very able, turned to me, the preacher standing behind him looking over his shoulder into my face, so that it was impossible for me to say a word without his hearing me, and asked me what I thought of his preacher. I said, "He is quite a talker, but I am sorry for him, for he cannot be saved, if what he preached to-night is true." The old gentleman seemed surprised that I should speak so, and turning his head and seeing the preacher, he stepped aside to let the preacher speak for himself. I told the preacher I was sorry for him, for if he had preached the truth to-night he never could be saved. I told him the only hope for him was that he had not preached the truth, and I thought that so far his chances were very favorable, for I did not believe he had preached he truth. He called on me for an explanation, and I asked him if there were no non-essentials in the Bible; he said there were not, and I asked him if the Bible did not say "Hope that is seen is not hope." He said it did. "Well," said I, "you stated that you doubted the existence of God, and the death, burial and resurrection of Jesus Christ, as much as you did the pardon of your sins, and Peter said, "Sanctify the Lord God in your hearts, and be ready always to give to every man that asketh you, a reason of the hope that is in you, with meekness and fear." Now, sir, will you please tell me how it is that you have a hope at all, when you already knew everything? He said it was growing late, and if I would come down to-morrow he would explain it to me. I did not go, and so he never explained it.

CHAPTER XVII.

In the spring of 1869, my wife being in very poor health, I sold out almost everything I had, except a team, and we took a trip to Wisconsin for her health. We were gone about six or eight weeks. We landed at Woodstock, Richland county, where we were acquainted with perhaps half a dozen families. There was no church in that country, that I knew of, but I was told of an old gentleman who lived some seven or eight miles away, up in the hills, who would preach some six or seven miles from Woodstock the following Sunday. A number of friends and myself went to his meeting, and when I was introduced to him, he insisted that I should preach, but I declined because it was his appointment, and I preferred not to say anything until after he was through. He did not preach a great while, neither did he preach very much. I could not have told from his discourse that he was a Baptist, because he did not touch upon any doctrinal points, affirmatively or negatively, by which I could judge him. When he was through, seeing that he had been very brief, I concluded to talk awhile, which I did, and the people seemed to be amazed, and at the same time they seemed to approbate what I said. I tried, in my little effort, as far as I went, to preach the doctrine that I believed, both affirmatively and negatively, and at the close of my remarks, I overheard a voice saying, "I could sit here all evening." I found that there were some people in that country who loved to hear the Baptist doctrine preached. At the little town, Woodstock, where I made my headquarters, there was no meeting-house to preach in, but there was a large school-house, and those who preached at all in that place preached there. I found that it was occupied every Sunday, so that it would be impossible for me to have an appointment even one Sunday in the month. But as I had no other place to go to, and no other brethren to visit, and could preach about as well at one time as another, I concluded to have meeting at this school house every Sunday at 5 o'clock P.M. This I did, as long as I remained in that country. At my meetings I had good, interesting congregations. Other people seemed to hold me at a distance, I thought, and I knew of no reason for it only that I preached a doctrine that they did not believe. I have learned, long ago, that the only way you can please some people, is either to preach nothing, or else preach their doctrine. I did not feel disposed to do either, and on one occasion, a friend of mine gave me word that the school officers who had conrol of the house, had made threats that they would turn me out, and not allow me to preach there any longer, after I filled my next appointment. This did not embarrass me, for I knew that when they turned me out of their school house, they would be turned out also. It was as much my school house as it was theirs. So I went on and filled my appointment the next Sunday evening to a crowded house, and the parties who were supposed to have made the threats were present, and when I got through, I published a meeting for the next Sunday evening, and no person said a word. I felt sometimes, that these were efforts to intimidate, as I have often felt during my life, especially when I was young. The next Sunday evening, there were two Methodist ministers present, and they sat up right next to me. I felt certain that they were brought there for the purpose of intimidating me, and I still think that was their object. But, instead of it having the desired effect, it seemed to arouse an ambition in me to be plainer, and to take my positions more boldly than if they had not been there. When I was through, they went away, and said nothing to me, and from that time on, I held my meetings as long as I stayed. There was an urgent request for me to remain and constitute a church at that place, but I felt that, while I might be able to find material enough for the constitution of a church, it would do no good, unless it had some one to keep it together afterwards. And as I did not intend to remain there, I did not encourage the organization of a church.

I heard of another preacher in that country, and I traveled three or four days, taking my wife and little children in a one-horse wagon on the hunt of him, but I never found him. When I gave up the hunt my wife had improved in her health a great deal, and as I was eager to get back among my people at home, I came back to Southern Illinois, sowed a crop of wheat, and went to work, preaching among my churches, until the spring of 1870. I then lived in the neighborhood of old Long Prairie church, and during the summer a revival broke out in that church, which lasted all summer, and during harvest, and through the busy times with the crops, we had meetings there every Wednesday evening at 5 o'clock, or at night, and it was astonishing, that right in the busiest time of the year, when we came in sight of that meeting house, to see the whole side of the hill covered with buggies, wagons and people, and when we met some of the old sisters, we would hear them say, "It has been a long week." During that summer there were quite a number of accessions to the church, among which were three brethren, who to-day, are ordained ministers of the gospel. I look back to that season as one of the bright spots in my ministerial life. Everything was lovely. The church was all in peace. Brethren and friends loved to meet and greet each other, and there was nothing to do but to preach the gospel, enjoy all its comforts, and obey all its injunctions. Surely we did sit together in heavenly places in Christ Jesus, during that time.

CHAPTER XVIII.

In the year 1873, I had three public debates—two of them were with the Campbellites, one at Paris, Illinois, with a gentleman by the name of William Holt, and one at Mount Pleasant Church, White County, Illinois, with a gentleman by the name of Stone, and the other with Elder Ed. Hearde, who denied the doctrine of the resurrection. From the day that our churches closed their doors against the non-resurrection doctrine, until 1873, Elder Trainer made his visits among the people in the bounds of our churches, and held his meetings at private houses and from what we could learn, he always challenged our brethren to debate on the subject of the resurrection. So finally Elder David Stuart, who was pastor of the Little Wabash church, hailed him, as he was passing his house one Monday morning, and told him that his challenge was accepted, and the result was that we debated two and one-half days, at Elder Trainer's Church, in Jasper County, Illinois. After that debate closed, Elder Trainer's visits to White County, among the churches in our bounds ceased. But I do not wish to dismiss this subject without giving a few hints, at least, of the character of the debate, and the man with whom I debated with at that time. Elder Ed. Hearde came to the debate with a written endorsement, signed by his church at home in the state of Indiana, (I believe Johnson County,) as a member of Bethlehem church of Predestinarian Baptists, and that Bethlehem church was a member of Bethlehem Association, and that Elder Hearde was the Moderator of that Association. At the time I debated with him, he was perhaps sixty years of age, and had engaged in a large number of debates. He was a very shrewd man, naturally. His advantages as to education, perhaps were limited. There was a circumstance told of him once, that I will relate. During the time of the Maine Liquor Law campaign, in the state of Indiana, in 1853, or '54, there were a great many stump speakers over the country, on both sides of the issue. It was said that whenever a man came into Elder Heard's country to speak in favor of the Maine Liquor Law, that Elder Hearde was in the habit of putting in his presence and replying to the speaker. This was his course until the temperance people got tired of him. But on one occasion, they were having an extraordinary meeting in that neighborhood, and Mr. Cary, of Ohio, who afterwards ran for Vice-President, with Peter Cooper, was to be the speaker of the day. When Elder Hearde arrived at the grounds on that occasion, he was met by one of his opponents, who told him that if he would reply to Mr. Cary, he would give him five dollars. He readily accepted the offer, saying, "Give me the money." The gentleman did so, and Elder Hearde told him that now he must come and introduce him to the speaker, Mr Cary. He did so with that degree of politeness and dignity customary on such occasions, the gentleman stating to Mr. Cary that Mr. Hearde was an old Baptist preacher, and would reply to his speech to-day. Mr Cary readily assented to the arrangement, and during his speech he frequently referred to the fact that he must be careful, because he was to be followed by a minister of the gospel, who, of course was well posted aud would scrutinize his speech very severely. While Mr. Cary made use of such expressions rather ironically, yet it was true that when he closed his speech, Elder Hearde arose with the five dollars in his hand, flourishing it in such a manner that the people could all see it, and told them that the way he came by that money was that a gentleman had given it to him to reply to the speech that we had just heard, and that all he had to say concerning that matter was that fools and their money soon part. So he put it into his pocket, and immediately began to review the speech. The result was that even Mr. Cary did not wait to hear him through.

Elder Hearde, in his debate with me, treated me very courteously, I being quite a young man while he was much older. He undertook to prove in his affirmation that the people of God are a seed which existed in heaven prior to the formation of the Adam man, and that they would all go back to heaven where they came from. I do not pretend to say that I have his proposition verbatim, but this is the substance of it, and he led out in the opening of that question, with a speech for one hour, in which he made a number of scripture quotations to show that God's people were a seed. He quoted this among others: "A seed shall serve him and it shall be counted to the Lord for a generation." And "In thee and thy seed shall all the kindreds of the earth be blessed." "I will put enmity between thee and the woman, and between thy seed and her seed. It shall bruise thy head and it shall bruise his heel." Quite a number of other texts of this character were introduced in his first speech, without a great many comments. He stated that he intended to merely lay his planks down loose, in this speech, and that he would come with his hatchet and nails and fasten them down in his next speech. In my reply to his arguments on these proof-texts, to prove the pre-existence of God's people, I simply admitted that I believed that the Lord's people were a seed, and that was all that he had proven by these texts. I was not here to deny that God's people were a seed, but that I was here to deny that they had an eternal existence, and that there was not a single text in all the catalogue of texts that he had quoted that said anything about the pre-existence of the people mentioned in his proof-texts. I thought then, and do yet, however, that he did about as well in proving that doctrine as any man could do. I felt very confident that he could not prove it by the Bible. He finally inquired where the Lord got his people, if they did not eternally exist. I replied that he made them. That I knew of no people as the subjects of eternal salvation, only the people that God made. That the Bible frequently spoke of the fact that God made his people. "Thy maker is thine husband," is one expression of Scripture, and the very idea of a maker is the best inferential testimony that they must have been made. Again, I do not believe that they had an eternal existence, because it was said that Adam was the first man, I could not conceive of the idea of there being a man before him, and not only was he the first man, but that he was made of the dust of the ground. This was the man that I believed had transgressed the law of God, and fallen under its curse, and became subject to death, and all the miseries consequent upon sin, and that they were the subjects of salvation. But I will not stop here to give a full detail of the arguments, any more than to say that I became more fully convinced during that discussion against the doctrine of the pre-existence of God's people than I had ever been. I believe that God eternally knew His people, and that it was as easy a matter for Him to know them before they existed as it was afterwards. I believed then, more than that, that God fore-knew His people, and how He fore-knew His people and they have an eternal existence I could not understand, for I thought to foreknow a thing was to know it before-hand, that is, to know it before it was, so if He fore-knew His people, He knew them before they were, and the Apostle says, "Whom He fore-knew them He also did predestinate to be conformed to the image of His son." It would be impossible for Him to fore-know them, or to know them before they were, if they eternally existed. He finally, however, made this remark, that if I would admit the pre-existence of God's people, he did not ask me any boot on the question of the ressurrection. So I say to-day, that the non-ressurrection doctrine is the legitimate consequence, and the inevitable result of the doctrine of the pre-existence of the children of God, or the doctrine of eternal children. Men may talk all they wish about the doctrine of eternal vital union, eternal children, eternal justification, and so forth, but I do not believe in the eternal existence of God's people; neither do I believe in eternal vital union. Now, if a man admits the doctrine of eternal children, he may as well admit the doctrine of non-ressurrection. We discussed this proposition a day and a half, after which I affirmed that there will be, in the future, a ressurrection of the bodies, both of the just and the unjust, of Adam's posterity, some to eternal life, and some to everlasting punishment. I give the substance of the proposition from memory, for I do not remember it verbatim. I argued that ressurrection meant to restore to life that which once had life, and that to put one man down and take another up in its place, would be no ressurrection, but to lay one body down in death, and then take that same body up alive, is a ressurrection, and nothing short of it is. I believed then, and do to-day, that it was the Adam sinner that was saved, the same man that was made of the dust of the ground. I did not then believe, nor do I yet, that any part of him came from heaven. I believe that the very same body that goes to the grave will be precisely the same body that will be raised from the dead and finally taken to heaven. I contended for that doctrine in this discussion.

As before stated, after this discussion was over, the visits of those men ceased among the churches in our part of the country, and as I will give another chapter concerning the doctrine of the ressurrection of the body, I will close this chapter, stating that on the question of the ressurrection, our churches have been blessed with peace in our section of the country ever since that debate.

CHAPTER XIX.

During the year 1871, and '72, I began to get acquainted with the brethren of Wabash District Association. I visited their Association once or twice, and visited a number of their churches, and found that among them and some of their correspondents, the question was being agitated as to what it is that is born again in the work of regeneration. Some of the preachers of that, and some other Associations, differed so widely about it that they were accused of taking positions that were very extreme. One man was accused of claiming that the body was no part of the child of God. Another denied any distinction of soul and body, claiming that the man that was born again, to use their own language, was the man that ate bacon and cabbage. There might have been other issues among the people, but about that time I met a man by the name of G. W. Paine, who denied the doctrine that the soul was born again in the work of regeneration, and made light of the idea that any part of the man went to heaven when the body died. The first hint that I ever had from him on this question, was in a conversation which I overheard between him and another brother in Paris, Illinois. As soon as I had an opportunity, I asked him if he believed that there was a distinction between the soul and body, and if he believed that the soul went to heaven when the body died. He held forth the idea that man went to the grave and remained there until the resurrection, and that if he went to the grave he did not go to heaven. He denied being a soul-sleeper, but at the same time in speaking of the state of the dead, he had the whole man in the grave. He said when the Bible said soul it meant man, and when it said man it meant soul. According to his own definitions, I sometimes called him soul-sleeper, and sometimes accused him of believing that man had no soul, the latter, I think perhaps is the most proper name. He also held forth the idea that the flesh and bones of Jesus Christ had existed from all eternity, and that no part of the body of the Savior was taken from the Virgin Mary except the blood. In conversation with him, I asked him this question: "Jesus Christ said to the thief on the cross, 'To-day shalt thou be with me in paradise.' Where is paradise of which the Savior spoke on that occasion?" He said it was the grave. I then asked him, "If the grave was paradise, why would not both the thieves be in paradise when they went to the grave?" This question he did not answer, if I remember correctly. He finally began to make visits among the churches and country where I lived, and as is always the case, when heresy is introduced among a people, he had a following. I opposed his doctrine, and I also opposed him as a man. Finally the churches refused to open their doors to him to preach, because he advocated the doctrine that I have already mentioned in this chapter. During the agitation of this question among our brethren, I became more discouraged in the ministry than at any other one thing that could have happened. I did not believe that doctrine. I believed that there was a distinction of soul and body in the man, and that the soul was born again in the work of regeneration, that it went to heaven at the dissolution of the body, and that in the resurrection, the body would be changed and taken to heaven, and that soul and body thus united would make a complete man, capable of enjoying heaven with all that heaven means. I still believe that doctrine. There has never been a moment of time when I thought on that subject that these have not been my sentiments, and so far as the pre-existence of the children of God is concerned, I never have believed that they actually existed. I have believed that God has known them from all eternity, and that it was as easy for Him to know them before they existed as afterwards. I believe that God made his people, both soul and body, and I have never believed that he brought any part of them down from heaven.

I also believe that Jesus Christ took everything from the Virgin Mary, his mother, that pertains to his humanity. I do not now, nor have I ever believed In the pre-existence of human nature. Because I contended for what I believed on these things, and opposed what I did not believe, some of the brethren thought very hard of me, especially the admirers of Mr. Paine. One man who had been, and is yet a friend of mine, spoke to me on one occasion concerning the matter about this way: "Let me tell you as a friend, that when you undertake to fight Elder Paine, you are killing yourself. You are jealous of him—that is the trouble. He can beat you preaching. He does not even leave you the bone to gnaw on, that is the reason you are opposed to him." I replied to him that if my opposition to Elder Paine and his doctrine killed me, to just let me die. I expected to oppose him and his doctrine as long as I was able to do so, and thought it necessary. His doctrine is heresy, and it is not good for the church.

CHAPTER XX.

There were a few occurences that took place between Elder Paine and myself that I wish now to notice. In he first place, when I first met him, and had the conversation with him in Paris, Illinois, I asked him if he preached that doctrine wherever he went. He said he did, and I asked him if it did not cause trouble wherever it was preached, and he said it had caused a great deal of trouble. I told him I did not want him to come into my country and preach that doctrine, for we had had all the trouble there on different doctrines that we cared about. He remarked that this was a free country, and that he had the right to go where he wished. I told him that if he would just admit that he was not a Baptist, and wanted to preach in my country, I would use my influence to get him a house and a congregation at any time. But for him to come there and preach that doctrine and claim it as Baptist doctrine was something that I did not want. He never had at that time been in our country. This was the first time I had ever seen him. Finally the first thing I knew, by corresponding with some of the brethren whose names he had gotten, there had been a list of appointments published for him, and he had filled them. I was away from home at one time some two or three weeks, and when I got back home, I found that he had been in a number of our churches, and had preached. The brethren all seemed to think that he was very able. I heard some of them speak of him, as to his ability, in the most favorable terms. None of them seemed to have discovered that he was not sound. I questioned several of them as to his doctrinal positions, but I found that they had not detected anything wrong. I felt that, perhaps, he was a policy man, and preferred to ingratiate himself into the good feelings and confidence of our people before he advanced his doctrinal ideas. But there was one good old brother in the ministry who had heard him, who, I felt confident, would be as likely to know whether he was all right or not as any man in our association. That was Elder John Hunsinger. I was eager to see him, so I finally went to his meeting. I arrived at his house on Friday night, and stayed over night with him, and had a good opportunity to converse with him concerning Elder Paine. I introduced the subject by saying: "Well, Uncle Johnny, I suppose you have had a new preacher visiting among you." He said, "Yes, we have had a visitor. Elder Paine has been among us." I asked, "Well, how do you like him?" I saw that he rather shook his head, and I felt happy to think that Uncle Johnny had detected him. I felt confident that he knew that Elder Paine was a heretic. He remarked, after shaking his head significantly, that we might as well open our doors to Elder Trainer or any other heresy, for the doctrine that Elder Paine preaches is no better than the doctrine taught by Elder Trainer. That afforded me a great deal of consolation. I have always had a great desire that our brethren dwell in peace, and that they advocate the doctrine of the Bible.

Among other things that Elder Paine preached, besides the no-soul doctrine, as I have stated in another chapter, was that the flesh and bones of Christ and his human nature had existed in heaven from all eternity. I had about as little use for this as for the no-soul doctrine, or the non-resurrection doctrine, and I had frequent conversations with him upon that subject. He seemed very ready to accuse me of being jealous of him because I was so bitterly opposed to the doctrine he was advocating. I could not conscientiously be still, and hold my peace, and let that doctrine overrun our part of the country. At one time when he came through, he had an appointment at my church in Grayville to preach one sermon at night. He came to my house that morning, and remained until the next morning. We had ample time for considerable conversation during the day. At the supper table he made the remark to me that he had one request to make, and that was that if he should preach anything that night that I did not endorse, I should speak to him privately about it, and say nothing publicly upon the subject. I told him that we had tried that course with some of those men who denied the resurrection until they had greatly the advantage of us, and that I had concluded that if a man preached anything in my pulpit, to my people, that I did not believe to be true, I should expose it at once publicly, so that the Baptists might be aware of the fact that I did not believe it. We went to church that night, and I felt confident of the fact that he was under the impression that if he should preach anything that I did not endorse, I would reply to him. It was the only time that I ever heard him preach. I had never heard him up to that time, and I have never heard him since. He took a text and preached a good discourse, which was very comforting to myself and my people. I felt so proud of it, that when he was through I arose and publicly endorsed it, and told the people that was just what my people believed. We sang a song and the people came forward and gave him the hand as an evidence that they believed his preaching. He said nothing about the controverted points of which we had been talking, but some time after that, on two or three different occasions, I was plucked to one side by my brethren, and asked if I had undergone a change upon that subject. I told them no, I believed just what I always had, but did not ask them at first why they asked me such a question, until it had been repeated several times. Then I began to make inquiries and was told that Elder Paine himself had gone away and told the people that he preached the eternal flesh and bones of Jesus in my pulpit, and that I and my brethren endorsed it, and that I called on them to come forward and give him their hand as a token that they endorsed his doctrine. I did not feel much surprised when I was told that Elder Paine had so wilfully misrepresented what I had said, for he had prevaricated so many times, while he was in our part of the country, on different occasions, that I had lost confidence in his veracity. I was not alone in that view. A number of other brethren soon found out that it would not do to depend too much on his word.

He was at Mount Pleasant Church on one occasion, and the brethren requested him to come out on those points plainly in his Sunday discourse, so they would know just where he stood, but he politely declined and preached a good sermon, that I suppose no Primitive Baptist would make any serious objections to. But afterwards he preached at a brother's house in the neighborhood, and in his discourse stated that he could prove by the Scriptures that Jesus Christ was on earth three times before he was born of the Virgin Mary, and that he ate meat, and after his meeting was over he walked around among the brethren, and seemed to feel very much elated, with the thought that all those brethren were going to take his doctrine. I think, however, that this was the last time that he was ever in our country, until the doors of our churches were closed against him. I was told that he thought very hard of me for opposing him in that country, but I feel thankful that his preaching, with all the zeal and ability that he possessed, did not effect a division among our people, and perhaps very few if any of the brethren of the Skillet Fork Association fell in with his doctrines, concerning what it is that is born again in the work of regeneration in time, and the pre-existence of the flesh and bones of Jesus Christ.

So far as preacher jealousy is concerned, I confess

that I was jealous of Elder Paine. It did hurt me to see good brethren falling in with him, and to see that they were his warm admirers. I think I would be jealous of any other man under the same circumstances, and I should do very little to encourage them to come among my people. I did not believe that man is all soul, nor that he is all body, but that he is possessed of both soul and body, I believe that still, and I think that is the doctrine held by the Regular Baptist people, as a denomination. I do not know how many sorts of criticism were made to the doctrine that there is a distinction between soul and body. One man, for instance, would ask, "What is the soul of man?" seeming to think that if we could not tell just what it is, that there certainly is no such thing. Another would ask, "Did you ever read in the Bible of a never-dying soul?" Of course no man ever read that expression in the Bible, but we do read in the Bible, in very plain and unmistakable terms, that the soul survives the body, and the fact that we are not able to find a Bible definition of the soul, in so many words, is not to be taken as an evidence that there is no such thing. Perhaps those same men would be just as badly puzzled, many of them, if they were called on to tell what the body of man is, and give all its parts and minutia. They would be just as badly puzzled if they were called on to tell what is the mind of man, and how is it connected with the body, and yet we know that man has a mind, and the fact that we can not explain anything, is no evidence against its truthfulness. The Bible says soul and boyd, and it always has said it.

CHAPTER XXI.

In the month of February, 1881, I held a three days' discussion with a gentleman by the name of Williams, in Franklin County, Illinois, on the following proposition: "The Scriptures teach that there will be a general resurrection of the bodies of all the sons and daughters of the first man Adam, or natural man, some of them to endless life, and some to endless punishment." Mr. Williams was a Universalist, and while he professed to believe in the salvation of "all men," as he said, he did not believe that Adam's posterity would be saved. In this chapter, I shall give an outline of the arguments I used in affirmation of the proposition stated above, without undertaking to give any of his arguments whatever. I will proceed:

Definitions: By the term Scriptures, I mean the books of the Old and New Testaments of the common version, known as King James' translation.

By the term teach, I mean to impart the knowledge of. I also mean by the term teach to give intelligence concerning; to tell impressively; to exhibit.

By the term general, I mean the resurrection will embrace all mankind.

By the term resurrection, I mean a rising again; resumption of vigor.

By the term bodies, I mean persons; human beings, I mean the body that God formed of the dust of the ground.

By the term sons and daughters, I mean the entire progeny of Adam, whether male or female.

By the expression first man, or Adam, or natural man, I mean the man who is possessed of soul, flesh and blood, that we see moving about here in the world, that sickens and dies, and that is a visible, tangible human being.

By the expression, some to endless life, I mean that in the future state they will be raised a spiritual body, which is that they will be made spiritual, and that they will not be natural then like the first Adam, but spiritual like the second Adam, and that their life in that spiritual and glorified state will never end.

By the expression, endless punishment, I mean a punishment that will never cease. As to the nature of the life or the eternal punishment, I shall have nothing to say, as that is not a part of the issue. The issue is whether they will be raised to eternal punishment or not, and that they will be, is what I am to affirm, and what he is to deny. The expressions of Scripture relative to this subject are, punishment, torment, death, damnation, shame and everlasting contempt, or separation, and while the term death is frequently employed I believe it to be death in the sense of separation, and not that they possess no vitality. This state will be a state of wretchedness and misery that will never cease.

My first argument is based on the fact that Adam, the natural, earthly man, is the man that God made or created in his image, and after his likeness, and that he is the man of the Bible, the man proper. To prove this I quote Genesis, ii; 7. "And the Lord God formed man out of the dust of the ground and breathed into his nostrils the breath of life, and man became a living soul." I Corinthians, xv; 45, 46, 47. "And so it is written, The first man Adam was made a living soul; the last Adam was made a quickening spirit. Howbeit that was not first which is spiritual, but that which is natural, and afterward that which is spiritual. The first man is of the earth, earthy: the second man is the Lord from heaven." Again, Genesis, i- 26. "And God said, let us make man in our image, after our likeness, and let him have dominion over the fish of the sea, and over the fowls of the air, and over the cattle, and over the earth and every living thing that creepeth upon the earth." Genesis, v- 1. "This is the book of the generations of Adam. In the day that God created man, in the likeness of God made He him." Male and female created he them; and blessed them and called their name Adam, in the day when they were created." I claim that these texts of scripture fully sustain tbe arguments that I have made, that Adam is the man proper, the man of the Bible.

My second argument is that the people of God

were made of the dust of the ground. To prove this argument, I quote Isaiah lxiv-8-9. "But now, O Lord, thou art our Father; we are the clay and thou our potter: and we all are the work of thy hand. Be not wroth very sore, O Lord, neither remember iniquity forever; behold, see, we beseech thee we are thy people." From this text we learn that these were the people of God. They were clay; they were the work of God's hand. They never came from heaven. Job, xxxiii-4-7. "The spirit of God hath made me and the breath of the Almighty hath given me life. If thou canst answer me set thy words in order before me, stand up. Behold, I am according to thy wish in God's stead: I also am formed out of the clay. Behold my terror shall not make thee afraid, neither shall my hand be heavy upon thee." I, perhaps, introduced several other scriptures in the discussion, in support of that argument that it would be impossible to crowd into this chapter. My object is to give an outline of my arguments so that the reader may see the position that I occupied.

My third argument is that the only people that ever inhabited this world as a people, are the earthy. Adam and his progeny, so when we read of man in the Bible, we read of the earthy man and his offspring.

My fourth argument is that the man that is already named, and his offspring are the subjects of God's address all through the Bible. It was to Adam that God gave his law. It was Adam that transgressed the law. It is the transgressor that is the sinner, and it si the sinner that is subject to damnation.

My fiifth argument is that it is the earthy man that dies. Job xxi, 32, 33. "Yet shall he be brought to the grave and shall remain in the tomb. The clods of the valley shall be sweet unto him, and every man shall draw after him, as there are innumerable before him." Psalm xxii, 29. "All they that be fat upon earth shall eat and worship; all that go down to the dust shall bow before him; and none can keep alive his own soul." Psalm lxxxix, 48. "What man is he that liveth and shall not see death? shall he deliver his soul from the grave?" Eccl. i, 3, 4, "What profit hath a man of all his labor which he taketh under the sun? One generation passeth away, and another generation cometh; but the earth abideth forever." Psalm ciii, 10, 16, "He hath not dealt with us after our sins; nor rewarded us after our iniquities. For as the heaven is high above the earth, so great is his mercy toward them that fear him, As far as the east is from the west, so far hath he removed our transgressions from us. Like as a father pitieth his children, so the Lord pitieth them that fear him. For he knoweth our frame; he remembereth that we are dust. As for man his days are as grass; as a flower of the field, so he flourisheth. For the wind passeth over it, and it is gone; and the place thereof shall know it no more." The last text quoted proves not only that man dies, but it proves that he is of the dust of the ground and also that he is the object of salvation. From the fact it is said that "As far as the east is from the west, so far hath he removed our transgressions from us." This is never done for a people who are not interested in salvation.

My sixth argument is that the earthly Adam involved his own posterity in sin and death by his own disobedience, and that death is the result of sin. For proof of this argument I call attention to Romans, v, 12-21. "Wherefore as by one man sin entered into the world and death by sin, and so death passed upon all men, for that all have sinned. For until the law sin was in the world: but sin was not imputed when there is no law. Nevertheless death reigned from Adam to Moses even over them that had not sinned after the similitude of Adam's transgression, who is the figure of him that was to come. But not as the offense, so also is the free gift: for if through the offense of one many be dead, much more the grace of God, and the gift by grace, which is by one man, Jesus Christ, hath abounded unto many. And not as it was by one that sinned, so is the free gift: for the judgment was by one to condemnation, but the free gift is of many offenses unto justification. For if by one man's offense death reigned by one; much more they which receive abundance of grace and the gift of righteousness shall reign in life by one Jesus Christ. Therefore, as by the offense of one judgment came upon all men to condemnation; even so by the righteousness of one the free gift came upon all men unto justification of life. For as by one man's disobedience many were made sinners, so by the obedience of one shall many be made righteous. Moreover, the law entered, that the offense might abound. But where sin abounded, grace did much more abound: That as sin hath reigned unto death, even so might grace reign through righteousness unto eternal life by Jesus Christ our Lord." In addition to this text, to prove my sixth argument; I quote I Corinthians, xv, 21. "For since by man came death, by man also came the resurrection of the dead." Again, Romans, vi, 23. "For the wages of sin is death; but the gift of God is eternal life through Jesus Christ our Lord." I claim that these Scriptures establish my sixth argument, which is that the earthy Adam involved his own posterity into sin and death by his own disobedience, and that death is the result of sin.

My seventh argument is, that in order to have a resurrection there must be a death first, according to the definition of resurrection.

My eighth argument will be the meaning of the word grave and resurrection as used in the Bible.

CHAPTER XXII.

Now I come to the second part of my proposition, which is that the bodies of the people, of whom I have already been speaking, will be raised from the dead.

My first argument in favor of this part of the proposition, is that the doctrine of the resurrection of the body is directly asserted in the Old Testament, either in relation to individuals, or in a general manner. I call attention first to Isaiah xxvi, 19. "Thy dead men shall live, together with my dead body shall they arise. Awake and sing, ye that dwell in dust: for thy dew is as the dew of herbs, and the earth shall cast out the dead." Again, Daniel, xii, 1-2. "And at that time shall Michael stand up, the great prince which standeth for the children of thy people: and there shall be a time of trouble, such as never was since there was a nation even to that same time: and at that time thy people shall be delivered, every one that shall be found written in the book. And many of them that sleep in the dust of the earth shall awake, some to everlasting life, and some to shame and everlasting contempt." Another text, Hosea, xiii, 14. "I will ransom them from the power of the grave; I will redeem them from death: O death, I will be thy plagues; O grave, I will be thy destruction; repentance shall be hid from mine eyes." Isaiah, xxv, 7-8. "And he will destroy in this mountain the face of the covering cast over all the people, and the vail that is spread over all nations.

He will swallow up death in victory; and the Lord God will wipe away tears from off all faces; and the rebuke of His people will He take away from off all the earth, for the Lord hath spoken it."

My second argument is that the inspired men in the Old Testament times, have expressed their utmost confidence in the resurrection of the body. In proof of this argument, I quote Psalm xlix, 12-15. "Nevertheless, man being in honour abideth not: he is like the beasts that perish. This their way is their folly: yet their posterity approves their sayings. Like sheep they are laid in the grave; death shall feed on them; and the upright shall have dominion over them in the morning; and their beauty shall consume in the grave from their dwelling. But God will redeem my soul from the power of the grave, for He shall receive me." Again, Psalm, xvii, 15. "As for me I will behold thy face in righteousness: I shall be satisfied when I awake with thy likeness." One more text in support of this argument. Job, xix, 23-27. "Oh that my words were now written; Oh that they were printed in a book. That they were graven with an iron pen and lead in the rock forever. For I know that my Redeemer liveth, and that He shall stand at the latter day upon the earth; and though after my skin worms destroy this body yet in my flesh shall I see God; whom I shall see for myself, and mine eyes shall behold, and not another; though my reins be consumed within me." From this expression of Scripture I claim that the man of God in olden times confidently believed that, although they should be mown down with the sickle of death and cast into the grave, yet that they would be waked up out of that sleep to a life of eternal happiness and joy.

My third argument in favor of this part of the proposition is that the doctrine of the resurrection of the body was taught in the Old Testament, because the Jews generally believed in the resurrection. I argue that if the resurrection had not been taught in the Old Testament, that the Jews would not generally have held to that faith. But as an evidence that they did hold to it I quote Isaiah lxvi, 14. "And when ye see this your heart shall rejoice and your bones shall flourish like an herb; and the hand of the Lord shall be known toward His servants, and His indignation toward His enemies." Again, Matthew, xiv, 1-2. "At that time Herod the Tetrarch, heard of the fame of Jesus. And said unto his servants, This is John the Baptist; he is risen from the dead; and therefore mighty works do shew forth themselves in him." This expression shows that Herod believed in the resurrection of the dead. John xi, 23-24. "Jesus saith unto her, Thy brother shall rise again. Martha saith unto him, I know that he shall rise again in the resurrection at the last day." This text shows that Martha believed in the resurrection at the last day. Why she believed that doctrine if it had not been taught her is a question worthy of notice. I claim that the fact that she did believe it is good evidence that it was taught by the Old Testament Scriptures.

My fourth argument in favor of the resurrection, is that the doctrine of the resurrection is true, because on various occasions it had the tacit assent of Jesus Christ when he was here in the world. Luke xx, 27-38. "Master, Moses wrote unto us, If any man's brother die, having a wife and he die without children, that his brother should take his wife, and raise up seed unto his brother. There were therefore seven brethren: and the first took a wife and died without children. And the second took her to wife and he died childless. And the third took her; and in like manner the seven also: and they left no children and died. Last of all the woman died also. Therefore in the resurrection whose wife is she? for seven had her to wife. And Jesus answering said unto them, "The children of this world marry and are given in marriage. But they which shall be accounted worthy to obtain that world, and the resurrection from the dead, neither marry nor are given in marriage. Neither can they die any more: for they are equal unto angels; and are the children of God, being the children of the resurrection. Now that the dead are raised, even Moses shewed at the bush, when he calleth the Lord the God of Abraham, and the God of Isaac, and the God of Jacob. For he is not a God of the dead but of the living; for all live unto him." It seems to me that if the Sadduces had been correct in their denial of the resurrection of the body, that Jesus would have told them so and he did not. "But they which shall be accounted worthy to obtain that world and the resursection from the dead neither marry nor are given in marriage, neither can they die any more. "There are two thoughts in those two expressions. One is that Jesus believed that somebody would be worthy to obtain that world and the resurrection from the dead, and another is that they had died once. Hence, I claim that Jesus did not only give his tacit assent to the doctrine of the resurrection, but he plainly and unmistakably taught it.

My fifth argument is that the doctrine of the resurrection of the body was positively affirmed by the Lord himself. Luke xiv, 13, 14, "But when thou makest a feast, call the poor, the maimed, the lame, the blind; and thou shalt be blessed; for they cannot recompense thee; for thou shalt be recompensed at the resurrection of the just." If there is no resurrection, when will they be recompensed? If there is a resurrection of the just, then it must be a resurrection of the body, for it is the body that dies, and there is no resurrection without a death first. John, v, 28, 29, "Marvel not at this; for the hour is coming, in the which all that are in the graves shall hear his voice, and shall come forth; they that have done good, unto the resurrection of life, and they that have done evil, unto the resurrection of damnation." Again, John, vi, 54, "Whoso eateth my flesh and drinketh my blood, hath eternal life; and I will raise him up at the last day."

Argument sixth is that the apostles affirmed in unmistakable terms the doctrine of the resurrection of the body. Acts xxiv, 13, 15, "Neither can they prove the things whereof they now accuse me. But this I confess unto you, that after the way which they call heresy, so worship I the God of my fathers, believing all things which are written in the law and in the prophets; and have hope toward God, which they themselves also allow, that there shall be a resurrection of the dead both of the just and the unjust." Romans, viii, 10-11, "And if Christ be in you, the body is dead because of sin; but the spirit is life because of righteousness. But if the Spirit of him that raised up Jesus from the dead dwell in you, He that raised up Christ from the dead shall also quicken your mortal bodies by his spirit that dwelleth in you." II Corinthians, i, 8-9. "For we would not, brethren, have you ignorant of our trouble which came to us in Asia, that we were pressed out of measure, above strength, insomuch that we despaired even of life. But we had the sentence of death in ourselves, that we should not trust in ourselves, but in God, which raiseth the dead." Philippians, iii, 20-21. "For our conversion is in heaven; from whence also we look for the Savior, the Lord Jesus Christ; Who shall change our vile body, that it may be fashioned like unto his glorious body, according to the working whereby he is able even to subdue all things unto himself." I claim that these texts prove, with a great many others of the same character, in the New Testament, that the Apostles affirmed the resurrection of the body.

My seventh argument in favor of this doctrine is

founded on the connection of Hosea, xiii, 14 and I Corinthians, xv, 54 to 56. The first reads, "I will ransom them from the power of the grave. I will redeem them from death. O death, I will be thy plagues. O grave, I will be thy destruction. Repentance shall be hid from mine eyes." This was a prediction of the resurrection of the body. If it was a prediction by the Prophet of the Lord, it was something that has taken place since it was predicted, or else it is still to take place, or else it must be a false prediction. If it has taken place already, the Scriptures have said nothing about it, and if it has it has been since the writing of the fifteenth chapter of I Corinthians. For in that chapter, on the text referred to, we have the following language: "So when this corruptible shall have put on incorruption and this mortal shall have put on immortality, then shall be brought to pass the saying, that is written. "Death is swallowed up in victory." "The sting of death is sin, and the strength of sin is the law." The Apostle in this language is quoting the Prophet Hosea that I have already quoted, so it is very evident that the prophesy had not been fulfilled up to the time that Paul wrote his letter to the Corinthians. I feel confident that it has never been fulfilled since that time, so I argue that the Scriptures teach that it will be fulfilled.

My eighth argument is based on three quotations from David. Psalm, xvii, 15, which reads, "As for me I will behold thy face in righteousness. I shall be satisfied when I awake in thy likeness." And

Psalm, xlix, 15, "But God will redeem my soul from the power of the grave, for he shall receive me." I claim that this was David's confidence, and that David did not go to heaven and enjoy all these things bodily, when his body died, and left the world. As an evidence of that fact, I quote Acts, ii, 29 to 35. "Men and brethren, let me freely speak unto you of the patriarch David, that he is both dead and buried, and his sepulchre is with us unto this day. Therefore, being a prophet, and knowing that God has sworn with an oath to him, that of the fruit of his loins, according to the flesh, He would raise up Christ to sit on his throne; He, seeing this before, spoke of the resurrection of Christ; that His soul was not left in hell, neither His flesh did see corruption. This Jesus hath God raised up, whereof we all are witnesses. Therefore, being by the right hand of God exalted, and having received of the Father the promise of the Holy Ghost, he has shed forth this which ye now see and hear. For David is not ascended into the heavens; but he saith himself, The Lord said unto my Lord, Sit thou on my right hand, Until I make thy foes thy footstool." In this text the Apostle Peter says, "For David is not ascended into the heavens, but he saith himself, The Lord said unto my Lord, sit thou on my right hand." It is very evident here that the Apostle Peter was arguing for the truth of the resurrection of Christ, and referring to the language of David in which he predicted the death of Christ and his resurrection, Peter lets us know that David did not have allusion to himself in this prediction, from the very fact that David had not yet been raised from the dead, for in the twenty-ninth verse he said "Men and brethren let me freely speak unto you of the patriarch David, that he is both dead and buried." What died of David, and what is buried? It was his body, "and his sepulchre is with us unto this day." Now, if he is both dead and buried, and his sepulchre is with us to this day, it is very evident that he is not yet raised from the dead, therefore he was not speaking of himself in this prediction, but of Jesus Christ. For he himself is not yet ascended into heaven which evidently has allusion to his body, because it is yet in the sepulchre, but David's hope was that God would redeem his soul from the power of the grave, and that he should be waked up in the likeness of God, and his hope either was disappointed or will be disappointed, or else he is yet to be raised from the dead, and when we say raised from the dead we mean his body.

CHAPTER XXIII.

I now pass on to the third division of my proposition, which is that some of these bodies are raised to endless life and some to endless punishment. I will notice them in their order. First, then I propose to show from the Scriptures that some of the bodies will have endless life. To prove this, I refer first to Dan xiii, 2, which reads, "And many of them that sleep in the dust of the earth shall awake, some to everlasting life, and some to shame and everlasting contempt." We have everlasting life in this text, which means endless life. This we never hear Universalists deny. They argue that everlasting life is endless life, or at least they concede that fact. Another point in this text is that those who are to be raised to everlasting life are those who sleep in the dust of the earth. That must be the body. Again, I call attention to Luke, xx, 36. "Neither can they die any more." This is on the subject of the resurrection of the body, and taking the two verses together, beginning with the verse 35, we have the following: "But they which shall be accounted worthy to obtain that world and the resurrection from the dead, neither marry, nor are given in marriage, neither can they die any more." If they cannot die any more, they certainly have endless life. There is no evasion of that conclusion, and the very fact that they cannot die any more signifies that they did die once, and that they have been raised to life again, and that now they shall not die any more. I claim that I have proved a point by this expression that will never be answered. Another text that I will introduce is Matthew xxv, 46. "And these shall go away into everlasting punishment, but the righteous into life eternal." I believe that I have, beyond the shadow of successful contradiction proven that the bodies will live forever. I will add one or two quotations and pass on. 1 Corinthians, xv, 51 to 55 inclusive. "Behold, I shew you a mystery; We shall not all sleep, but we shall all be changed, in a moment, in the twinkling of an eye, at the last trump: for the trumpet shall sound, and the dead shall be raised incorruptible, and we shall be changed. So when this corruptible shall have put on incorruption, and this mortal shall have put on immortality, then shall be brought to pass the saying that is written, Death is swallowed up in victory. O death, where is thy sting? O grave, where is thy victory?" I argue from this text that the bodies will be glorified with incorruption and immortality," that is, the bodies of the righteous, and if they are incorruptible and immortal, they will never die. If they will never die it will be because they have life that is endless. They cannot die any more.

I now proceed to notice the last part of the proposition, that some of these bodies will suffer endless punishment. My arguments upon this part of the question will be founded upon Scriptures which I shall introduce to prove that there is a future and endless punishment. First, I call attention to Mark, iii, 28-29: "Verily I say unto you, All sins shall be forgiven unto the sons of men, and blasphemies wherewithsoever they shall blaspheme; but he that shall blaspheme against the Holy Ghost hath never forgiveness, but is in danger of eternal damnation." I claim that eternal damnation is endless damnation, the same as eternal life is endless life. And notice, the sons of men are spoken of here, which must be Adam's posterity. I quote again, Luke xii: "And I say unto you my friends, be not afraid of them that kill the body, and after that have no more that they can do, but I will forewarn you whom you shall fear. Fear Him which after He hath killed hath power to cast into hell; yea, I say unto you, fear Him." From this text we find that the hell here is not death. It does not matter how Universalists may undertake to evade the conclusion this text says it in so many words, and the thing killed in this text is the body, and we are warned to fear Him that after He has killed the body, is able to cast it—the body—into hell. Hence there is a hell after death into which the body is certain to go. Again, Matthew x, 28, "And fear not them which kill the body, but are not able to kill the soul, but rather fear Him which is able to destroy both soul and body in hell." Now, notice it is not only the soul that goes to hell according to this text, but it is the body as well, and from the language recorded by Luke, it is after the death of the body. Again, Mark ix, 42 to 48 inclusive. "And whosoever shall offend one of these little ones that believe in me, it is better for him that a mill-stone were hanged about his neck and he were cast into the sea. And if thy hand offend thee cut it off: it is better for thee to enter into life maimed, than having two hands to go into hell into the fire that never shall be quenched: Where their worm dieth not, and the fire is not quenched. And if thy foot offend thee, cut it off: It is better for thee to enter halt into life, than having two feet to be cast into hell into the fire that never shall be quenched: Where their worm dieth not, and the fire is not quenched. And if thine eye offend thee pluck it out: It is better to enter the kingdom of God with one eye, than having two eyes to be cast into hell fire: Where their worm dieth not and the fire is not quenched." That is all the argument I make from that text.

This discussion, as I have already stated, lasted three days, and I spent one day on each division of the proposition, in which I amplified my arguments more extensively than I have here, and during the time of the discussion, my opponent denied that any human body ever went to heaven, stating that if I could have proved that one human body ever went to heaven that he would yield the point. I quoted the text in the second of Acts, where it is said, "Neither did His flesh see corruption." In speaking of the body of Christ, if His flesh did not see corruption, it must be incorruptible, and whether it ever went to heaven or not, it saw no corruption and never will. According to this text, if it should have been left in the grave, it is in an incorruptible state but the fact that it saw no corruption is the very best evidence that it certainly went to heaven. The last time that it was ever seen it was going up, until a cloud received it out of the sight of the apostles.

I have given this brief account of the discussion as an evidence that I believe in the doctrine of the resurrection of the body of all the people, and that the Scriptures teach that doctrine. I think it is a mat- of vital importance, for upon the doctrine of the resurrection hangs the destiny of men. It has been said that Mr. Williams, my opponent never came into that vicinity again.

CHAPTER XXIV.

I am now in my thirtieth year in the ministry, and my experience is such that I often think if I had my time to go over, I could make many improvements, but it may be if I had my life to live over again, that under the same circumstances, I would do no better than I have. My experience as a minister has been one peculiar to myself. I have found that no other minister I have ever heard talk, has had the same experience that I have had. When I first began to exercise in public, my recollection is, that I was more willing to try to preach than was becoming. I thought many times that I would be glad to have an opportunity to try to preach. I was well aware of the fact that propriety would dictate for me to remain silent, and occupy an humble seat, when there were older ministers present; yet that did not suit me all the time, for my desires to exercise in public were such, that if I was invited, I was rather too willing to get up. I frequently feared that the brethren would notice this in me, and I was well aware of the fact that it would be against me if they did. I very well knew that nothing would hurt a young minister quicker in the estimation of his brethren in the ministry, as well as the people generally, than for him to be too anxious to preach. Yet I was distressed frequently in my mind to keep my feelings concealed in this particular. I do not know just how many years I had this evil to contend with, but if the brethren did notice it in me, they seemed to treat me well, and encouraged me to exercise my gift, and invited me to their meetings, as if they did not notice anything wrong. They seemed to put me forward, fully as much, or more than they ought to have done. I still think that I had as much encouragement from the brethren generally as was due me, and that this has been the case all my life. I have traveled over a great portion of several states and preached among the brethren. I have been received cordially everywhere I have been. After I had been preaching a few years, there was quite a change in my feelings, so that I became as unwilling to preach as I had hitherto been willing. I thought for a while that if the brethren would not meet me with solicitations, and urgent appeals to come to their meetings, I could remain at home very well satisfied, not to preach at all. I had the care of churches, and when I went to meeting, I really dreaded for the moment to arrive that I should begin services. I often felt while on my way to church, that it would be a great relief to me, if some brother in the ministry would happen to come, who would do the preaching. I suffered a great deal in mind from this state of feeling. I often wished, that as I must preach, I were more willing. I sometimes took my case to the Lord, and begged him, that if it was my duty to preach, it should not be such a burden to me. Frequently, when I went to meeting and found some other brethren in the ministry there, I would almost become impatient with them, if they insisted on me doing the preaching, and when trying to preach, I often looked at my watch to see if I had not been talking long enough to call it a discourse, and quit. This was a fearful state of mind to be in while having to engage in the ministry almost every day. I frequently saw brethren in the ministry who seemed willing, and who on the first intimation that they were to preach, were ready. I sometimes wished that I felt that way. I think I know what it is to wish very much to preach and not have an opportunity, but I also know what it is to be compelled to preach when I do not wish to. This frame of mind oppressed me for a few years, I do not remember just how long, and then my mind underwent another change. I have since felt perfectly passive in the hands of the brethren, and perhaps as easy upon the subject of preaching as any man among our brethren. If I go to meeting and there are other brethren present, it is all right with me to try to preach if the brethren say so, and it is all right with me to listen to other brethren preach, if the brethren say so. I am perfectly willing to try to discharge my duty and live at the feet of my brethren, and serve them, when they ask me to, in the best manner I can. I seldom in late years make any calculations how I shall preach. When I was younger I often contemplated a big sermon for special occasions, and about as often I failed to do any preaching at all. I have, many times, arose to preach when I did not think I could say a word, and it seemed I was blessed with the presence of the Lord, and the power of his might to preach to the edification and encouragement of his people. In fact matters have seldom ever worked out in my experience, either as a Christian, or as a minister, according to the plan that I have arranged. I have even taken texts thinking that I would present certain points or arguments or thoughts during the course of my remarks, and would spend my time on an entirely different line of thought. I am reminded many times of what I have heard other brethren in the ministry say, and that is that they never could learn how to preach. I think what I have learned might be profitable to younger men in the ministry, provided they will study carefully what I have said, and examine themselves carefully. I have studied a great deal about preparing notes, or as some men call it sketches, or skeletons of sermons, but I have never tried such a thing, and I think that I would be very awkward at anything of that kind. I feel confident of one thing, that if I were to write out a sermon and read it, I might be as able to read it at one time as another, but I do not think I would be a very good judge as to whether the Lord was in that matter or not. I have written speeches and read them, and my judgment is that if I speak extemporaneously, I can tell better whether I really have the presence of the Lord or not. I take it as an evidence that the Lord is with me when I feel a deep and abiding interest on the subject of which I treat, and that he is not with me when I feel no interest in the subject I am trying to talk about. Be that as it may, there is one thing certain, and that is that I cannot live contented and neglect the ministry. I have tried that, and it does not take a great while of running after the world, until I begin to feel guilty that I am neglecting my duty as a minister of the gospel, and as to impressions where to go, I am governed by two things. I have visited churches where I had no liberty whatever to preach and had no particular enjoyment religiously with the people in those churches, although they were good, kind and godly people and seemed deeply interested in my welfare and comfort, and would insist that I visit them again. I never have as great a desire to go to such places as to others. Again there are places that I have visited, that from the very start, it seemed that I was blest with excellent liberty, and the people were built up and edified under my little efforts, and I was made to feel that the Lord was present and that surely it was right for me to be there. I would rather feel impressed in my own mind to go, than to have invitations from the brethren. However, when it comes to going and visiting among the brethren, everywhere, I am inclined to go more where they invite me than where they do not. And I would advise brethren in the ministry who feel that it is their duty to travel a great deal, to be governed more by the invitations they get from the brethren than by merely the desire to travel. I have at times thought that a man might possibly be mistaken about it being his duty to go. The fact that a man desires to preach is not always an evidence that God has called him to the work of the ministry. Many men have been called to preach who have been unwilling to go. In fact, this seems to be the rule, that when the Lord first impresses them that it is their duty to go and preach, they revolt against it until the Lord makes them willing. It is a matter of necessity that a minister of the gospel should leave his home and travel about the world to preach the gospel. It never was intended of the Lord that men should volunteer to preach the gospel but that He Himself would call them forth.

CHAPTER XXV.

There are two or three things in the work of the ministry that I have noticed among our brethren, and I would love to see them abandoned by our people. While I have been what our brethren usually term a doctrinal preacher, yet I am opposed to the idea of our brethren in setting forth and defending their distinguishing principles, pursuing a course that will wound the feelings of people of other denominations. I have heard men preach who, I thought, were very rough in their expressions about other people. The idea of telling a man that the reason he does not understand the doctrine of the Bible as we do, is because he has no grace, is, in my judgment, a mistake. And there is nothing in such a course as that to edify our people or convince our opponents as to the truth of our opinion.

I visited a little town, not long since, where our people had held an Association a few months before, and it was said that the different denominations in the little village opened the doors of their houses to our brethren and invited them to preach especially on Sunday, and that some of our brethren preached in such a manner, as to so offend the people who owned the house in which they were preaching, that they refused to stay and listen to them. Whenever a minister drives his congregation away, by being rough, he is doing no good for the cause of Christ. The ablest defenders of our doctrine are men who draw crowds to them, instead of driving them away, and I should take it as an evidence that I was wrong either in sentiment or in spirit, if good people would arise from my congregation and move out. Reasonable people, who are intelligent, will stay and listen to a man preach even if they do not endorse him, if they are respected as they should be by the speaker. I do not think that it is an evidence of soundness in doctrine to call people by hard names who oppose what I believe, and I think that our ministers should preach for some other cause than to try to establish the fact that they are sound in the faith. I would love to call the attention of the reader to this fact, that I think I have seen men who rejoice more under the voice of that minister who abuses other people, than of the one who describes the dependence and helplessness of the poor sinner, in his lost and ruined state, and the all-sufficiency of God's grace through Jesus Christ, as a remedy for the disease of sin and its plague in the heart. I do not know that it is always an evidence of grace in the heart, that a brother will smile and sanction me more when I am fighting Arminians than he will when I am preaching on experience or practice. The Apostle says, "If ye live after the flesh ye shall die, but if ye through the spirit do mortify the deeds of the body ye shall live." I have been afraid many times that our brethren live after the flesh too much, in wanting to hear a great deal said against their religious neighbors, by the minister in his sermon, and rejoicing at it when it is said. The Apostle Paul said "I determined not to know anything among you save

Jesus Christ and him crucified." I am of the opinion that every sentence of gospel must have Jesus in it, and every word be seasoned with grace if it does good to the people of God's cause and kingdom, and the glory of his name. I once heard of a minister who was preaching for a church, only a short distance from a church of another denomination, and they got to reviewing each other's remarks, and the Baptist minister was so rough that when he would refer to the other man he would say "That abominable hypocrite." His brethren would chuckle and laugh at the idea of his "peeling" the other preacher so. My judgment is that there was no gospel or Spirit of Christ in that kind of a course. Perhaps Jesus was not at the meeting at all, and when the congregation dispersed if they had anything to say about the sermon at all, it was to rejoice at the manner in which our preacher had "skinned the other man." Brethren in the ministry, suppose we abandon that kind of a course, if we have ever been guilty of it, and if we have to make any reference to any other minister, let us not treat him as if he were a criminal, and set him down with thieves, liars, hypocrites and everything abominable. I think brethren make a wonderful mistake in that line.

There is another thing I have noticed in my life, and that is when we have an able minister, come to see us we think we would like to have him to preach in our little town. He is so able and so smart that we would love for our Arminian neighbors to hear him, and I fear it has often been the case that some of our preachers have been called on to go to a town to preach more to show the town people that the Old Baptists had a preacher that they were not ashamed of, than to have the gospel preached to those people. I am opposed to a course of that kind, and would admonish the brethren never to undertake to make an exhibit of their preacher. The idea of a preacher going to a place for no other purpose than to make the people think he is smart, is very foreign to the calling of a gospel minister. I think it is time for our brethren who have been inclined to things of this sort, to stop and think, "Is this right"? Am I living after the flesh, or is this the doings of God's holy spirit"? I once heard of a preacher who took for his text, "Beware of dogs." He told the congregation that there was a wonderful difference between a dog and a sheep, and his application of the two seemed to be that the sheep were Old School Baptists, and that the dog was the Arminian. He said that a sheep loved grass and could live on grass, that it could not have anything better, and he seemed to think that grass in his application was the truth, or Old School Baptist doctrine. He said a dog did not eat grass unless he wanted to vomit, and that was the way the Arminian was by the truth. He never swallowed the truth unless he wanted to vomit, and he was certain to vomit if he swallowed it. The brethren under his voice chuckled and snickered and were ready to say at the close of his sermon "I tell you, he is a good one. Did you ever hear a man that could beat him? Wonder what that Methodist man thought about it? If I was him I would go home and crawl into my hole." Reader, what do you think of that kind of a course for Christian people as they go home from their house of worship? The Lord deliver us from such a course of preaching as that. It is all wrong. My judgment is that there is more of the flesh in such a meeting as that than anything else, and I feel to thank the Lord that, although my brethren have accused me of being rough and severe on the Arminians, I have never called them hypocrites, neither have I ever unchristianized them. While I do not believe their doctrine, I believe they are as good as I am; and while I do not believe their institutions are of God, nor their doctrine true, yet I believe they do great good in the world, and are Christian people, and I believe they should be treated with all the respect due intelligent Christian men and women by our people. No reasonable man will expect our preachers to preach to please him, neither will a reasonable man fall out with one of our preachers if he, in the right spirit preaches the Baptist doctrine, and presents, in the right kind of a manner, his objections to the doctrine of their people. I am aware of the fact that a great many people seem to think that it is very wrong to say anything about other peoples' views of religion, at all. I think that is a mistake. The truth is worth contending for, and if it is preached in its purity, and simplicity, it will commend itself and its preacher to other men's consciences in the sight of God, and it is certainly unnecessary to abuse those who do not believe it. It is too late to undertake to convince a man that he is wrong, and that you are right, after you have insulted him, but to gain his good will and confidence, and then you have his ear, and if he is never convinced, he is as good as he was when you found him, and as long as he acts the gentleman, he deserves to be treated as such by you. These are my convictions about fighting, but I am far from believing that, in order not to offend other people, we should keep our doctrine to ourselves. I believe that I have the right to preach the doctrine I believe and oppose the doctrine I do not believe, no matter who does believe it and the man who falls out with me for it simply meddles where he has no business to meddle. This is a free country, and I do think that an Old Baptist preacher is in the very poorest business that he could be in, to go about apologizing to the Arminians for preaching the Baptist doctrine. If it is the truth and he believes it, there is no apology due for preaching it, and if it is not the truth and he does not believe it, he should not preach it, so in either case apologies are out of place.

CHAPTER XXVI.

In the foregoing chapter I have said that I thought it was wrong to fight other denominations by abusing them. I think there are extremes both ways. There are some of our brethren who seem to have an idea that if a man preaches doctrine at all, and distinguishes between his own sentiments and those of other people, he is skinning some one. This class of our ministers are very eager to discourage the idea of preaching doctrine, at all. They seem to think the best way to do, is not to treat on doctrinal differences between us and others. They frequently encourage people of other denominations to think that a man who will preach doctrine is a fighter. It is often the case that impressions are made against our brethren on the minds of our Arminian neighbors as fighters, because they set forth the doctrinal differences between themselves and others. I have been told that certain men have said they would not go to hear me preach, because I always got up with my arms full of clubs. Men who are acquainted with me do not talk so much this way about me. I do not feel disposed to manifest egotism upon that subject, but I never did preach a congregation away. As a general rule, where I have preached the longest I have the best congregations. I never thought it was fair for one preacher to want to dictate to himself, and then to another preacher, how they should both preach. I have always been willing for my brethren to exhort, or to talk about experience, or anything they saw fit, so long as they preach the truth, and I have thought that some men object to my manner of preaching, simply because I do not preach as they do. That I cannot help.

Another thing on the subject of preaching, that is worthy of notice, is that our brethren have neglected reading more than they should. However, I think of late years that there is an improvement in that direction. There has been a great deal of improvement since I first began the ministry. When I was young, it was very common for our brethren to throw out insinuations against a man who would read a great deal in other books, aside from the Bible. I have known some of our old ministers, who were really able, to have no other library but the Bible, and brethren have said when they would find a minister reading and studying the Scripture, that they had no confidence in a man who had to study what he was going to say. I am of the opinion that our brethren, who talk that way concerning a minister, are very much mistaken as to what our ministers can do. The Apostle told Timothy to study. Study the Scripture, and be as well informed on everything else as he possibly could. A good store of general information will not hurt a preacher. I have seen men arise to preach and heard them announce their text and then make the remark that they had no idea what they were going to say. I think that is true many times, that a minister does not know what he will say, because he may think that he is going to say something, and not say it, or he may think that he is not going to say certain things, and yet say them. But no minister is very well qualified to handle any subject before his audience, in a manner to teach them, unless he has some knowledge of the subject himself. We must be masters of what we teach, and one Bible qualification of a minister of the gospel is to be apt to teach. The man who knows nothing, can teach nothing. It is true that a man may know a great deal, and yet not be able to teach anything, but we know that it is true that if he knows nothing he cannot teach. "Study to show thyself approved of God; a workman not to be ashamed, rightly dividing the word of truth." This is the language of the Apostle Paul to a young minister, who had known the Scriptures from a child, and if it was necessary for Timothy to study, it is also necessary for ministers to study nowadays. I think that many times if a minister would take pains to acquaint himself with the state and condition of his church and the condition of its members, he might many times be impressed to take a text and preach on a subject, that he would not think of taking without such a knowledge of his people. A minister should look around and see what is going on and what his people are doing, and then he will be more likely to have something profitable to talk to them about than he otherwise would. It is not always an evidence of soundness to see a man afraid of doing what other people do. I remember I once attended the ordination of a minister. I was called on to deliver the charge and, because I had something to say about propriety, I was accused of having read the Methodist discipline, before I got half a mile from the meeting-house. I have always claimed that if the Methodists had anything good, I wanted it. If the Missionary Baptists have anything good or if any other people have anything good, I think we ought to have it, and I never saw any good reason for rejecting anything simply because somebody else, of a different denomination had it. I have heard good songs many times, that are found in the hymn books of other denominations and that are sung by almost every denomination, and some of them are sung by most of our people, but to some people among the Old Baptists such songs are very much out of place. I have spoken of or recommended a song many times, and have been answered by this remark: "I have heard that song sung so much by the Methodists that I do not like to hear it sung; or "The Methodists sing that song; or "That song belongs to the Methodists;" as if Baptists must not sing it, if the Methodists do. I have thought that if we are never to do anything that other people do, we will have to quit preaching, praying, and going to church, for other people do all these things. Besides all those good things that other people have, we had first; and we should not give them up. We should never refuse to use a good thing religiously simply because the Methodists or any other people use it. I have been told many times that such and such things were not Baptist usage and I have almost always replied that Baptist usage is not a standard. When we come to quote Baptist usage on anything religiously, we find ourselves lost, for there is no one church that can be a standard for other churches. Each Baptist church is an independent organization of its own, and each one has rules and usages of its own. I have seen things practiced in some churches, that I am satisfied would be very bitterly opposed in other churches, of the Old Baptist order. I believe if one church can practice a thing and be good Baptists, any other church may practice the same thing and be good Baptists. I also believe that if one church can do without that practice and be a good Baptist church, any other church may do the same; but the fact that my church never practiced such a thing, is no reason that your church should not. If a church is pursuing a course that is contrary to the Scriptures, either in doctrine or practice, she should quit it, and no Baptist church should give countenance to the doctrine or practice. I have seen a great many Baptist churches of our faith and order, who at their meetings, took up public collections from their congregations just like the Arminians and other denominations in this country, by passing the hat. The Baptists of the Ketockton and Ebeneezer Associations of Virginia and perhaps all other Baptists in the east have that practice among them. I visited Elder Chick's church in Washington city and they took up a public collection and I am told that all the Baptists in the east and northeast practice that course. If the Baptists in this country should undertake such a thing, there would be very serious objections raised to it; but I think those eastern people are good Baptists and they have that practice. If they were going to quote Baptist usage, they would be in favor of public collections, but if we were going to quote Baptist usage, we would simply quote what we are used to here. In no case can we take usage as a standard for all Baptists everywhere, neither should we say that people who do those things or do them not, are not Baptists. We have no right to say that. I mention the subject of public collections as an example, because there are many other things in which churches differ from each other as to their customs, that are too numerous to mention here. I believe that almost all our people are agreed on the subject of receiving members by experience, but while this is true, they differ in their practices in different localities in their manner of receiving members. Some of them count a man a member of the church from the time he has related his experience to the church and the church has voted his reception. Others receive them into the church formally, after baptism. Both are Baptist usages but not in the same locality. Thus, a practice is not necessary to soundness, neither is the omission of a practice necessary to soundness. Again Baptists differ about shaking hands with each other. In some places they seem to think it is an Aminian practice, but among our people in southern Indiana, southern Illinois and farther south it is a common practice, and one which the brethren seem to enjoy very much. A minister would be in poor business, if everywhere he goes, he objects to and fights every new practice he comes across. I speak of this from my own personal knowledge.

CHAPTER XXVII.

As it is often thought that we ministers have an easy time traveling about from place to place to preach and visit among the brethren. I believe I will devote one or two chapters to that subject, in order that the reader may form an idea as to what easy times we do have. I believe that I will give an account of one or two trips, as samples of several that I have taken in my life.

In about the year '71 I was requested to make an appointment at Lynn Church, Moultrie County, Illinois, in connection with Elder John Shields, who then lived in Coles County, Illinois. The meeting was to be on Saturday and Sunday, including the fifth Sunday in November, if I remember correctly. The brethren who invited me instructed me to get off the train at Sullivan, Illinois, and that I would be met and conveyed to the church, which was south of Sullivan a distance of four miles. I left Grayville, my home, on Friday morning and went to Olney in a stage, a distance of some thirty-five miles. I arrived at Olney in time for a train on the O. & M. railroad going west about five o'clock in the afternoon. I went from there to Odin and changed cars for Mattoon, at which place I arrived about midnight. There I remained until the next morning which was cold and frosty. Then taking the train for Sullivan, I landed there about nine o'clock in the morning. No person met me, but as it was cool and pleasant I thought I could walk four miles and it would not hurt me. So I started and I feel confident that if I walked one mile I must have walked six or seven. When I arrived at the church, the people were beginning to gather and there was no one there who knew me, nor did anyone come until late that I had ever seen. I stood around playing the part of a stranger, not being very communicative, and listened to the brethren and sisters talking to one another, until finally a man came up who paid more attention to me than the others. While he talked to the other people, he would frequently cast his eye at me, as if he thought he had seen me. I had no idea who he was, but he finally came up to me and asked me if my name was not Potter, and when I told him it was, he said that he had seen me at an Association some time before that. He did not live in that neighborhood, and there was no person present that had ever seen me except him. He introduced me to a few of the brethren and sisters present, but they did not seem to take much interest in trying to get acquainted with me. I was quite young and looked fully as young as I was and had more the appearance of some strange, green boy, away from home than of a minister of the gospel. Finally an Elder came by the name of Watson. I had an introduction to him and after we had been in the house a few minutes and the brethren had sung a few songs, this Elder Watson arose from his seat and started toward the pulpit, saying to me, "Brother Potter, it is meeting time. Come into the stand." Elder Shields had not arrived. Elder Watson walked up into the stand without saying another word to me, and I saw if I did not go on that invitation, from all appearances, it seemed that I would get no other, so I got up and took a seat in the stand. He took his books, selected his hymn and text, arose, introduced services and went to preaching without saying anything to me. It seemed that the people there had no knowledge of any appointment for me, or if they knew that there was an appointment, they had no idea that I was the the man for whom it was made. Elder Watson had not been preaching a great while until I began to feel eager to preach. I have a few times in my life heard men try to preach, whom I thought I could beat and I thought, after hearing Elder Watson a few minutes that I could beat him. I suppose this was all of the flesh, for he was a very good preacher. When he was through, I took the book and read my text from the eighth chapter of Hebrews, some expression in the New Covenant, but I do not remember what part nor what expression and I suppose that I occupied about forty-five minutes. When I was through, the brethren and sisters seemed more anxious to make my acquaintance than they had been before and from that on I enjoyed myself very well, but it was very embarrassing to find no one at the train when I got off whom I knew, and then to find no one at the church who knew me. However after meeting on Saturday, I enjoyed myself very well among those strange people. I think that they were good people, but I have no idea that they had ever heard very much about me, if anything. Elder Shields came in during the afternoon and we had meeting at a private house that night. On Sunday we met again at the church and had a pleasant meeting, and on Sunday night we had meeting at another private house, an old Brother Wagoner's, who lived about ten miles west of Mattoon. Elder Shields and Elder Dalby were two leading men of their respective Associations. Shields was a member of the Wabash district, and Dalby a member of the Okaw Association. They differed very materially on the subject of the new birth. Elder Dalby was said to be the originator of the no-soul doctrine, which I have already mentioned in connection with Elder Paine. Elder Shields fought that doctrine, and at the time of this meeting the two men were on very unpleasant terms. Elders' Dalby and Paine had held a meeting a few miles away that day, and in the afternoon they came to old Brother Wagoner's where we were to preach that night. These two brethren had been accused by each other of taking very extreme positions against each other. Elder Shields has been accused of denying that the body was any part of the child of God. Whether he was guilty or not, I do not remember his ever saying so, but I do know that he claimed to believe in the resurrection of the body. Elder Dalby had been accused of denying that there is anything about man except the physical part of him. He believed that it is the man that is born again in the work of regeneration. It seems that this controversy was so hot between the two that it was impossible for one of them to preach in the presence of the other without referring to it. Elder Shields preached first that night and in the course of his remarks he took hold of his coat and drew it around him, stating that he had said that John Shields did not believe The Bible. I was very much surprised at that statement, but I felt that he intended to be understood that John Shields was the outer man, or body, and that it had not yet been regenerated, but that the soul had and was a believer. I felt that it was an extreme position for a man to take and I still think it was. When he was through, I followed him, and Elder Dalby seemed to sanction very heartily what I said. When I was through, Elder Shields suggested that the brethren sing a parting song and, as I was going to start home from there, that we extend the parting hand. Elder Dalby started the song and on that account Elder Shields took a seat near the fire-place and shook hands with no one. His conversation, after meeting was over and the people were gone, convinced me that the reason he would not was because Elder Dalby started that song. This was indeed, a very unpleasant state of affairs. But these are some of the experiences a man may have in traveling about and trying to preach the gospel among strangers. Not only will he have hard times so far as bodily exercise and exposure are concerned, but unpleasantness among the brethren and cool treatment from those with whom we are not so well acquainted are very well calculated to make a poor minister feel that it would be more pleasant to be at home with his family, where he will be more kindly received, and where the people know him better.

CHAPTER XXVIII.

At another time, I think it was in 1875, I started on a tour through the northern part of the state of Indiana, into a portion of the country where I never had been before. I was living at Grayville, and I was to take the train at about ten o'clock in the morning going to Vincennes, to make connection with the train from there to Terre Haute and thence to Greencastle and from there to Bainbridge, my first appointment being at that place. I was to arrive there at six o'clock in the evening. Elder G. M. Thompson had arranged the appointments for me. When I left home and boarded the train it was about thirty minutes late and its time in Vincennes was precisely the time of the E. & T. H. train, on which I was to go to Terre Haute. When I gave the conductor my ticket, he inquired if I wanted to go farther north than Vincennes. I told him I did and asked him if he thought we would make the connection. He said he thought we would although we were thirty minutes late. We had about forty miles to run and to make thirty minutes' time in a forty mile run required a considerable gain. About a mile and a half south of the depot at Mt. Carmel our train wrecked. No one was hurt seriously, but the idea of meeting the train at Vincennes was preposterous now. The conductor however recognized the passengers and said that there would be a train here for them, as soon as they could despatch to Vincennes and the train could come. Some of the men and myself walked on up to the depot to await the arrival of the other train. I waited there until late in the afternoon and no train came and it was a hard matter to get any information from any of the railroad employes. I began to get hungry and thought if I had an opportunity I would go to a hotel and get my dinner, but I hardly knew whether to leave the depot or not for fear the train might come and I would miss it. I do not think there was a hotel nearer the depot than a quarter of a mile, but I finally started to go up town to get my dinner, and about fifty yards from the depot, I met a stranger walking in a hurry and he asked me if the train had come. I told him it had not and I doubted if there would be any train. "O! yes," he said, "there will be a train here now in five minutes. I heard some railroad men say so a few minutes ago." I concluded that if the train would be here in a few minutes I had better not leave, so I turned back and waited till about four o'clock. I finally concluded that the best thing I could do would be to take what is now known as the Air Line train over to Princeton and catch a train there for Terre Haute. So I went to the other depot and it was so near train time that I did not have time to get anything to eat, but I thought I would get my supper when I got to Princeton. When I got there, however, the connections were so close and there were no arrangements for meals near the depot, so I had no opportunity to get anything to eat. It was after dark and I was hungry. I boarded the train and went on to Terre Haute, arriving there at about ten o'clock in the night. I then went to a lunch counter and got a cup of coffee and perhaps a sandwich. After a while my train came for Greencastle and I boarded it and went on, arriving there at about three o'clock in the morning. When I landed, there was no person about. The depot was all closed up, no hacks, no street cars at that time in the night, and one man and little boy, who got off the same train that I did, were the only persons that I saw. I inquired of the man where the other depot was and he told me that it was at the extreme northern part of the city. The depot where I got off was at the extreme southern part. I asked him how I would find the way to it. He showed me a street car track and told me that it led directly to the other depot and if I would follow it, I would get there. I started and all the light I had to walk by was the starlight. Sometimes the mud hindered me from seeing the track, from the sidewalk and, as the track turned once in a while, I would perhaps go on until I missed it and then wade out into the street and find that I had left it and then I would have to go back until I found it. I went on and, when

I got into the main part of the city, the first thing I knew I was within two feet of a policeman, who threw his light on me from a dark lantern. I did not know whether he intended to molest me or not; however, I was not afraid. He remarked, "You are traveling, are you?" I told him that I had just gotten in off the train. He said, "All right. Go ahead." I went on to the depot and when I got here, at perhaps four o'clock in the morning, there was no one about the station. Everything was dark and silent as the grave and I knew nothing about when there would be a train. It was ten miles to Bainbridge, where I was to preach that day. I saw a house near by that was lighted up and had a hotel sign by the door. I concluded I would go in there and sit by the fire until the train came or until I could learn something about it. I walked in and as the room was warm and a good cheerful fire burned in the stove I took a seat. There was no one in the room, but I had not been seated long before a man opened the door and looked in saying, "This is no hotel." "Well," said I, "what did you say it was for? The sign out here says hotel." He remarked that he had only been there but a short time and had not taken the sign down. I told him that I did not want a hotel, that I was waiting for a train and saw no place to wait and just thought I would come in there until train time. "Well," said he, "you can not stay in here," and I got up and walked out and waited out in the cold, frosty weather, until finally I heard a train coming, but it proved to be a freight train. I ran immediately to the first man I saw with it, and asked him if that train went to Bainbridge. He said it did and if I wished to go there to get right in the caboose. I made my way to the rear end of the train and entered the caboose, where there was a good warm fire, so I lay down upon a bench and the next thing I knew we were on our way to Bainbridge, at which place I arrived at about sun-up. I had had nothing to eat since the breakfast before, had been up all night and had an appointment to preach at eleven that day, also that night. Of course I was in a grand plight for preaching. These are some of the blissful experiences a minister has in traveling to preach.

CHAPTER XXIX.

While out on this trip, I met with several of these brethren in central Indiana, who have since separated from our fellowship on account of means and instrumentalities. I was at Elder J. W. Shirley's church one day and night and I felt confident, from all that I saw and heard, that he was not well pleased with the manner in which Elder Thompson and I preached. When we arrived at the church, he took us into the back part of the house and requested us not to preach doctrine. I have felt for many years that those people, who claim to be Primitive Baptists and are opposed to doctrinal preaching, have their reasons for their opposition. I am also of the opinion that the reason they have for opposing the doctrine is that they do not believe it. Elder Shirley did not believe the doctrine that I was preaching at that time. As an evidence that he did not, he told me at Lebanon, Indiana, when I was there attending court during the noted trial for the property of Mount Tabor Church, that he had known that he and I had differed ever since the first time that he saw me. I took that as a plain admission on his part that he never did believe what I preached.

I went from there on up into Clinton County, and there a little circumstance occured at the late and beloved Brother William Oliphant's, of which I wish to give an account. After preaching at Little Flock Church on Saturday, a Mr. Oliphant and his wife, who had been and who were Methodists, went back with us to old Brother Oliphant's for dinner. When we arrived there we found Elder John Kinder, who was to preach a funeral at the church the next day. This Mr. Oliphant, who was a Methodist, began to ask me some questions concerning my discourse on that day, and the positions that I occupied. I thought that, as Brother Kinder was an old man and at home, and better acquainted with Mr. Oliphant than I was, he would take the controversy off my hands, if it was necessary to have anything like a controversy. So I answered his questions as easily as I could, until finally Elder Kinder made a remark which gave me to understand that he did not endorse the positions that I occupied. Then I began to talk very plainly to him, so that he would not mistake me as to what I did believe, and in a very short time he made the remark to me: "If that is what you preach you had better go home, for you are doing no good preaching." I told him that I was a comparatively young man and that I was a long way from home, and that I had no other business there than to preach the gospel and get acquainted with the people. I also told him that if I could not show good reasons for preaching as I did, I was ready to start home at any time, but that I now wished to ask him a question or two. I do not remember the question I propounded to him, but I soon saw that he was disposed to evade it. This I would not allow him to do, so, when he saw that nothing would do but an answer to the question I had asked, and that it was rather hard to answer, he made the remark, (I thought a little crusty), that we differed so far that he did not think we would ever come together, and that he could not give me any information, and that he would rather not talk to me. I said "All right, I hope there is no hard feelings about it." He said "No," so Mr. Oliphant and I went on with our conversation, and I really felt that Mr. Oliphant was more consistent than Elder Kinder, but I was not allowed to say anything to him about it. At the supper table, our conversation still being kept up, Mr. Oliphant made the remark that he was no preacher, and that he wanted it understood that he could not hold his own with all of us preachers. I told him I thought they were all on his side but me, when Elder Kinder spoke up and said "Yes, I like his positions better than I do yours." I thought that was the case, but I was not allowed to say anything. The matter passed on, but I thought very little of Elder Kinder as a Baptist. I had no doubt that he was a good man, but I felt confident that he was not a Baptist. On Sunday morning, when I got ready to start to meeting, Elder Kinder was also ready, and as it was only a little ways to the meeting-house, he and I started out on foot. When we got out on the road I said to Elder Kinder that I was aware that we differed, but to what extent I did not know, and, in order to find out, I would love to ask him a few questions if it would not be an intrusion on his feelings. He said it would be all right, so I asked him if he believed Christ died for all the race of men. He refused to answer. I remarked that if he would not say, I would not be able to find out whether we differed or not. I told him I did not believe he died for all the race. I then asked him if he believed in election. He said yes, but not as some men held it. He said, "I believe just as the Apostle Peter did; God is no respecter of persons, but in every nation he that feareth Him and worketh righteousness is accepted with Him." Elder Kinder gave this text just about such an interpretation as the Arminians usually do, when they quote it in reference to the doctrine of election. He said that he believed that there was a sufficiency of grace given to every sinner in the world, that he could accept salvation and be saved if he would, and if he did not it was his own fault.

"Well," said I, "that is your position, is it?" He said it was, and that he would preach that if he had to stand alone. I told him I thought he need not be uneasy, for he would have plenty of company, for the whole Arminian world believed it. Those men. that is Kinder and Shirley, are now among those who have left our people and gone off with Burnam and others, who have favored the doctrine of human instrumentalities and means in giving the sinner eternal life, and the practice of Sunday Schools, Missions, and other so-called means of grace for the Evangelization of the world of mankind. From that day to this I never saw the time that I thought very much of those brethren as Baptists. I noticed during my stay among the churches where those preachers were, that they did not approve of what we call negative doctrinal preaching very much. Some of them undertook to talk to me about it, and said that the people did not understand the doctrine if we did preach it to them, to which I replied that if we did not preach it to them, they were certain never to understand it. I feel confident that those brethren have not become unsound since that time, for they were already unsound.

CHAPTER XXX.

After I had visited several churches on this trip and had wound up my tour and was ready to start home, I went to Wabash to take the train for home on Monday morning. The weather was cold and the snow in that part of the country was about eight or ten inches deep. I had been away from home some five or six weeks and was very eager now to get started home. When I came to the station at the city of Wabash, I found a number of passengers waiting for the train, also that the train would be perhaps an hour late. It seemed dreadful to me to think of waiting an hour for the train when I was ready to start and anxious to be on the road. I walked the floor, without any conversation with anyone, for I did not feel very communicative. Finally I noticed a man come in, whom, for some cause or other, I took to be a preacher. I did not pay any attention to him especially but, when I stepped up to the ticket window to get my ticket, I noticed he was getting a clergyman's ticket. While I was standing around a young gentleman recognized and approached me and commenced conversation with me. I did not know him, but he said he had heard me preach at one of my appointments in the past week. After I had procured my ticket and had a few words with this young gentleman, I began my walk back and forth across the room again, waiting very impatiently for the train to arrive. Finally, this gentleman, who I thought was a preacher, hailed me as I was passing him and invited me to a seat with him. I sat down and he remarked, "You are a minister, I suppose?" I answered "Yes, sir, I try to preach some." "What church are you preaching for?" he asked. I said "The Baptist church." "The Missionary Baptist church?" I said, "No, the Old School Baptist church." "O, well, it don't make much difference what church a man is in, so that he is doing good." I told him I was doing the best I could, preaching the gospel to the people and baptizing occasionally. I found that he also was a minister and that he belonged to the United Brethren. This was about the amount of our conversation, as I did not feel much like talking to him. Presently the train came and we boarded it for home. After taking a seat in the car, the aforesaid preacher looked around and saw me a few seats back of him and he arose and came back and took a seat with me. He asked me what the difference was between the Old Baptists and the Missionary Baptists. I told him I could give him a few thoughts of what I believed and our people believed and, if he was acquainted with the Missionary Baptists, he could draw the contrast himself. I told him that our people believed in the doctrine of the absolute sovereignty of God in all cases and that God chose his people in Christ Jesus to salvation before the foundation of the world and that Christ came into the world to redeem them exclusively and that all that He redeemed would be saved. That the Holy Spirit quickened them into divine life and that there was no such thing as final or eternal apostasy of a saint. "Well," he said, "you don't believe that Christ died for all men, then?" I told him, yes, I believed He died for all men, but I did not believe He died for all the race of men. He said "Is there not a text that reads this way?" "He is the propitiation for our sins and, not for ours only, but for the sins of the whole world." I answered, "Yes, there is just such a text as that in my book." "Well, what does that mean?" I told him I could not tell him for the life of me, unless it meant what it said "Well," said he, "I understand it to mean just what it says, too." "We are together then," said I. He said he believed it meant all the race. Said I, "It does not say all the race." But he said he understood it to mean just the same as if it had said all the race, for it said all the world. "Very well," said I, "Let us read it that way." "He is the propitiation for our sins and not for ours only, but also for the sins of all race of Adam." In addition to being the propitiation for our sins, He is the propitiation for the sins of all the race of Adam. Agreeable to that, we are not of the race of Adam. Another text I referred him to: "We know that we are of God, but that the whole world lieth in wickedness." Suppose we say that the whole race of Adam lie in wickedness, then who are left of God out of that race? The apostle did not say, we know that we are of God and all the balance of the race lieth in wickedness, but he says the whole world lieth in wickedness. From this time, he seemed to lose his temper and began to talk loud. He became very much excited and said he would not give a cent for the Bible without common sense with it. "Very well," said I, "your position has neither the Bible nor common sense." That did not seem to put him in any better humor, but he began to talk so loud that he attracted the attention of the people all over the car. I did not try to argue with him, for I saw that he was not in a suitable frame of mind to argue. When I would begin to speak and tell him what I did believe, he would pitch in and undertake to tell it for me, until I finally suggested to him that one speak at a time and that we time ourselves. I took my watch out of my pocket and told him to go ahead and make his speech and I would reply to it. "Well, you speak first," said he. So I began and quoted about a dozen different texts, without any comment whatever, and said, "Now I will give you thirty minutes to reply to what I have said." Said he, "Do you think I am going to reply to the Bible?". Said I, "That is what you have to reply to if you reply to me, for I stand right on the Bible." He hesitated and said he knew the people used to believe that old doctrine away back in the dark ages, but he did not know that anybody believed it now. "Well," said I, "Did they have the Bible when they believed it back in the dark ages, or were they heathen people?" He hesitated a moment and finally said "I thought that since Dr. Clark's Commentaries had been introduced, men had quit believing that old doctrine." "Oh," said I, "When they had the Bible they believed as I do, but when they got Dr. Clark's Commentaries, they believed as you do." "Now," said I, "You can have Dr. Clark if you want him, but I will still hold to the Bible." The poor fellow seemed very much away from home in the seat with me, but he did not have the courage to get up and go back to his seat, until the train stopped at Lafayette, where he got off. Then he arose, put on his wraps and walked away, without telling me goodbye, or saying that he wished me a safe trip home, or that he hoped to see me again, or anything of the kind. The train stopped for dinner, and, while we were waiting, I noticed that a number of gentlemen who had listened to us on the train seemed very sociable and friendly to me after he was gone. I went on and soon arrived at my home, I felt that during that trip I had gained several important items which perhaps I would never forget.

CHAPTER XXXI.

I have always argued in favor of the doctrine of substitutionary atonement, and that all for whom Christ died would be eternally saved. I have also taken the position that the death of Christ did not affect any others, only the elect. I have had several discussions on the atonement and I feel satisfied, from the efforts of my opponents on that subject to refute the doctrine of a limited or definite atonement and also the doctrine of the vicarious sufferings of the Son of God, that the doctrine that I have advocated is the doctrine of the Bible. I went on a visit to Sulphur Springs Church, in Simpson County, Kentucky, a few years ago and when I stepped off the train at Franklin, I was met by the pastor of the Methodist Church of the city. When he found out where I was going and that I expected to return to Franklin on Sunday evening, he invited me to preach in his pulpit on Sunday night. His invitation seemed to be cordial and so it was readily accepted. As soon as I arrived in Franklin on Sunday evening, he called on me and seemed very genial and I enjoyed his company very much. Before we arrived at the church, one of his brethren came to me and said that I was requested to preach on the atonement that night. I very readily consented to do so and, in the the course of my remarks, I took the position that nothing short of perfect satisfaction for sin could be atonement. I stated and argued that Jesus Christ either satisfied the law for sin, or else he made no atonement whatever. If he did make an atonement it was by making such an offering and suffering such a penalty of the law, as would be equivalent to the demands of the law for sin. If he thus atoned for all the sins for the whole race of men, then, it must be unjust to send any of them to eternal perdition. For if Christ had made perfect satisfaction for their sins no just law would ever ask more. For proof of the positions for which I argued, I referred to Rom. v, 6-11. "For when we were without strength, in due time Christ died for the ungodly." I took the position that to die for the ungodly, in this text, was to die in the place of the ungodly. The preposition *for* is from the Greek *huper*, which means instead of, or in the place of. "For scarcely for a righteous man will one die; yet peradventure for a good man some would even dare to die." If any man loved a good man so dearly that he would die for him, he certainly must have the welfare of the good man in view in such a death. He would not die for him just for fun nor merely for the sake of dying. It must be that this good man is exposed to some terrible disaster from which he cannot escape, unless one die for him; and then it is not argued here that he has a friend that would die for him, except with the most certain assurance that such a death would save him from the disaster. For a man to make such a sacrifice as to give up his life for the benefit of his friend, when he knew it would not benefit him, would be unwise. For him to die for his friend, in order to keep his friend from dying, and at the same time know that his friend would die too, just as if he had not died for him, would be to give up his life for nothing. Did Jesus Christ give up his life for nothing? "But God commendeth his love toward us, in that while we were yet sinners Christ died for us." His love for us was so great that he died for sinners, not for good men. "Much more then being now justified by his blood, we shall be saved by his life." Who are justified by his blood? I answer, "Those for whom it was shed." For whom was His blood shed? I answer, "Those for whom He died." The apostle here couples together the death of Christ and the justification of those for whom He died. Will justified men go to hell? I answer, "No." If the Savior died for all the race of men, then what will be the result? I answer, "All the race of men will be saved if He died for them. "For if, when we were enemies, we were reconciled to God by the death of his Son." Notice. Reconciled to God by the death of his Son. Who were reconciled to God by the death of his Son? I answer, "Those for whom He died." If He died for all the race of men, then He reconciled all the race of men to God by His death. "Much more being reconciled, we shall be saved by His life." Who shall be saved by His life? I answer. "Those who are reconciled to God by the death of his Son." All for whom He died were reconciled. If that was the entire race, then they will all be saved. I then quoted from Heb. x, 1. "By the which will we are sanctified through the offering of the body of Jesus

Christ once for all." How are they sanctified. I answer. "Through the offering of the body of Jesus Christ." Who were those sanctified? I answer. "All for whom His body was offered." If it was offered for the whole race, then the whole race are sanctified by that offering. Sanctified people never go to hell. He did not only sanctify those for whom He was offered, but He perfected them forever. They who are sanctified and perfected forever, will most assuredly be saved. "For by one offering He hath perfected forever them that are sanctified." Verse 14. I of course quoted many other Scriptures from which I argued as above and when I was through the minister arose and said to his audience. "If we admit Brother Potter's premises, we cannot escape his conclusions,"

After dismission we walked out together and I told him that my premises were the plain readings of the Bible, and if you admit the Bible to be true, you cannot escape my premises, and if you admit my premises, you say you cannot escape my conclusions. I am glad to hear your frank admissions. But he said that there could not be such a thing as a substitutionary atonement. I have felt confident for years that the ablest men, among those who believe in a conditional salvation, have been able to see for some time if they admit a universal atonement, they cannot consistently deny a universal salvation. I was once in a conversation with a Mr. Tennison, a minister of the General Baptist Church, and I told him that I was not a Primitive Baptist just for fun and that

I might just as well be something else, if we were not right. I told him that I wanted to read some Scripture to him and tell him how I understood them and then I wished him to tell me wherein I was wrong, I then turned to Rom. v. and Heb. x, and read and commented as I have done in this chapter, and when I was through, I called on him to tell me my mistakes. He simply said he could not do it. I was not disappointed, for I felt sure he could not before I asked him, but I think he thought he could until I was through and called on him to do so.

CHAPTER XXXII.

When I first joined the church and commenced trying to preach, I was a member of a church which belonged to the Skillet Fork Association, in Illinois. The churches of that Association were not as strong as they are today. The Birk Prairie Church only numbered five members when I first knew them. Other churches in the Association were very weak and I think that the Association, at that time, numbered about three hundred and fifty members. She now almost doubles that in point of membership. This is clear evidence that the prediction, that has so often been made by our opponents, that the Old Baptists would soon all die out is a false prophesy and, if any person feels comforted by the thought that our people will soon die out, let me disabuse such a mind, for instead of dying out they are on the increase and there are more of our people in the United

States today than there ever was before. I remember visiting what was then called Mount Sterling Church, in about the year 1872. This church, at that time, held its meetings in a small log house about two miles west of Carmi. The present Carmi church was then the old Mount Sterling Church. After meeting was over on Saturday, I was invited by a brother to go home with him to dinner and, when I asked him how far it was, he said about six miles. I thought I would not go that far, for I had already come twenty miles and it was getting late and the weather was very warm. But, before I left the meeting house, I found that it would be the best that I could do, so I went home with the brother, who lived in the neighborhood of where Little Zion Church now is, in White County, Illinois. I stopped near what they called Number Four School House—I think there were about four or five members of the Regular Baptist Church, living within three or four miles of this school house. The people throughout the whole country, as near as I could learn, that belonged to any church at all were Campbellites and a gentleman by the name of Logan was holding a protracted meeting at Number Four. I went out to hear him on Saturday night and had an introduction to him and he asked me if I would not preach there on Sunday night. I told him I would not object but for the reason that he was holding a meeting there and that it was against my rule to make appointments that would interfere with the meetings of other people. He said it would be no interference, for he would do his preaching during the day and would have no night appointment and that he was anxious to hear me preach and requested that I make the appointment. I finally consented and the appointment was published for me to preach at Number Four on Sunday night. When I came back from Mount Sterling meeting on Sunday afternoon, I was told that he had held meeting that day and had baptized three or four and that he had made the remark that if I did not "toe the mark" he would reply to me. This made me think that he intended to fight, so I concluded to be very plain in what remarks I made. I took for a text, "Except a man be born again, he cannot see the kingdom of God." I went on to give the doctrine of the new birth, according to the New Testament, the way I understood it, also to show that not only was baptism not essential to it but that no other creature condition was, for it was the work of God. During his sermon the night before he had made several misquotations and I took the pains to correct some of them, during the course of my remarks. The house was full and a large number of people were outside at the windows, so anxious were they to hear what I had to say. It was my first sermon, in fact, my first visit to that neighborhood. When I was through Mr. Logan arose to make a reply and the first thing he did was to thank me for correcting his mistakes. In his reply he soon made another mistake by making this statement: Said he, "Let me make a correction," and he turned to me, saying, "You quoted, 'Which were born not of blood, nor of the will of the flesh, nor of the will of man, but of God.' Now," said he, "it does not read that way, but it says 'by the will of God' and that means by doing his will." I knew he was mistaken as soon as he told how he thought it read. I opened the Testament, put my finger to the verse, held it up before him and told him to read it. He looked at it, saw his mistake and confessed it, stating at the same time that he had plenty of other Scriptures. This seemed to expose him in a manner that was very embarrassing to him but he rather recovered and, after talking some time, remarked, "But let me correct another mistake." Said he, "Where is that text of Scripture that says, 'He is exalted at the right hand of God to be a prince and a Savior, to give repentance to Israel and the forgiveness of sins?'" I answered, "Acts, v-31." "Well," said he, "it does not say to give repentence to Israel, it does not say to whom." I told him to turn to it and read it. So, as he turned to it, he kept repeating, until he found it, that it did not say to Israel. Finally he found it and I told him to read it out, so that we could all hear it. He read it and left out the words "to Israel." I told him to read the whole verse. Said he, "That is all the verse." I told him if he did not read it all, I would; so he went back and read it as I had quoted it. His dishonesty was so plainly seen by the people, that I thought it unnecessary for me to say a word. He had read the Scriptures wrong with his eyes upon the verse and claimed that he was reading it just as it was. Such dishonesty disqualifies a man for common respectability, much less to be a minister of the gospel. What can we expect of a man, who is so dishonest as to read the Scriptures wrong with his eyes on the very thing he is reading? If the souls of men and women were in the hands of such a preacher, they would certainly stand a good chance of missing heaven. It is a great mercy to sinners that the Lord has never put the souls of men into the hands of preachers or into the hands of the church that they may be saved, but He has given them to His Son, and His word has taught us that "God was in Christ reconciling the world unto Himself." After Mr. Logan got through with his review of my sermon, I got up and announced that I would be back there in a few weeks, setting the time, for I felt that surely this people ought to have the truth preached to them. He wanted me to reply to him, but I told him that I did not think it was necessary. Matters were just as good as I could make them. The people had seen what he had done and it was not necessary for me to say anything. He did not seem to be in the best humor and, after I dismissed the congregation, I told him that he had made one more mistake last night, that I had not corrected and that I would correct it now. He asked me what it was and I told him that, in speaking of repentence the night before, he had stopped and asked this question, "What is repentance?" and that he said, "Some men say it is godly sorrow for sin, but I do not know where they got it unless they got it from men. The Bible does not say so," and then he said that repentance worketh a godly sorrow. I asked him if he did not say that last night and he said he did. "Well," said I, "it does not read that way." "Well," said he, "I will find it for you by the time you come again." I told him I did not believe in going on credit and I wanted it settled now. I took my testament from my pocket and turned to the text, for I had it marked out and, instead of reading that repentance worketh a godly sorrow, it said "A godly sorrow worketh repentance." "Now," said I, "that is the way with your whole theory; it is just the reverse of the truth." And he, in rather a gruff manner, remarked, "Well, it don't read the other way, anyhow," and turned away and I have never seen him since. I went back and filled my appointment and the brethren began coming in occasionally to preach, and some of the Baptists moved in there and finally there was a church constituted that is now called Little Zion Church and today it numbers sixty or seventy members and the Campbellites seldom, if ever, hold any meeting there.

CHAPTER XXXIII.

After I moved to Grayville in 1870, I made the acquaintance, during the ten years that I lived there, of a great many different preachers of the Campbellite, Methodist, Presbyterian and other denominations. When a new preacher came to Grayville and his brethren took him around to introduce him to the citizens, it was frequently the case that I would meet him in the rounds and get an introduction to the new preacher. The most of them treated me very well except, perhaps, when they tried to pick at me a time or two, on first acquaintance, for being an Old Baptist. When I was young, they would often puzzle me with their questions, which caused me to study a great deal. I always respected a man, even if he differed from me on very important matters, so long as he treated me as I thought he should, but if I thought he felt himself smarter or wiser and was the least inclined to make light of me for being what I was, I had no mercy on him. I took care of myself, under those circumstances, to the very best of my ability. During my stay there, a Methodist minister came to town whose name was Whitaker. I had an introduction to him soon after he came into Grayville, which was perhaps in the month of September. From that time on during the fall and early part of the winter I never saw him to speak to him, until a day or two before Christmas. He was almost a total stranger. I knew nothing of what kind of a man he was, but as I was going down the street one morning, not thinking of anything unpleasant or pleasant either for that matter, between Reverend Whitaker and myself on the subject of religion, I met him. When I came within a few feet of him, he began to call out and ask me how I was, saying that he had not seen me lo these many days and wanted to know where I had been keeping myself all this time. I told him I had been preaching the gospel, as the commission said, "Go ye into all the world and preach the gospel," and I had not stayed in Grayville all the time to sponge a living off the people. He kept his talk up very loud, to draw a crowd. He said, "Every church in town is going to have a Christmas tree, but the Baptist Church." I said, "Yes, so I understand." "Well," said he, "why don't the Baptists have a Christmas tree?" I told him I had been away from home and was not here to make the arrangements. "Well," said he, "why don't your brethren fix it?" "Well," said I, "we would not have had one if I had been at home." "Well, why don't you have a Christmas tree and Sunday schools and class meetings?" I replied, "Because we do not want them. Now, let me ask you that many questions. Why do you have a Christmas tree? Why do you have Sabbath schools? Why do you have class meetings?" and the only answer he could give was "Because we want them." "Well," said I, "we are even. You want them and have them; we do not want them and do not have them." He said the Old Baptists would soon all be dead. I said they would, or some man had told a falsehood. Said I, "Do you know what they did with false prophets in olden days?" He said he did not know. I told him they used to stone them to death and I believed it would be a good idea in this day. I told him that he was not posted, anyway, that the Methodists were dying out, that I had been all over the country, traveling all winter, and I had not heard of a revival among the Methodists and of only one effort to have a revival, and that was a failure. I told him that I had a brother-in-law who was a Methodist and that I had been to see him in my rounds and he said their church was dead. He replied, "You say you have a brother-in-law who is a Methodist?" I replied, "Yes, sir." "He is a pretty fine kind of man, is he not?" I told him he would be if he were not a Methodist. He then began to tell an anecdote which he applied to the Old Baptists and their doctrine, on which he seemed to think he had made a good point, but what it was I do not remember. But I told him one to offset it, concerning the darkey, who went to hear a Methodist preacher. He listened very attentively to the preacher, who started out by preaching the doctrine of total depravity. Said I, "You know that is the doctrine of the Methodist Church." He said, "Yes." The preacher then began preaching about joining the church on six months' trial. Said I, "You know the Methodists preach that way." He said, "Yes." And he wound up by preaching the doctrine of final apostasy. I said, "You know that is the doctrine of the Methodist Church." He said, "Yes." The darkey noticed all these things and listened so attentively that he attracted the attention of a gentleman in the crowd, who was anxious to know what the poor colored boy thought and who sought an opportunity, after they were out of the house, to ask him what he thought of the sermon. The poor fellow said, "Why, dat man is a fool, or else de God he preaches is dishonest, one or de oder. He says that God Almighty say if you work for Him six months he will give you religion and den if you don't work for him all de balance of your days, he will take it away from you. You know dere is no honesty in dat. You agree, if I work for you six months, you will give me a horse and I work de six months; de horse is mine. I don't have to work for you all de balance of my days so you won't take de horse away from me." He then started away and I walked along by the side of him to the post office and remarked to him, " Whitaker, I can tell you what is the matter with you. You Methodists love for me to whip the Campbellites, because you know that I can do it, but the Campbellites can whip you. You call them "water ducks," because they believe that baptism is essential to the remission of sins and yet you believe it yourselves. I have it from one of your ministers in black and white in his notes on your Articles of Faith, that baptism is in order to the remission of sins. You think more of water than they do, for it only takes a spoonful to do the work for you and for them it takes enough to cover a man all over." The next morning he came running up to me on the street, saying "Brother Potter, I want you to show me that article of our faith that says that baptism is in order to the remission of sins." "All right, sir," said I, "Your Article of Faith does not say it, but one of your ministers, in his notes on your Articles of Faith, does say it." "Oh, well, we are not responsible for what our ministers say," he remarked. I told him it might be that a Methodist minister was not accountable for what he said and that, if I was certain that none of them were, I would not have a great deal to do with any of them. So we parted, and that is about the amount of sociability that ever occurred between myself and Brother Whitaker.

CHAPTER XXXIV.

I have always believed since I became interested on the subject of religion, that there is a divine reality in the Christian religion. Concerning this I have never been troubled with doubts. I believe, from what the Bible says, and from my own experience, as well as the experience of others, that the Lord Himself comes down by His spirit, and takes up His abode in the hearts of men; so that, as the apostle said to the Corinthian brethren, "Your bodies are the temple of the living God." While I believe so confidently in a revealed religion, I have contended for years, that no person could give an account of why he turned away from sin, and began to serve the Lord, from love of the cause of Christ, without felling what we call an experience.

While I was living at Grayville, a gentleman by the name of Gaff came there to preach for the Campbellite Church, being hired by them, for one thousand dollars a year. From the price he got for preaching, it seems that he should have been capable of doing a great deal of good for the people to whom he was hired. This same man, Gaff, one morning in the winter time, came into the printing office where I was at work, setting type, and, after walking around through the office awhile, as if it were his own concern, and he wished to see that everything was in its place and moving along satisfactorily, he finally came to me and began to talk on the subject of the operation of the Spirit. He said that he believed in the operation of the Spirit but that the Spirit used instrumentalities in its operations. To illustrate, he took his cane, and remarked that he might strike me with his cane, and said he, "It would be me who does the striking and yet I really do not touch you myself, but the cane does. Just so the Spirit of God uses the word as the means through which it operates upon the hearts of sinners, and the Spirit itself does not come in contact with the sinner's heart." After talking along in that strain upon the subject of the operation of the Spirit, he said: "You Baptists claim to have an experimental knowledge of the Lord, and that when you were under conviction you prayed and begged and cried, and even went so far as to hide out in the woods behind a stump or brush-pile, and expected the Lord to pardon your sins before you obeyed

Him. Now" said he, "that is all a delusion." I laid my composing stick down and took a seat on a little bench by the stove, and said: "Brother Gaff, sit down here. The Apostle Peter says, "Sanctify the Lord God in your hearts, and be ready always to give to every man that asketh you, a reason for the hope that is in you, with meekness and fear." I understand from this text, that if I am called upon, especially by an opponent, for a reason of my hope, I am under obligations to give it. What do you think of that?" He said he understood it the same way. "Well," said I, "I want a reason for your hope, and in order that I may understand you, I will ask you a few questions, that I want you to answer." He said, "All right," and I asked him if he had the love of God in his heart. He said, "Yes," he professed to have it. "Well," said I, "I am not going to say that you haven't, for I presume you have. Was the love of God always in your heart?" "No," he said, "it was not always there." "Well," said I, "how did it get there?" He said it was shed abroad by the Holy Ghost. I told him that must be a part of his history; it was an event that had occurred some time in his life. "Now," said I, "what I want you to tell me is, when did the love of God enter into your heart, and how did you feel at the time, and what makes you think it is there?" "Now," said he, "you want my experience." I told him he need not call it an experience if he did not want to; he might call it what he pleased, or not at all, I just wanted the facts in the case. He said when he was a boy he was a great sinner, and, when he arrived at the age of manhood, he saw himself a condemned sinner in the sight of God, and he concluded he would repent of his sins, and, said he, "I did repent." "Now," said I, "just one little interruption right here. When you saw yourself a sinner, justly condemned, in the sight of God, did you feel comfortable, or did you feel wretched and bad?" To this he made no reply, and he told me no more of his experience. I told him that if there was such a thing as a man seeing himself a justly condemned sinner before God, and at the same time feeling comfortable, I wanted to know it, and that perhaps he could tell me. That all the persons with whom I had ever talked on the subject, who had felt themselves justly condemned, had told me that they felt miserable. But I could learn no more from Brother Gaff, and I felt convinced, from this little circumstance, that it would be impossible for him to give a reason of his hope without telling what we call an experience of grace.

While I have been a firm believer in the doctrine of experimental religion, I have also believed in a personal call to the work of the ministry, by the Holy Spirit. I remember a conversation with another preacher, of the Campbellite persuasion, whose name was James, in which he had something to say about a call to preach, and, after making some few remarks about it, he asked me the question, "When the Lord called you to preach, what did He say to you?" I told him that if he would answer me four questions, I would tell him my call to preach. They should be fair, and to the point, and the crowd would witness that what I had to say must be fair. He said he would do it. I asked him first,"Do you believe that it is the duty of men to preach the gospel?" He said he did. That is one. I asked him second,"Do you believe that it is the duty of all men to preach the gospel?" He said he did not; that there were some men whose duty it was not to preach the gospel. I asked him third, "Who makes it the duty of men to preach the gospel?" He said the Lord did. I said,"That is three; now one more question, and when you answer it, I am ready to tell you my call to preach, and if you can answer it as readily as you have the other three, I will soon be telling you." I asked him fourth, "How did you find out that the Lord had made it your duty to preach the gospel, and not some other man?" I have never told him my call to the ministry, because he never answered that question, and I feel confident that it is impossible for any man to answer the first three questions as he did, and then answer the fourth one consistently, without telling what we term a call to the work of the ministry. I believe that the preaching of the gospel is a matter of great importance, too much so to be left simply to the voluntary actions of men, because the Lord has a great and noble purpose to accomplish by the preaching of the gospel, and it is a matter of too vast importance to be left to the voluntary actions of men. So

He calls men to the work of the ministry, and they are to preach with the ability that God giveth, and to preach as of the oracles of God.

CHAPTER XXXV.

About the year 1872, I commenced visiting the church at Paris, Illinois, and I attended their meetings occasionally, for some two or three years. My first meetings at that place were held in a hall above a saloon. Of course, this was not a very inviting place for people to come to, but our brethren and friends attended our meetings. Sometimes I would preach in the Court House and sometimes in the Missionary Baptist Church, but the most of our regular meetings were held in this hall. I baptized a few people during my ministry at Paris. The church was weak, when I commenced going there, but revived considerably and seemed to have the respect and sympathy of the good citizens of the city of Paris. Even those, who did not believe the doctrine of the Baptist Church, attended our meetings and seemed to speak very encouragingly of our little interest there. Finally I was challenged for a debate by a Mr. William Holt, of the Campbellite Church. This debate began in the city of Paris, on the twenty-fifth day of June, 1873, and lasted three days. It seemed that, whether or not I maintained my positions during that debate, I had the entire sympathy of the people, outside of Mr. Holt's own brethren.

I have never flattered myself that I did anything great in that debate, for I was both young and timid and had had only a few debates up to that time. In fact, I never thought I was as great a debater as my brethren sometimes seemed to think me. After this debate was over the citizens of Paris, business men and others, told our brethren that if they would undertake to build them a house of worship in the City of Paris, they would assist them. Accordingly our brethren went to work and in a few months had a nice house built, but not all paid for. After this house was built and church matters were moving along very nicely, I quit preaching for them and there was a period of two or three years, in which I was not there. In that time, trouble had gotten among them and they had become divided. The church or part of it headed by Thomas P. Mullens, and a preacher by the name of Dodimeade were known as the Mullen's party. They excluded seven members. These seven members claimed to be the Mount Pleasant Church, in Paris and contended that the Mullens party, as I shall call them here for convenience, was in disorder and was not the church. These seven members set up to keep house; and both parties represented themselves by letter and delegates before the Association. They were members of the Wabash District Association. The Association, however, rejected both letters and advised them to go home and be reconciled to each other and return in order. They had meetings from time to time for the purpose of trying to become reconciled, and in the mean time the Mullens party shut those seven members out of the house, got new locks and put on the doors, and refused to allow them any use of the house whatever. The house, not being paid for, a suit was entered and judgment was obtained against them for the balance due. One Sister Darnell paid off the judgment and got a title to the house, which gave the house to those seven accused members, who occupied the same until they finally sold it to the United Brethren. During this unhappy season among the people at Paris, whom I loved dearly, I went to see them. In the first place I went to see Brother Mullens, who told his story about their trouble and division. Elder Joe Skeeters who had married one of the Mullens party, was living in Paris at that time and in sympathy with the Mullens party. Brother Mullens, Elder Dodimeade and I visited Elder Skeeters after supper. This was the first time I had seen him since he had moved away from Posey County, where he had lived and where I first met him. He was in warm sympathy with the Mullens party, though not a member of that church. Everything I heard in conversation that evening, was in favor of that party and against the seven members who had been excluded. Elder Skeeters told me that he had made a proposition to those seven members, like this: that if they would come to the church and request the church to rescind the act of there exclusion, not withdraw the charges from them but rescind the act of exclusion, and ask for a new trial and then, if they could not settle it themselves, call a committee of brethren from sister churches and let them settle it for them, he would go the security for the church, that she would grant the request. Brother Mullens and Elder Dodimeade sat by and heard him make that statement to me. I was totally ignorant of the whole affair and I asked him if they had done so. He said they had not but had refused to do so. On the next morning, I went to Brother Darnell's house. All the seven members were there and their trouble was the topic of their conversation, and during this conversation they frequently referred to an instrument of writing, which I knew nothing about, and to the fact that they had received a letter from an old brother at Oblong, whose name was Odell, and who had visited them recently. I finally became curious to know what was in that letter and what the instrument of writing was, to which they so often referred. When I inquired, they told me that they had gotten up an instrument of writing, requesting the church to rescind the act of their exclusion, and give them a new hearing, and that all seven of them had signed their names to it, and presented it to the church at the last meeting and that the church refused to hear them. They had kept this instrument and sent it to Brother Odell, and he had written them a letter, regretting very much that the church had refused to grant their reasonable request, which Brother Mullens and others had pledged their words to him and Elder W. H. Smith, when they were there, that they would do. When I read this letter and the instrument of writing to which the names of those seven members were signed, I immediately thought of what

Elder Skeeters told me the evening before, in the presence of Mullen's and Dodimeade, and I asked them if they would loan me that letter from Brother Odell and that written request that they had signed, until I could go to Elder Skeeters and back. Of course they said they would, so I put the papers in my pocket and started directly to Elder Skeeters' house. When I got there I found one of the brethren of the Mullens party there and I was truly glad he was. I said "Brother Skeeters, please repeat to me that proposition you made those seven members, as you did last night in the presence of Mullens and Dodimeade." He stated the matter again, just as he had the evening before, that, if they would request the church to rescind the act of their exclusion and give them a new trial, he would insure the church to grant it. I told him that I had understood him to say the evening before, that they had refused to do it. He said yes they had so far, but that they had come to the church he had been told, with a request for the church to rescind the act of their exclusion and withdraw the charges, and that the church of course had refused to do. That was not what he had told them to do, for if the church withdrew the charges, there would be nothing to try. I told him that perhaps I had some information for him that he knew nothing about, and I drew their petition from my pocket, and told him that I had seen all seven of the members and they had told me that they presented this petition to the church, with all their names signed to it; then I read it over to him. "Now," said I, "Brother

Skeeters, there is not a syllable in this about their wanting the church to withdraw the charges, and if there is any difference between this instrument of writing and what you told them to do, you will do me a favor to point it out to me. Elder Skeeters failed to make even an effort to point out any difference, for he knew there was none. The brother present stated that the instrument was presented to the church just as I read it and he thought the church ought to grant the request, and he made a motion to that effect, but no one seconded it. I became satisfied that some people were willing to misrepresent to the great hurt of innocent parties. I read to Elder Skeeters, Brother Odell's letter which corroborated what Elder Skeeters had told me, that they had agreed to grant that request if it was presented. I then went to Brother Mullens with the same papers, and gave them to him and requested him to point out the difference between the contents of that paper, and what they had proposed to do. He read it and every once in a while would say, "There is a difference," but he did not, neither could he, tell what the difference was. I soon became converted to sympathy with the seven excluded members. I felt confident that truth and justice never required false statements and misrepresentations to vindicate them. I then visited those seven members and preached for them at their houses occasionally, whenever I visited at Paris. I felt then and still believe that they were abused, and that perhaps some doctrinal heresies had been the cause of the whole thing. For Elder Paine, a man whom I have noticed before in this book, had been there preaching and was heartily endorsed by Mullens and Dodimeade. Elder Skeeters, also, was an able preacher of the doctrines of the regeneration of the whole-man, also of the eternal flesh and blood of Christ. A few weeks before I made the visit to Paris, of which I have already given an account, I met an old sister Huffman, known by her people familiarly as Aunt Cassie, of Bethany Church, in Posey County, Indiana, where Elder Skeeters had once lived. She was a cousin of Elder Skeeters and thought a great deal of him. She asked me if I had seen Cousin Joe Skeeters lately. I told her I had not seen him since he left Posey County. She then wanted to know whether he was preaching the Arian doctrine or not. I told her I knew nothing about what he was preaching, for I had never heard him. I told her that I had heard that he had preached that the flesh and bones of Jesus Christ came down from heaven and that he took nothing from his mother only the blood, but I did not know whether he believed it or not, for I had never heard him say anything about it. She said, "You preachers ought to see each other and talk matters over before you go about accusing each other." Such talk as that ruffled my feelings just a little, and I told her in plain terms that I had just informed her that I had neither seen nor heard Elder Skeeters preach since he left here and that I did not know what he preached and that I never had said I knew. I also said to her, "Before you accuse a man in such a style, you had better find out whether he is guilty or not."

She said that he did not preach that doctrine when he lived in Posey County, and that if he was preaching it now, he had changed, and she had no use for him or that doctrine, if he was preaching it, and that she intended to write to him and tell him so. When I saw him at his home, I asked him if he had received a letter from her lately, and told him the conversation we had, and that she told me if he believed that doctrine and preached it, she had no use for him. She knew he did not preach it when he lived in Posey County. He replied that he had preached it in that pulpit, that is, at Bethany Church, Posey County, Indiana, a hundred times. He said that in the sixth chapter of John, the Scriptures say in so many words, in speaking of Jesus Christ, that his flesh came down from heaven. During that conversation, we began on the subject of the new birth. He said that man never was known to have an "Inner man" until after regeneration. Of course, the Scriptures perhaps do not say anything about an inner man until after regeneration, but in taking his positions he made this remark, that the apostle commanded us to pray, lifting up holy hands; "Now," said he, "Where do you get holy hands, unless they are made so in the work of regeneration?" So I became thoroughly convinced as to where Elder Skeeters stood doctrinally, on those two points. In our conversation, however, the question of the pre-existence of God's children came up as a topic of conversation, and I told him that I did not believe in the pre-existence of God's children. He said he was aware of that, for he had seen in my paper the CHURCH ADVOCATE, in giving my account of the debate with Elder Hearde that I did not believe in the pre-existence of God's people in any sense whatever. He thought that was an extreme expression for a Baptist to make. I told him I had never said that in the ADVOCATE. He contended that I had, for he had read it. I told him he had read more than what was there. I ought to know what was there when I wrote it myself, and I know that was not in it. I told him that I had heard before, that some of his brethren had made the accusation against me, but that they had done so without any foundation, for it was not in the paper. He remarked that if it was not, he was badly mistaken. I reminded him that such a thing as that might be possible. The next morning I was at the house of Sister Leonard, who was a subscriber to the paper, and I came across the number referred to, and when I went to Elder Skeeters' with those other papers, I took that along, handed it to him, and told him I wanted him to point out, in my account of the debate, the expression that he accused me of using the evening before. He took the paper and looked over it carefully. About the time he gave it up he began to talk on some other subject, folding the paper up and handing it to me. I interrupted him long enough to ask him, "Brother Skeeters, did you find in that paper where I said that I did not believe in the pre-existence of God's children in any sense of the word?" He said, "No, it was not in this paper." "Well," said I, "you said last night that you had seen it. Now, let me tell you again that you have never seen it. It is possible that very positive men may be mistaken. I knew when you were talking to me that you had never seen it."

The church at Mount Pleasant, that is the church in Paris, battled along for a few years in their divided state, the Mullens party claiming to be the church and the seven excluded members also claiming to be the church, until finally the Mullens party quit meeting. There were only a few of them, and they moved away or died away, until they were not able to keep house. There were about fifteen members who had been neutral and had not expressed themselves for either party. While the Association refused to accept these seven members as the church and wished them to go to the church and be reconciled, there was no church for them to go to as long as the Mullens party was recognized as the church. One of the old brethren finally said to me, at my house, concerning the affair, that he did not know how to remedy the trouble there. He thought the seven members had done wrong in setting up as the church and that they ought to come to the church and make an acknowledgement of it, before the Association could have anything to do with it. I told him that was all right, that he should go and call all those members together, who had never taken any part in the trouble, and let them organize as the Mount Pleasant Church, independent of Mullens and Dodimeade, and let these seven members come and make their acknowledgement and be restored; then that would be the Mount Pleasant Church. That plan was adopted and a reconciliation was brought about and they were received again by the Association, and held their regular meetings for a few years, but I think that they do not meet regularly now.

CHAPTER XXXVI.

I have been accused many times in my life, together with my brethren in the ministry, of being anti-mission, and men have gone so far as to accuse me of refusing to obey the commission which says, "Go ye into all the world, and preach the gospel to every creature." I have always denied that charge. I claim to be a Bible Missionary. While some of my brethren, in order, I suppose, to meet the idea of the Missionaries concerning the carrying of the gospel to the heathen world, have contended that the apostolic commission is not in force to-day, I believe that it is. I have never felt disposed to say that the apostolic commission ended with the apostles, for I do not believe it did. I never could see the necessity of denying the commission in order to oppose modern Missionism, from the fact that I believe the commission suits me as it reads, better than it does our modern Missionaries. They claim that the commission was given to the whole church, while the text itself shows that it was given to the eleven. The reason the Missionaries want the commission so interpreted as to mean the whole church, is, that they claim that it is the church's duty to send Missionaries to the whole world. The commission says, "Go ye into all the world." It speaks to the eleven apostles personally, and it does not say to the church, "Send into all the world and preach the gospel," which certainly would be correct if that was what it meant. I believe that it is the duty of a man to go and preach, if the Lord calls him to that work, and then if he does not go, he is disobedient. When the Lord calls a man to the work of the ministry, he does not call him to go to school a series of years before he begins to preach, but when the Lord calls a man to be a minister, it is his duty to go to the work immediately. I have always opposed the idea that the preaching of the gospel is a profession. I am aware that some men claim that the preaching of the gospel is a profession, just like the practice of medicine or the practice of law or any other profession, but I do not believe that. I believe that when the Lord calls a man to preach, he impresses his mind in some way, which causes that man to think of going. Sometimes his mind is directed to a time and locality. I have already stated in a previous chapter, that when I was first impressed to preach, my mind was directed to the vicinity of Grayville, Illinois, when I did not know a single member in that church. After I had been exercising in public about six months, I concluded I would go to the Grayville meeting. I understood that their meeting was held on the third Sunday and Saturday before, in each month. Although I had never been there, I had a great desire to be, so in October, after I had begun exercising in January, I hurried up with my work during the week, in order to be ready to go to Grayville on Saturday. When everything was ready I saddled up a two-year-old colt that was hardly bridle-wise, and rode it down to Grayville, a distance of eighteen miles from where I lived. When I arrived in town I took my colt to the livery stable, watered it and had it fed, as I thought its trip that morning would be hard on it. I then went around to the meeting house. A panel was knocked out of one of the door shutters, and I looked through the opening into the house, to see how things appeared in there. I wandered around on the streets, in sight and hearing, thinking that they would meet after a while, and that when they did, I would be on hand. I waited around in that manner until about three o'clock in the afternoon, I did not know any of the members, and might have passed them on the streets and would not have known them, neither would they have known me. I finally went to a house and made some inquiries about the Baptist meeting, and was told that this was the time of their meeting, but, perhaps, their preacher had not come, as their bell had not been rung that day. They told me of a gentleman living in town whose wife was a member of the church; also where they lived. I went to their house and found that the old people were out in town somewhere, but, when I mentioned Baptist meeting to the children, they started out, and in a few minutes the lady of the house came in. I told her who I was and where I lived, and that I had come to attend their meeting. She asked me if I was a minister. I told her I talked some in public. She asked me if I had a horse in town. I told her I had, and that it was at the livery stable. She had me bring it around, saying that I should stay all night with them, and we would have meeting Sunday morning. I remained over night, and, after breakfast the next morning I sat around until about nine o'clock, when she came to me and told me the key to the meeting house was out in the country about three miles, and none of the brethren knew anything about the meeting, and there was a great deal of sickness in the country, and that it would be very inconvenient to have meeting that day, as no one knew anything about it. Strange as it may seem, with all these excuses, I took the hint, saddled my horse, and went home. This was my first visit to Grayville Church, that was in October, 1865. I was then twenty-four years old. Of course this good sister was not acquainted with me, and from every indication she thought it would not pay to call the people together to hear me preach, for I could not preach. In this I often think, she was just exactly right. I did not then, nor do I yet, when I consider the matter, think hard of her for taking no pains in trying to get up a meeting for my accommodation. In fact, I think that the poorest business that Baptist people can be guilty of, is to try to get up a meeting merely for the accommodation of a minister, when they themselves are not interested in the matter. It is certainly a kind of business that is all the way across the grain, and I would advise brethren and sisters everywhere, on all occasions, to be more faithful than that, and to let the preacher know, that if they would have meeting, it would be purely for his accommodation, and not because the people want it.

CHAPTER XXXVII.

I think it is very unjust on the part of any who have been acquainted with my life as a minister to accuse me of being opposed to preaching the gospel to every creature, for I take the commission just as it reads. When it says go, I believe in going; when it says preach, I believe in preaching; and when it says preach the gospel, I believe that is what ought to be preached; and when it says to every creature, I believe it means to everybody who will listen, saint or sinner, rich or poor, black or white, great or small, it makes no difference. Preach it to every creature. I have tried to the best of my little ability to do this for about thirty years. I have been governed in more instances by my impressions of mind, in selecting a place to preach, than by any other one thing. It is pleasant, to be sure, to have invitations from brethren to visit them but, if I had no impressions to go to a place and no other reason for going than that the brethren had invited me, my experience has taught me that it might possibly be a mistake for me to go. I have been in places many times, where I had no liberty to preach, and it seemed I had no religious enjoyment during my meeting at such places. The people were all right and appeared to be fond of me and of my company. It seemed they failed to see that I did not enjoy the ability that I should. When I thought of visiting those places again, it seemed to me to be contrary to every indication that good would be accomplished. At other places I have visited, I thought I was blessed with good liberty and that I enjoyed religion and the fellowship and confidence of the brethren in a manner that was very pleasant. This made me very desirous of revisiting these places. I have tried to tell my people during my little ministry, that there is no place nor time when the gospel should be suppressed, but that we should preach it or be willing to preach it at all times and under all circumstances if it is necessary to do so. Why should a minister of The Gospel not talk about Jesus and his goodness in his conversation among strangers, as well as other men talk about their callings or business among strangers? I have noticed in my travels that men, who travel about with shows and musical instruments and dances, do not hesitate to go into a hotel or car and play their music or sing their foolish songs and dance, without ever asking if there is a person present who opposes those things and has no taste for them; but if a minister should go into such places and sing or pray or preach or talk about Jesus and his goodness, even religious people would set him down as a crank and his influence would be weakened, because the people would decry him everywhere as a fanatic on the subject of religion. I have thought that this was unfair.

I am reminded of a little circumstance that occurred once at Farmersville, Indiana. A friend of mine, whose name was Cox, went to Farmersville one night to church and one of his neighbors, a dutchman, went with him. It was shortly after the presidential campaign of Blaine and Cleveland. As they went home, the Dutchman made some remark to Mr. Cox about the music they had there and inquired why they did not have an organ and a choir. Mr. Cox replied that they were poor and not able to afford such things, but that they did the best they could under the circumstances. "Well," said the Dutchman, "I was shust thinking tonight that Cleveland, he hav' a glee-club, and Blaine, he hav' a glee-club, and it seemed strange to me that Jesus Christ could not hav' a glee-club." I have thought many times that the remark of the Dutchman was well timed. Why not talk and sing in favor of Jesus Christ and his cause, as well as for other causes? My doctrine has always been, that a man who is a Christian at all, should be one wherever he is. At home in his own family, out on the streets, in the shop, on the farm, at the hotel, on the steamboat, in the railroad car or street car, or wherever he is, he should be a Christian. And a minister of the gospel should let it be known that he is a servant of Christ and a minister of the gospel under every circumstance.

In August, 1888, through the invitation of the brethren in the states of Maryland and Virginia, I visited the Ketockton and Ebenezer Associations. It was my first trip east and I enjoyed it very much. I took my son Lawrence with me, who, as well as myself, saw a great many things new to us during the trip. After our trip was over, and he had been over the city of Washington, through the Capitol, the patent office and the museum, the Smithsonian Institute and the treasury building, and then had hired a bicycle by the hour for two or three hours, and had run up and down some of the principal streets of the city, had gotten acquainted with a great many people during the trip at the Associations we attended, it seemed to be a good trip for him as well as myself. We started home on Monday morning from Luray, were up all night Monday night traveling and arrived in Cincinnati for breakfast the next morning. Then we came from there on home that day. I was tired and not paying very much attention to anything as we passed along, but he, boy-like, was still wide awake and noticing everything as we traveled trough the country. Late in the afternoon our train pulled into the depot at Princeton, Indiana, and while we were stopping, Lawrence came to me and said, "Pa, this man over here is crying. I wonder what is the matter with him."

I looked around and saw a young man, nicely dressed, intelligent looking, and all alone so far as associates or company was concerned, weeping bitterly. No person seemed to pay any attention to him, so I went up to him and said, " My friend, can you tell me the nature of your trouble?" He told me that he had left his home a few days ago in Evansville and had gone to Chicago on business. There he had received a telegram that his sister had died. He had her picture on the seat and was shedding bitter tears over it. I saw by the picture that she was young and beautiful, and had been called away in the very bloom of youth. Her young brother was so broken up that it seemed he could not be reconciled to his loss. I commenced trying to comfort him by preaching the gospel to him. I inquired if she was interested on the subject of religion, He said she was, that she had a good hope in the Savior, had been a member of the church for some time, and that he had no regrets in regard to her death in that direction. I tried to console him with the thought that she was called away from the troubles and temptations of this life, to a better home in heaven; that Jesus was the great antidote of death and it was evident that he had taken her away. As I thus tried to preach Jesus to him for his comfort and consolation, other passengers gathered around and seemed to be very much interested in my talk to him. I felt that it was as much my duty to comfort the distressed one place as another. I did not hesitate to talk to this strange young man in this manner and feel that

I should do so again under similar circumstances. I believe that there is a time when even wicked men will listen to a man talk about Jesus and his goodness to sinners, and that is the time of their afflictions, bereavements or death. In order to be prepared to talk to such, we should cultivate the habit of talking to people on that subject at any time. I have thought perhaps the apostle meant that, when he said to his son in the ministry, "Be instant, in season and out of season; reprove, rebuke and exhort with all long suffering and doctrine."

CHAPTER XXXVIII.

In order that the reader may see that it has been necessary for me to defend myself against the accusation of Anti-missionism, I clip the following from an old file of the CHURCH ADVOCATE, of July 15th, 1878, of which the reader can be his own judge. It is as follows:

MR. EDITOR:—I see by your issue of June 5th, that Elder Potter has published a challenge, and since this same Elder Potter did denounce my doctrine from the stand, with your consent I will ask the Elder a few questions.

Elder Potter, what is the difference in the meaning of the two words, *apostle* and *missionary?* The one comes from a Greek term, and means to send—to send forth. The other from a Latin word, which means to send—to send forth. The blessed Jesus is called an apostle; then was He not a missionary? Heb. 3;1. The apostles were all sent to preach the gospel. Were they not all missionaries? Was not the Apostolic Church a missionary church? Elder, is not the Anti-missionary Baptist Church, of which you are a member, divided into factions? First, the two seed party; second, the anti-means party; and third, the means party? To which of these parties do you belong? Which is purely Apostolic? Is there a man in your denomination that could translate the Bible from the original Hebrew and Greek into English? If so, who is he? Do not the missionaries print the Bible for your people? Elder, your church refuses to obey the Son of God in the great commission given, "Go into all the world and preach the Gospel to every creature," and you refuse to fellowship those who do! On what ground, then, do you claim to belong to the only true church of God? Elder, when was the commission given by Jesus Christ repealed? By whom?

Yours,

R. C. KEELE.

Salem, Ill., June 9, 1878,—(*Baptist Banner.*)

Editorial reply.

There is certainly as much bigotry and ignorance in the above as we have seen lately in the same amount of reading. Elder Keele, (we suppose he is an Elder, we have no recollection of ever having heard of him before), says, "And as this same Elder Potter did denounce my doctrine from the stand," etc. This is quite likely if he has any doctrine. We undertook to get Elder Throgmorton to tell us what his doctrine was, when we debated with him, and even asked him, when he was contending that Christ died for the race of men, if He died for them to save them, and he refused to answer. But perhaps Elder Keele has a doctrine, as he says we denied his doctrine, but what it is we know not. But because we denied his doctrine, he asks us the above questions.

On the grounds that "apostle" and "missionary" mean "to send—to send forth," he seems to claim that the apostles and Missionary Baptists of the present age are just the same. Then we are to understand that the Apostles of Jesus Christ, and the Mission Baptist ministers are just alike because they are sent. We may conclude that God's ministers and the devil's are alike, for they are both sent. The Lord sends His though, and the devil sends his. There was a missionary sent to Nehemiah on one occasion, with a message; but Nehemiah says, "And lo, I preceived that God had not sent him; but that he had pronounced this prophecy against me: for Tobia and Sanballat had hired him!" Neh. vi, 12. He is a missionary, if being sent constitutes one; and especially if they must be sent and hired. The apostles were sent, but they were not hired and sent by a "Mission Board," as the Missionary Baptists are, for God sent them. The Missionary Baptist preachers, and the apostles are both sent, but each being sent by a different authority, makes all the difference between them in the world. But he seems to think we are opposed to the name "missionary." The main ground our enemies have for thinking we oppose the name is that they call us "Anti-mission." It is rather hard to call a man by a name that he denies, and then kill him for having such a name.

Another word on being sent. The apostles were not only sent of the Lord; but he told his disciples to "Pray the Lord to send laborers into the harvest." He did not say, get up Mission Boards, and make and send them yourselves. We claim to be missionaries, but we believe the Lord will send laborers, or He would not have told us to pray for Him to. The difference between us and the Missionary Baptists, is that we believe in the Lord sending His ministers, and that He will do it, and they are fearful He will not, and they must send them. "Is not the Antimission Church, of which you are a member, divided into factions?" etc. "To which of these parties do you belong?" Show us the parties you mention, divided off to themselves under those different heads, or names, and we will answer; provided we belong to either, and if we do not, we will say so.

But he asks if we can translate the Bible; and if the missionaries do not print the Bible for our people. If we had a thousand men that were able to translate the Bible, we see no necessity for such a work, as it was translated by the king's translators, and suits us in that translation first-rate. Is that what the missionaries are educating men for? We are not dependent on the missionaries for Bibles, as there are quite a number of publishing companies in the United States that print them, and they are not all connected with the "Bible Society." We did have Bibles before there were any missionary organizations in the world, and we know of no reason why we could not have them now. But he says our church refuses to obey the Son of God in the great Commission. This is a grave charge, indeed, and if Elder Keele had to be our judge, we presume he would cast us off without mercy, for disobedience. But we deny the charge, and feel thankful that he is not our judge. We will compare notes with him so far as that is concereed, and see who comes the nearest to obeying the Commission, and before we undertake that, we want to know if he is a minister, and to what denomination he belongs, and where he preaches, and if he is hired, and how much he gets. Of all these things we are ignorant, but we will venture the assertion that if he is preaching at any stated place or places, that he is hired for a stipulated salary, in which case he is making no sacrifice at all for the Lord, or His people. Hence, he comes nearest repealing the Commission by waiting until the contract is closed before he goes to work. Come again, Mr. Keele, and let us know who you are, what you are, and all about it, so we will know who it is that asks us so many foolish questions, and is so willing to misrepresent us by making the impression that we do not believe in preaching, and therefore consider the Commission repealed. We are willing to take some pains with you, and by the time you become informed on the subject of the modern plan of Missionism, and Apostolic Missionism, and able to draw the contrast between the two, you may be of some use; especially so if the grace of God should make its way into your heart.

Tell us what "my doctrine" is that you heard us deny on the stand, and when and where it was done. Ask us a few more questions, and we will give you all the information we can.

CHAPTER XXXIX.

At the October meeting of the Bethlehem Church, in Posey County, Indiana, in 1875, I was elected to the pastoral care of that church. I was then living in Grayville, Illinois. I served that church as pastor, with the exception of an intermission of two years, seventeen years. During that time I baptized a large number of people, the church seemed to get along in peace, and it was very pleasant for me to be associated with them. I became familiarly acquainted with almost all the people, young and old, in that part of Posey county. Very little unpleasantness ever existed between myself and any of the members of that church, and I think that I have seen and felt as many evidences of my call to the ministry in my labors at that church, as I have at any other one church. During the time of my ministry there, they met with the misfortune to lose their house by fire. They were abundantly able and perfectly willing to build a new one. So they appointed a committee to superintend the work, and set immediately about it. In a few months they had erected on the same spot of ground a large frame building, which speaks well for the community in which it stands as a house of worship. One thing about it is that the building committee never made but one report to the church, and that was after the house was built and they were using it. In that report, they made a statement of how much money they had received, how much they had paid out, and that now the house was built and seated, every dollar of its cost was paid. I think that it is not often the case, that a church appoints a committee to superintend the building of a meeting house, and one report is all that it ever makes. There were no festivals, nor church dedications, nor anything of the sort gotten up for the purpose of building the house. It was paid for entirely by voluntary subscriptions, from members and friends in that part of the country.

In December, 1876, I was called to the care of Big Creek Church, at Cynthiana, Elder Hume having been the pastor of that church before I was called. I attended that church fifteen years in succession and lived in the immediate neighborhood eight years of the time. There was never any serious unpleasantness between myself and any of the members of that church. It is the church of my membership to-day, and is indeed a pleasant place for me to visit. I gave up these two churches of my own accord, recommending Elder Schultz as a man whom I thought they would be glad to have. He is now their pastor, and is highly esteemed by them for his work's sake.

In July, 1881, I was called to the care of Bethel Church, at Farmersville. This church was in a cold state when I took charge of it, having had considerable trouble among themselves, which they perhaps have not yet gotten entirely over. The congregation was small, and it seemed that there was not a great deal of interest manifested among the members of that church, at that time. I had not made very many visits, however, until I thought I could see that the interest was growing. I began to tell the brethren of other churches, that I believed Bethel Church was going to revive, but I was sometimes met with this reply: that they thought Bethel Church was about done, that it had been on the down grade until it had about got to the bottom, and they had concluded it never would revive. The second year that I preached for them, I baptized between twenty and thirty people, and have baptized during the time that I have preached for them, thirty-five or forty, and perhaps more than that. We have had some glorious meetings at that church, and no unpleasantness ever occurred to amount to nonfellowship between me and any of her members. Perhaps there is not a member in it, now, who would object to my being pastor of their church, if they had no pastor and were going to elect one. I gave that church up, after preaching for it most of the time for about ten years, because I had too much else to do and could not attend it regularly. I recommended Elder Willis, who is their present pastor and with whom they are well pleased. His labors have been abundantly blessed in that church. In the year 1883, at the July meeting, I was called to the care of Bethany Church. That gave me four churches in Posey County. I preached for that church seven years, without any intermission, and in that time baptized upwards of thirty-five people. This church had been in some trouble years before that time, which it had hardly gotten over, and it had some little troubles in the year after I commenced attending it. It numbered about sixty members when I took it, and when I gave it up it numbered about eighty-five members. The congregation was large and interesting, and I have certainly enjoyed some as bright evidences of my call to the ministry, both at Bethany and Bethel Churches, as I ever have anywhere. Those churches are dear to me, and their members seem to-day as if they were my own children. Elder Schultz is the pastor of this church and it is in a good, prosperous condition so far as I know. For the first few years after I began preaching for these four churches, it was no trouble for me to go into the neighborhood on Friday before their meetings, and visit from house to house over the neighborhood, during the two days I was there. I could start out on foot as soon as I had my breakfast, cross fields and fences, and call at half a dozen houses before meeting time in the morning. My object was to be at as many of their houses as I possibly could. I enjoyed visiting them in their homes and talking to them on the subject of religion. If any troubles arose among them, I made it a point to try to get them adjusted as soon as I could. By having the care of those churches so long I came as near being personally acquainted with the people of Posey County, and especially the portion of the county where those churches are located, as any one man, perhaps, who ever preached in the county. The people seem near to me, and I certainly do feel at home among them. I moved to that county from

Grayville, on the first day of December, 1880, and have been living in the state of Indiana ever since.

In 1885, I was called to the care of the church at Owensville. They elected me at their November meeting, which was on the fourth Sunday and Saturday before, in the month. Before their December meeting rolled around, I engaged in a six days' debate with Mr. Yates, of the Cumberland Presbyterian Church, at Owensville, on the subject of "Foreign Missions." We debated six days to a very large and enthusiastic crowd of people. Mr. Yates is a man who is well posted, and he has extraordinary ambition and ability. During the discussion, I made the statement on the first day, that I did not believe that all the missionaries, with all their friends and all they had ever done, had been or would be the cause of a single soul being saved, that would not have been saved without them. When I made this statement, quite a number of his brethren jumped to get their note books to note it down, as if they were very much surprised at me for making such a statement. I put the same question to him and he refused to answer, until the fourth day of the debate, in the afternoon, when his moderator suggested that he was under obligations to answer it. During that discussion, I had an eye all the time to future work among the people of Owensville and vicinity. While I believed that I was capable of defending the doctrine that I believed on the subject of missions and the preaching of the gospel, I felt that I had the good will of the community. After the debate was over, I held my first meeting in December. At the January meeting following, the church received one member for baptism; at the February meeting, I commenced on Saturday before the fourth Sunday and continued meeting until the next Sunday a week at night, and during that time received nineteen members for baptism; at the April meeting, the church had received twenty-six members. This caused great jealousy on the part of other denominations. As the Regular Baptists were the only people in Owensville or even in that part of the country anywhere who practiced strict communion, the preachers of other denominations began to argue the communion question with my people and with anyone who they thought was likely to join the Regular Baptists. A Mr. Hale, of the General Baptist denomination was publishing a paper there, in which he had a great deal to say on the question of the communion. I finally called on him at his office and asked him to meet me at the Regular Baptist Church and discuss the question of the communion, which he refused to do, stating that he was opposed to debates, and thought that the time for public discussions on the subject of religion had passed away. I then made the announcement that I would lecture at Owensville, on the subject of the communion, commencing on a certain Monday night, and continuing until I was through, and that any man who would undertake the other side of the question should have half of the time, if he would come on at that time. No man saw fit to do so and I delivered my four lectures on the communion at Owensville, and those are the circumstances that brought them about. So this is a brief history of my labors among the five churches that I have already mentioned in Indiana. These churches are all prosperous and have the labors of good, efficient and earnest young men, who are their pastors, sound in faith and zealous for the cause of Christ.

CHAPTER XL.

During the time I was preaching for the churches that I have already mentioned in the preceding chapter, I became impressed to visit the Mount Pleasant Church, in the neighborhood of where Griffin now is. I was deeply impressed for at least a year and a half to go to that church and preach, before I had an opportunity to do so. I had the care of five churches and frequently told Elders Hume, Strickland and Oliphant that if I could be released from one of them, I believed that the Lord would revive that little church, if I could go there and preach. Mount Pleasant Church was very weak, having only perhaps a dozen members. They had no preacher and it seemed that the last one or two preachers, they did have, left them in a worse condition than they had found them. I suppose fully eight years elapsed after the time I had preached in that neighborhood, before I went back. During that time a great change had been made in the membership of the church and also in the citizenship of the neighborhood. A railroad had been run through the neighborhood and a little town built up. I did not know who lived there. After studying the matter over and feeling so deeply impressed, I finally met with a friend of mine who lived in that vicinity. I told him that I had thought for some time that I would love to go down and preach at Griffin. That was the name of the little town which had sprung up. He was a member of another denomination, but a personal friend of mine, and he spoke rather favorably of my coming down to preach. The Regular Baptists had no house in that neighborhood. The old house that they had formerly occupied had become so dilapidated that it was not fit for meetings, but there was a house built in the little village by the people, which seemed to be a union house. It was controlled by the Campbellites but was free for the use of other denominations when not occupied by them. After talking the matter over with my friend, I finally told him that I would be at Griffin on the next Tuesday, at eleven o'clock, and that he might have it announced for me. I told him to tell the people that I did not know how long I would stay. The next Saturday, after the Tuesday my meeting began, was Christmas day, and the people in that neighborhood loved to have a great deal of fun about Christmas time, as is common with a great many people, who are located back in the river bottoms. Griffin had the name of being a hard place at the time, and was very commonly known as the "Blind Tiger." There were two or three saloons in the little place, and they were well patronized.

On Tuesday morning, when I was preparing to start, I told my wife that she might put a change of clothing in my satchel, for I expected to baptize some while I was gone, and I would need them if I did. She thought I was rather too sanguine about the matter, and replied to me that if I found anybody that wanted to be baptized, I would also find clothes to wear. So I went and commenced my meeting on Tuesday at eleven o'clock, and continued it for four days and nights. In that time the church received four candidates for baptism. I was not surprised at that, for I had been deeply impressed before I left home that the church would certainly revive if they had regular preaching. In a few weeks I went back and held meeting a day or two, and received three more members. I visited them frequently as opportunity offered, until other brethren began going there to preach, and occasionally there would be one or more added to the church. Finally they elected a regular pastor, and they have had regular preaching ever since. I believe that I attended them as pastor one year. Other brethren have visited and preached for them, and to-day they number in the neighborhood of fifty members. They have built a nice house to worship in, in the little town, at a cost of nearly one thousand dollars. I regard this as an evidence that I was impressed by the Divine Spirit to go to that place and preach, and I have noticed that to follow such impressions is almost infallibly to see the same results that I saw there. The churches are in good condition throughout this country.

After a while there seemed to be a great interest at Wadesville in favor of the Baptists, and I became very much concerned in favor of a church at Wadesville, provided we could obtain a house at that place. Matters finally adjusted themselves in such a way that our people bought a controlling interest in the house at Wadesville, and we constituted a church there with seventeen members, in the year 1891. I have had the care of that church as her pastor all the time since her constitution, and she now numbers forty members. We have had very interesting times at that church, as well as at all the churches of which I have had the pastoral care. The churches of Posey County are as strong numerically, as they were when I first began to preach for them, and some of them are considerably stronger. The Baptists of these churches are sound, faithful brethren, none of them that I know of being the least tinctured with Armenianism or anti-nomianism, but primitive Baptists, who love to hear the doctrine and practice of the Baptists vindicated.

Before dismissing this chapter, I will state that the churches I have mentioned heretofore were the churches among whom Elders Hume and Strickland labored most of their ministerial lives. Those churches never did divide on missionism, two-seedism, no-soulism, non-resurrectionism, nor the means question, nor any other "ism." Some of them date as far back in their constitutions as 1806, and there is not a Missionary Baptist Church in the County, nor in the bounds of the Salem Association. The General Baptists, who are full-fledged Armenians, and free-communionists, are the only body of religionists in the bounds of the Salem Association who claim the name of Baptists, except our people. The difference between our people and the General Baptists is so great, that there never was much danger of a man being mistaken and joining one of these denominations when he intended to join the other. This is not true in every case where there are Missionary Baptists, for I feel confident that the Missionaries to-day have in their churches hundreds and thousands of our people; and the way they get them is by telling the people that there is really no difference of importance between us, and that their churches are flourishing. They get a great many people to join them, who in heart are really our people.

CHAPTER XLI.

In my efforts to preach, I have had a great many pleasant times in trying to proclaim the gospel to a dying world. There is nothing more pleasant to me than to be blessed with ability and deep personal interest while I try to proclaim life and salvation through a crucified and risen Redeemer. I have thought many times during my ministry that I could do better and realize the presence of the Lord more sensibly, if I could keep self out of my discourses. That has been one of the hardest things for me to control, and I have suffered a great deal because I could not be farther away from self in my efforts to preach, in my prayers, and in my exercises generally in the service of the Lord. While I have had many pleasant times among the brethren, I have been made to feel frequently that the brethren were ungrateful for my services and did not appreciate me as I deserved. At times, on that account, I have been very miserable. I think, however, that this was a temptation from the evil one, for I know when I look back over my life that the brethren have been kind to me. They have treated me better than they have a great many others, who perhaps are as good as I am in every way and more able to preach the gospel. I have many times in my life made complete failures when I expected to preach well, and I wish to give one or two instances of my experience in that direction.

When I was very young in the ministry, I think it

was in the year 1870, I lived in the neighborhood of Long Prairie Church, in Illinois. I worked on a farm in those days and tried to make my own living. One time, while I was out in the fields at work, a text of Scripture came into my mind and I thought a great many good things in connection with it. I could see more beauty in it than I ever had before and thought I understood some things about it that I had never heard anyone say anything about. I felt certain that the ideas I had upon it were correct, although I had never thought of them before. With these ideas in my mind, I thought if I were going to preach now, that would be my text. And, working along, the text remained with me until finally the thought occurred to me that, next Saturday being our meeting time, I would certainly preach from that text some time during the meeting. There were two or three other preachers, who were members of the same church, and we usually divided the time among us at our regular meetings, so the probabilities were that I would not get to preach just when I would like to. It would suit me best to preach from this text on Sunday, as more people would be likely to be present then, than at any other time during the meeting. From this time on until meeting time, I studied about this text and felt confident that I would try to preach from it the first opportunity I had before a good congregation. I felt that I would not preach it to a small crowd. If I was called on to preach on Saturday, I would use some other text and save this one until I had a large crowd, for it would be too good a sermon for just a few to hear. I went to meeting on Saturday, and we had our ordinary attendance, and some of the other brethren preached. I was glad of that, for it was a pretty fair indication that I would get to preach on Sunday; and I felt that when I did get up, the people would hear something. We had meeting Saturday night, and, as I went to the meeting house, I thought that if there was a pretty fair crowd out and I was called on to preach, I might preach my sermon that night, lest I might not have an opportunity to preach it on Sunday. When I entered the house and looked around, I thought to myself "This crowd will do very well, and if the brethren insist on my preaching to-night, I will only be just a little backward, enough for good manners, and I will preach my sermon." So, when the time came for preaching, the brethren insisted that I must preach. I went into the pulpit, asked one brother to introduce services for me, took the Bible down off the stand, and was going to turn to the text, but by the time I had gotten the Bible down, ready to open it, I had forgotten where the text was. Then I studied a moment to try to call to mind where it was. Then I studied a moment to try to think what the text was. I could not call it to mind. I then tried to call to mind some of the things I had thought about it and I could not. By this time I began to be wretched. I raised up and looked over the pulpit, (it was one of those old-fashioned pulpits, closed up in front,) and I looked at the congregation and thought "I do wish there were not so many people here." I wished that I were out of the stand and that I did not have to try to preach. My text was gone, my sermon was gone, everything that I had ever thought about that text was gone, and I had no message for this people. I never have known from that moment to this what that text was, nor anything I had ever thought about it. I may have used it many times since then as a text, but if I have I do not know it. I took some other text and whiled away a portion of the time. When I went out of the stand that night I was as completely whipped as was ever a poor servant of the Lord, which at that time I could not think I was. I abominated the thought of depending upon myself and felt that I ought to apologize to the people for ever offering to talk to them on the subject of religion. I never could make any calculations about preaching and then work up to them.

Another circumstance that occurred in my ministry was later in life. I was still living in Illinois, and Elder Lewis Hon and myself were the delegates to the Little Wabash Association. I had not been with the Little Wabash Association for two or three years. When I was younger I had been in the habit of going about every year, besides visiting among the churches at other times in the year. When we got there I met a great many old brethren and sisters, whom I had met many times. They seemed so very glad to see me that they made use of such expressions as these: "I am glad to see your face once more," "It seems like old times to see you among us again," "Why did you stay away so long?" "I am eager to hear your voice again," which were very pleasant. I finally began to be anxious to preach to them, and thought that if I had an opportunity to preach they would think of old times, more than simply to see me. To my satisfaction, there was an appointment made for me at the house of a Brother Sands, for Friday night, which was the first night of the Association. I was glad and a great many people assembled at Brother Sands' before night. Although there were other appointments in the neighborhood not far away, yet it seemed that most of the people had come to my meeting. By this time I had lost what little sense I had ever had about preaching. When the hour drew near for the services to begin, I made ready without any hesitancy whatever, selected my text and song to introduce services, and when the time came, I was ready. There were several ministers present sitting around me, but I did not think to invite any of them to take any part. When I was ready to begin. I told some of the brethren to be ready to conclude the meeting when I was through preaching. I did not ask them to preach any after me, for I expected to do all the preaching that would be needed that night. When I commenced reading my song, it seemed that my voice was in an unnatural key, and that I could not get it toned down to a natural, easy key. During the prayer it seemed that I had no voice, but I felt that when I got to preaching I would be all right. I read my text and commenced talking. In a few minutes I found myself talking in a very uneasy, low, dragging, unnatural monotone. As I could not change my voice from that way, I concluded that I would begin anew and see if I could not start out better. In the course of twenty minutes or so, I made about three efforts to start and "Failure" was written on each one of them. By this time I came to the conclusion that I could not preach, so I quit, saying to the brethren, "Brethren, some of you preach, for you see I cannot preach a bit." Brother Hon arose and commenced preaching. I felt that he thought it would be a good time for him to beat me preaching, also that he would make use of the opportunity. I did wish that he could not preach a word, and felt that I wanted him to quit every moment of the time. But he did not do it; he went on and preached and labored hard. Toward the last of his sermon a young sister was very deeply affected, and I concluded that he wanted her to shout before he quit. I was not in a spirit of mischief, for I was feeling sad and almost out of humor, but I did wish the girl would shout so he would quit. I felt almost confident that he wanted her to shout, and did not intend to quit until she did. Finally I thought he gave the matter up, for he closed his discourse; (a man you know can think anything but what is right, when he is in such a frame of mind as I was.) I do not know how many brethren remember that occurrence, but I am satisfied that there are ministers living to-day, as well as many other brethren, who, if they chance to read this page, will remember the whole circumstance. I give these two instances to show that I, for one, cannot preach every time I want to. I am still as dependent on the Lord for ability to preach, as I ever was in my life. I know that it is wrong for me to calculate that I am going to preach a big sermon, because I never did make any such calculations without being disappointed in the arrangement. I would say to the brethren generally, that perhaps the admonition of the apostle is as applicable to my case in such circumstances as to any other man in the world; that is, "He that standeth, let him take heed lest he fall."

CHAPTER XLII.

In the summer of 1880 I made a trip down into the state of Alabama, at the invitation of Elder Purifoy. I left home about the 28th day of July. The weather was intensely warm, and on the way from Evansville to Nashville the train came to a broken bridge about thirty miles north of Nashville. It was about five o'clock in the afternoon when we got to this bridge. When the train stopped and the passengers learned of the trouble, as is natural, we all went out to see the damaged bridge and what must be done in order to insure our safe crossing. The train finally ran back to a station at Springfield, Tennessee, and took a position on a side track to wait for the bridge to be repaired, so that we could pass over. Some time after sunup the next morning found us still waiting and we did not dare to leave the train even to get refreshments, for fear of being left, for we were not likely to receive any notice of the starting of the train. During the night I tried to sleep, but I had no better bed than a seat in the car. There were so many of the passengers awake and talking all the time and so much moving and stirring about that it was impossible to sleep. There was a gentleman aboard the train who was a minister of some branch of the Presbyterian Church and he was a good talker. He came aboard the train, I think, at Hopkinsville, Ky., and I soon learned that he was a preacher, for the people seemed to be well acquainted with him. When I found that I was not likely to get to sleep any, I felt that the hours whiled away very slowly, and I did wish I had some person to talk to, but there was not a person on the train that I knew or that knew me. I thought that if I could get acquainted with the Presbyterian minister, I would not be so lonesome, for he seemed to be good company; but I had no one to introduce me to him, and I did not wish to be forward in introducing myself to strangers in a place like that. I noticed him and another gentleman in conversation and I overheard the other man tell him that he would love to hear him give his reasons for infant baptism. He agreed to do so, and they sat down, and I moved near them so I could hear. He began to tell the man that God always takes families by their representatives, as He did Adam, Abraham, Jacob and so on. If the father or the mother of the child is a believer, or if they are both believers, then the child is to be admitted to baptism. He said that if the Baptist doctrine were true, that the child was to be denied baptism because it was not a believer itself, and no one believed for it, then the same thing that cuts it out of baptism would cut it out of heaven. I listened to him until he got through, and I saw that the other man did not seem disposed to differ from him, so I told him that I would like to ask him a question, if it would not be an intrusion. He looked at me somewhat suspiciously, and said, in rather a gruff manner, I thought, "What is it?" I told him that in the second chapter of The Acts, we read: "And as many as gladly received his word were baptized, and there were added to them that day about three thousand—— what?" he said, "three thousand souls." I told him that I did not know but what it should have been families. He sprang to his feet and pranced around somewhat like a horse with sore feet, and said, "If that is the way you are going to treat the Bible, like an Irishman would a pile of rock, take up one at a time and throw at an opponent, you can prove anything." I said, "You are a preacher, are you not?" He said he was. Well, I told him that I did not think he would be likely to convert many people, if that was his manner of talking to them. I told him that I had permission to ask him that question, and that I now asked him to sit down here and talk to me; for I had done nothing to deserve such treatment as that. He came to his seat in as fine a humor as I ever saw a man, and from that moment he was so polite and gentlemanly, that it was a complete apology for the way he had acted. I called on him to give me his reasons for infant baptism, and he began as he had done before, saying about the same things. He repeated, that according to the Baptist doctrine, that the infant was not to be baptized on the ground that it did not believe itself and no one believed for it, the very same thing that would cut it out of baptism would cut it out of heaven. After passing some words and quoting a few texts of Scripture, I asked him if he baptized all infants. He said he would baptize any infant whose father or mother or guardian was a believer. I asked him if he would baptize a child whose parents or guardian were not believers. He said he would not. I asked him why. He said, because they do not believe and no one believes for them. I told him that I had heard him say twice that if infants were to be cut out of baptism on the grounds that they do not believe, and no one believes for them, that the same thing that would cut them out of baptism would cut them out of heaven. Now, Sir, said I, according to your rule, some infants are cut out of baptism because they do not believe and no one believes for them. You say that if that is what cuts them out of baptism, the same thing will cut them out of heaven. I claim, Sir, that in your doctrine, some infants are cut out of heaven. He did not fight for his position, nor did he take it back, but I was confident that he felt the weight of his own argument when it fell back upon his own head.

CHAPTER XLIII.

I have heard all my life that the Regular Baptists are long-winded. It has been said many times that if they have a half dozen ministers present they must all preach. People have said many times that they did wish they had their dinners with them. I was at a meeting at Middle Fork Church, called Webb's Prairie, Franklin County, Ills., on one occasion, and after services were over on Sunday, arrangements were made for me to go to a house not far away for dinner. A surrey was going to that place, in which there was room for me, and I was instructed to ride. I took a seat in the surrey with a lady, who was a total stranger to me. In fact, the entire crowd were strangers to me. I do not even know their names now. But we had not gone far before the lady sitting with me began to complain of the "Hardshells" for preaching so long. I had conducted the services myself that day, and there was no other minister there and she knew it. Yet, as if she thought I did not have any better sense than to allow her to abuse me to my face, she indulged in her strictures to her friends in the surrey as we went along the road. I asked her if she was a church member. She said she was a member of the Missionary Baptist Church.

I told her that I did not think that the Missionary Baptists had any right to complain of us, or any one else for long services; for they begin a meeting in the fall of the year and run it through the most of the winter, sometimes, and they often begin their night meetings at an early hour, and run them until ten o'clock, or later. We had never held such meetings, and I thought that it was unjust to blame us for long services. I told her I did not think it looked well, especially for the Missionary Baptists to speak of it in such a manner.

"Oh!" she said, "Our minister never talks more than thirty-five or forty minutes, and we think that is plenty long enough for a sermon." I told her that I thought so too, for the sort of stuff he preached, I would not want to listen to it any longer than that myself. "But," I said, "if he had good news for you, and you loved what he preached, you would not get tired of hearing him even if he should preach an hour or more." She seemed willing to drop the subject, so I said no more about it, and we went on and had a very pleasant time.

CHAPTER XLIV.

I once took a trip to the churches in the bounds of the Little Wabash Association in Illinois, and when my tour ended I was conveyed by a good brother to Odin, a station at the crossing of the O. & M. and I. C. Railroads, in Marion County. It was late in the afternoon when we got there, and the brother had to return home, so I was left alone to wait until about ten o'clock for my train. There was no one about the station that I knew, and a great portion of the time there was no one in the room but myself. I never was much of a coward about traveling, as I have never seen many times that I was scared or even uneasy when away from home. I have gone several times in life two or three days at a time without seeing any one that I knew. I have arrived in strange cities and towns in the night, have landed off of steamboats, and have gotten up at hotels at all hours in the night, at strange places, to meet trains or boats, and I never did feel the least uneasy under such circumstances, except a very few times in all my travels. I am not of a very excitable nature, and have always been slow about being suspicious of danger. On this occasion, some time after dark, three or four men entered the waiting room and acted very strangely. They passed all around me, and seemed to gaze at me as if they thought they knew me. They seated themselves in the room, and they all seemed to have their eyes steadily fixed upon me, but they did not say a word to me, nor to each other.

After sitting awhile, they arose and walked out, and in a short time they returned and took their seats again, as they had done before, still looking at me very suspiciously. I did not feel uneasy, and yet I felt confident that I was the special object of their attention. I had heard before of Odin, that it was rather a hard place, and that travelers had been molested, and some of them robbed there. I thought of these things, but the room was well lighted up, and the Agent and Operator were in their offices. I did not fear that they would undertake any foul play with me, if I remained in the room. They again left the room and I was alone. Some time after, I discovered one of them in the ticket office, gazing at me through the ticket window. In all this time not a word was said by them to me nor to each other. Before the train came, I found out that it was the sheriff of the county, and a posse that he had with him, who were on the hunt of a horse thief. When I heard all this I felt certain that I was in great danger of being arrested, for if I had offered to leave the room while they were watching so closely, they would have been very apt to have laid hold of me. It is a wonder that I did not get up and walk around, for I am of such a restless temperament that I hardly ever sit still very long at a time, when I am waiting for a train, especially if I have been away from home several days, and am trying to get back. I feel almost certain that if I had made an attempt to walk out I would have been arrested by this company; that is before they became satisfied that I was not the man they were on the hunt of. They, however, did not interrupt me, and I bought my ticket, and when the train came I was permitted to board it as usual and go home. I felt thankful to the Lord that I was not a horse thief, and I adopted the language of the great apostle to the Gentiles, "It is by the grace of God that I am what I am." If I am any better than others, it is not by nature, but it must be that grace has made the difference. So, the Lord should have all the glory, while I get all the benefit of his mercy and grace.

CHAPTER XLV.

One time, at an Association, I met a lady who, I was told, belonged to the Methodist Church, and was not in the habit of hearing our people preach. She was not acquainted with our ways and customs. I felt confident that she had heard that the Old Baptists were selfish and clannish, and that if she could not learn better about us, she would not enjoy herself very well at our Association. She had come some distance with a family of our people, who lived out of the immediate neighborhood of the Baptists. In the afternoon I thought I would converse with her on the subject of religion, if by that means I might make her feel more welcome among us. So I began by asking her some questions, and she began to object. She said she was not going to argue with me. I told her that I did not wish to argue, but that I preferred to talk about matters upon which we agreed. I told her that I thought we might talk about our experiences without differing, and if we could I would enjoy it very much. She said that she had no objection whatever to telling her experience, if that was all I wished to talk about. She stated that she had an experience and not only that, but she thought she had the most singular experience, perhaps, that I had ever heard. She then proceeded to relate her Christian experience, which was good, and she said that she had realized that experience when she was very young. After that she joined the Methodist Church, and finally she married a good man, and became the mother of two or three sweet little children. She said she thought that she ought to be the happiest woman in the world. She had everything to make her happy. She had a good hope in Jesus, was a member of the church, was blessed with a pleasant home, a good, kind husband and a sweet little family.

But soon the terrible wrecker of homes, the grim monster, death, invaded this lovely home, and took one of her children. She said that during her grief and mourning over the loss of her darling child, once in a while the thought would suggest itself to her, that God was unjust, to treat her so; but she would not allow herself to harbor such a thought for a moment. She went on and tried to feel reconciled, and finally another of her loved ones sickened and died. After this one was gone, the same thought would come into her mind that surely God is unjust. Under this weighty cross of affliction and the loss of her family, she gave up her place in the church and tried to conclude that there was nothing real in religion. She tried for ten years from that on to be an infidel, but she said that there was a dissatisfaction in her mind about it all the time. She would speak out against religion and in favor of infidelity, yet she could not feel clear in her conscience, in denying the Lord. However, she went on in this way for ten years, trying all the time to be an infidel, but she could not. At the end of ten years she gave up her infidelity and went back to the church. Since then she had gotten along about as other people, sometimes up in her feelings and sometimes down, but down most of the time. She often thought that if she was a Christian she was just a little one.

I said to her that I thought her experience was very interesting, but I thought she was indeed a child of God. I asked her if she went back to the Methodist Church. She said she did. I asked her if she believed the doctrine of the Methodist Church. "O yes," she said, "I believe their doctrine." I asked her if they did not believe that a saint could apostatize, fall from grace and be eternally lost. She said they did. Well, said I you do not believe that doctrine, do you? She said, yes, she believed it. Well, said I, how long does it take a Christian to fall from grace? You said that you tried it for ten years and could not fall. She said she had never thought of that. She became very much interested in our preaching during the Association, and seemed to be free and at home among our people. I was glad that I had accomplished my purpose in trying to make her feel that our people were her friends, even if they did differ in their views.

CHAPTER XLVI.

While I lived at Grayville, Illinois, my county town was Carmi, the county seat of White county. I sometimes had business there and would usually go down on the train, after the railroad was built through there. At one time I went down on a little business and after I was through, having nothing else to do, I walked over to the depot and arrived there an hour or more before the train was due. There was no one in the waiting room, and thinking an hour would be a long time for me to sit there alone, I walked out. Over the way I noticed a company of men sitting around on the doorstep of a store, so I went over there. I knew none of them, and I am satisfied that none of them knew me. The most of the crowd were rather young, but one of them was an elderly looking man. The topic of their conversation was the election of township officers in the county, which had taken place very recently. I took a seat in a chair just inside the door, and listened to them. Once in a while I would join them in their conversation. Finally we saw a man coming past with a load of hay on a wagon, and his team consisted of three animals, two horses at the tongue and a mule in front, or two mules at the tongue and a horse in front, I am not certain which. A boy was riding the front animal, and a man was up on the load of hay. The novelty of the outfit had its attractions, and if I had noticed it, I would have known the old gentleman. After he had gone out of sight, one of the crowd remarked, "I thought that was a preacher." "Was he a preacher?" said the old man. "Who is it?" "John Haynes," said the other. I was well acquainted with Brother John Haynes, but he was gone and I said nothing. The old man asked what sort of a preacher he was, and the other answered that he was a Baptist. "What, a Missionary Baptist?" "No, a Hard Side Baptist," the young man replied. "O well," said the old man, "that is enough for me, if he is a Hard Side Baptist, I have no use for him. They preach infants to hell, and I do not like them. I do not like the Methodists either, for they preach falling from grace, and according to that doctrine, I think when they do get good, they should get some one to kill them, so they will not have to run the risk of falling from grace." I said to him, "What do you like?" He said, "The Missionary Baptists." "What objection have you to the Methodists?" I asked. He said, "They believe in falling from grace, and infant baptism, and infant church membership, and I do not believe in any of those things." I asked, "What did you say the man was that passed with the team?" (I did not want him to know what I was yet.) He said, "He is a Hard Side Baptist." I asked, "What are your objections to them?" He said that they preached infants to hell. I asked him if he ever heard one of them preach that. He said he had. He had heard a man preach it by the name of Hume. I asked him where he had heard him preach it. He said at Mt. Pleasant Church, I knew where Mt. Pleasant Church was. I asked him what Hume said, and he replied that Hume said it was his opinion that there were infants in hell. "And you heard him say it?" I said. He said he did, and that he could prove it by as good men as there were in Wayne County. I told him that I did not doubt that he could prove it, for that matter. He stormed out, "May be you do not believe he said it." I told him that I knew he did not say it, that I did not believe anything about it. I told him that I was acquainted with Elder Hume, and I had heard him preach many times, and that I had heard him say often that he had never preached it, for he did not believe it, and I knew that he had never heard him say it. I told him that I was pretty well acquainted with the Hard Side Baptists, as he called them, and that I knew that they did not preach anything of the sort. He asked me if I was a Hard Side Baptist, and I told him that it was no difference to him what I was, and that he had never heard them preach infants to hell. He got up, looked up and down the street, brushed himself, and said, "Boys, let us go," and they left me alone, but in more agreeable company.

CHAPTER XLVII.

On one occasion, I took a trip to New Hope Church, in Hamilton County, Illinois, to attend a funeral, or rather to preach a funeral discourse. I got off the train at McLeansboro, and preached there on Friday night, and then went out ten miles into the country on Saturday morning, with a company of brethren from town. At my meeting at McLeansboro, there was a Campbellite preacher by the name of Baker, with whom I got acquainted after preaching, and who took some exceptions to some of my remarks because I had accused his brethren of quoting the commission as given by Matthew, "*into* the name" instead of "*in* the name." He seemed rather disposed to deny it, but I referred him to some of his own authors who I knew had done so, and with whom he was not acquainted, so we parted and I saw him no more until on Sunday afternoon, as we came back to town from our meeting. As we were on the road back to town, Sunday afternoon, we passed a meeting house, and seeing that there was a collection of people at the place, and that there was preaching going on, we stopped and went in; and when we got into the house we found that the same man was there that we had met at McLeansboro, as we came over. In the course of his remarks, he spoke some on the subject of prayer. He said that he had often heard men pray prayers that he could not say amen to. He said that we should never pray the Lord to do for us what he had commanded us to do. He told us that he had heard men pray to the Lord to visit the widow and the orphan and that he never said amen to that prayer, because the Lord had told us to visit the fatherless and the widow, and that we should do it, and not pray for him to. He said he had heard men, in their big meetings, pray for the Lord to come right down here, and be with us; but he said, "I always say, Lord, don't do it." He said the Lord was there already, if two or three had met in his name, and that we should not pray for Him to be there, if he is already there. He said that he had heard men pray for the Lord to send the gospel where it is not, but he said he never said amen to that prayer. The Lord had made it our duty to send the gospel, and if we wished the gospel sent where it is not, we should dive into our pockets and send it and not pray the Lord to do what he had told us to do.

When he was through we went on, and on the next morning, before train time, I met him on the street and told him that I had the pleasure of hearing him awhile the evening before. He seemed glad, and was ready, of course, to hear what I had to say about his sermon. I told him that I only heard a portion of the preaching, but what I did hear was interesting, but that if he was correct I had always been under a mistaken idea about prayer. I told him that I had never thought of the idea that we should not pray the Lord to do what He had told us to do, until I heard him the evening before. I had read the language of Jehovah to Adam, "In the sweat of thy face shalt thou eat bread," and I had always thought from that that if a man wanted bread he must work for it, and that the Lord had made it our duty to work for our bread. I asked him if that was not his understanding of it, and he said it was. I told him that I had always understood it that way, but the Savior taught his disciples to pray, "Give us this day, our daily bread," and I always thought that it was right to pray for bread, although it is our duty to work for it, and I never knew any better until the evening before. I said to him that I believed that it was our duty to "Abstain from every appearance of evil," because the apostle had given us an exhortation to that effect, and yet the Savior told his disciples to pray, "Lead us not into temptation, but deliver us from evil." I never thought of such a prayer being wrong, until the evening before, but I suppose that I was mistaken, if he had taught us correctly on the subject. On the subject of preaching the gospel, it had never entered my mind, that, notwithstanding it is our duty to go and preach, and assist those who do go, yet the Lord had instructed his disciples to pray the Lord to send laborers, which we all believe means ministers, and I always thought that such a prayer was all right until I heard him the evening before. It was certainly good for me to be there, and I told him that I was glad I had met him—good bye. He asked to wait a moment. He said he wanted to read something to me. He drew out of his pocket a small copy of the New Testament, but as I had one of them, and could read it as well as he could, I told him that he had better go home and read to himself, and being in a little hurry, I left him to reflect on his wonderful sermon on prayers that he could not say amen to.

CHAPTER XLVIII.

I believe that I will give an account of my first visit to the Soldier Creek Association of Kentucky. I had met some of the brethren of that Association, a few weeks before, at the Muddy River Association, in Illinois, and had arranged with them to go. They instructed me to take the train to Cairo, on Thursday evening, and that I would connect with a boat at that place, going up the river to Paducah, and that some of the brethren would be on their way from Illinois, and that they would come down the river, and that we would all meet at Paducah on Friday morning, and go on from there together. But, just as the train was going into Cairo, I saw a boat starting up the river. That was the boat that I was to connect with, but it was gone, so I went to a hotel, and told the host that I wanted to go to Paducah on the first boat. He said there would be no regular boat going up the river until the next evening, at that time; but he said that some transient boat might come at any time. He told me that he would be up all night, and that I could go to bed, and he would watch the river, and if he saw a boat coming he would call me. I went to bed, and was not molested, and when I got up next morning, he told me that no boat had come yet. Of course, I had no idea when I could go, for there was no one who knew of a boat that was likely to go before evening. I remained there the whole day, until about four o'clock in the afternoon, when a boat came in sight, and when she landed I boarded her for Paducah. She had a heavy load, and she stopped at every landing on the way, and it was about nine o'clock that night when we got to Paducah. The brethren who were to meet me there on Friday morning were gone, for it was now Friday night, and the meeting was to begin on Saturday morning. I did not know the way any farther, and I knew of no one to inquire of who did know. I went to the hotel, where I had to stay all night, and while there I looked over a railroad time table, and as I thought that I should take a train from there, I was solicitous about which road to take, and at what station I should get off. In looking over the time card, I saw Viola mentioned as a station. It sounded familiar to me, and I felt confident that it was on the road that I should take, whether it was the station for me to get off or not. I asked the host what time the train went out on that road in the morning, and he said it would go out at four o'clock in the morning, so I told him to call me for that train. At four, the next morning, I bought my ticket for Viola, and boarded the train, not knowing whether I would be in fifty miles of the Association when I reached Viola, or not. As the train moved out the conductor came through for tickets, and I asked him what sort of a place Viola was. He asked me if I had never been there, and when I told him that I had not, he told me that I would never want to be again, and he passed on, and I wondered if I was right, and if Viola was the place for me to get off, even if this was the road. I noticed an elderly gentleman and his lady on the train, and I thought they might be going to the Association. I made up my mind that I would ask him if he knew anything about it before we parted. So, when the train stopped at Viola, a little after sun up, I noticed that they were getting off at the same place, and as the gentleman stepped off the car, I asked him if he knew anything of an Old Baptist Association that was to meet that day, anywhere in the country. He said, yes, that there was to be one about nine miles from there. I asked him if this was the place for me to get off the train to get to it, and he said it was; that I could not get any nearer the Association on this train. I asked him if he was certain that it was an Old Baptist meeting, and not a Missionary Baptist meeting. He seemed to be very confident that it was an Old Baptist Association. I told him to mention the names of some of the ministers, and then I could tell whether it was the one I wanted to go to or not. He said they had as preachers Parson Worrell, Harrison, Dalton, Perkins, &c. I told him that would do, it was the meeting I was making for. I then inquired for a hotel, and they told me there was none there. I then asked if there was a livery stable in the place, and they told me there was no livery stable. I thought it would be rather trying on a man to have to walk nine miles without anything to eat.

While I was wondering what to do, and talking to the agent about it, there was an old colored man came up, and found out what I wanted, and he told me of a man about half a mile out who had plenty of horses, and he felt sure that I could get one. While I was talking with the colored man, the old gentleman who had gotten off the train, came back to me, and said, "I will tell you what you had better do." I told him that was just what I wished to know. He told me that I had better come over to his house, and get my breakfast, and that he had a horse and buggy, and that he had nothing for them to do but to carry me over to the Association. Unreasonable as it may seem, I accepted his proposition, and went over to the house, where he had built a fire, for it was a cool October morning, and I made myself at home until breakfast. I was not very full of talk, for the delays I had suffered, and the disappointment in not meeting my brethren at Paducah, on Friday morning, and being thrown out alone, had discouraged me so much, that I did not feel a great deal like talking. My friend, however, was a great talker, and seemed to realize the circumstances, and he did everything he could to make me feel at home. He proved to be what we call a Dryland Baptist, and was well acquainted with our brethren, in that country. His wife was a Methodist lady, and she did her full share, by her christian kindness and hospitality to make me feel at home. After breakfast, we started to the Association, and the gentleman had a great deal to say as we went along, and, among other things, he spoke freely of his interest in the Savior, and said that if he was only worthy, he would go to the church at the very next meeting, and that he would take up the cross at once; but he said he was not fit, and for that reason he could not think of such a thing. When we got near the meeting grounds he told me that his horse and buggy were mine during the entire meeting, and that he would be the driver and the hostler. I thought that with all my disappointments in the trip, I had been very fortunate, in finding friends. I was a total stranger to him, and I could see no reason why he should take such an interest in me.

There was an appointment made for me to preach that night at a Brother Baker's, in the neighborhood, and we got into the buggy and drove over to the place, and found a number of the brethren there, some of whom I knew. The Moderator of the Association, Elder Hutchins, was present, and as I had never met with him before, I invited him to preach first, and the brethren present seemed to be agreed with me on that question, so he went forward and preached a real good sermon, and when he was through I followed, using for a text, " Go ye therefore, and teach all nations, baptizing them in the name of the Father, and of the Son, and of the Holy

Ghost." I was blest with about as much liberty as I ordinarily am, and I suppose I talked about an hour, and there were only a few present that had ever heard me, and this was my first effort to open my mouth to preach in that part of the state. After I was through and the people were dismissed, my hostler acted very strange toward me. He did not speak to me again that night, nor the next morning, until he got ready to start to meeting. He would pass around and gaze at me as though he did not understand me. I discovered that he seemed to act very strange, as I thought, but I did not let on that I noticed anything. I thought to myself that I had, perhaps, taken the last ride in his buggy. I felt eager to know, but would not ask. I finally overheard a brother ask him what he was going to charge that preacher for hauling him around. He answered that the bill was already paid now. That relieved my mind, and I did not think much more about it. When he got his horse and buggy ready to start to the meeting house, the next morning, he came to me and said that he was ready to go. This was the first time he had spoken to me since before services on the evening before. I went out with him and we got into the buggy and started, but he seemed to be in a deep study about something, and I said nothing to him, and he finally turned to me and said, "You did not fool me so very badly. I had heard of you before. Now," said he, "you seldom ever preach any better than you did last night, do you?" I told him that was a question that would be hard for me to answer for I was a very poor judge of my own preaching. He seemed to be very much overcome over my little effort, and from that on he seemed at home with me again, and I felt thankful to the good Lord for affording me such a friend in time of so great need. This instance made me know that even in this country, with all the modern conveniences, a minister does not always have sunshine. Many times he will find himself surrounded in such a manner, that the most successful weapon he can use to fight the battle with is prayer.

CHAPTER XLIX.

Our people have often been accused of being selfish and bigoted because we refuse to affiliate with others, as they say "in the good work." I have always denied the charge, and claim to be as liberal as any of my religious neighbors. I think it was in the year 1873, that I made my first visit to the state of Kentucky, during which I had meeting a time or two, in Madisonville, in the Methodist Church. The last night that I preached there, I met a Missionary Baptist preacher by the name of Lacy and he gave me an introduction to a Mr. Baker, who, he said was a missionary from Georgia, and who had an appointment also, at the same house on the same evening, and that he hardly knew just what to do, as my appointment was the oldest, I had the first right to the house. It seems that all denominations occupied the one house in Madisonville, at that time. He said that Brother Baker would love to have about fifteen minutes after I was through if I did not object. I told him certainly I would not object, but if it would suit him as well, he might go before and I would take what time was left, as I was somewhat tired anyway, having been traveling and preaching several days. He refused to go before, but insisted that I should preach first and he would follow me. The Methodist minister came in and I had an introduction to him. He told me that the house was mine for the evening and that he wanted me to feel at home and preach my sentiments freely and not feel intimidated nor trammeled in the least, for he had a desire to hear me preach my doctrine. So, as the appointment was made for me, and the people had gathered to hear me, I consented to go first and comply with the wish of the Methodist minister, as well as I could. I do not remember the text I used, but the idea of teaching was in the subject. I told them that the Lord, in the New Covenant, had said that He would write His laws in their hearts and put them in their minds, and that I and my brethren believed that the Lord did this work for the sinner, and that it was exclusively the Lord's work by His Spirit, and that He was not dependant on human help in the affair. I had taken that position, and had heard men undertake to establish the doctrine of means and instrumentalities in this text, by saying that penmanship was the figure used to illustrate the Lord's work in the writing of His laws in their hearts.

I told them that for the sake of argument, we would admit the use of means, and that as was claimed, we would admit that the preacher was the pen, and that the Spirit was the ink, and that the parchment or paper upon which the writing is to be done was the sinner's heart. Now if I understand the matter, God is the penman. In the art of penmanship, who is the sovereign? Is it the pen, or the ink, or the paper, or the penman? Of course all must agree that it is the penman. In writing, then, the penman takes up the pen (preacher) when he pleases, does he not? Does the pen ever object, and complain that it is not getting enough pay, and that it will not write a word unless the pay can be made certain? The preacher does, and to make the figure fit in this case, we should see some independence on the part of the pen. But in the figure we do not; but the writer takes up his pen at his own pleasure, and applies it to the ink as he wishes, and then when he comes to the paper, the (sinner's heart,) it does not resist, and begin to oppose the work of the writer, saying to him, "You cannot write on me." If we were to see such things as that in nature, we would be surprised. But we are told that in many instances, the sinner will not allow the Lord to write in his heart. I argued that the penman took up his pen when he pleased, and dipped it into the ink when he pleased, and then he wrote on the paper when he pleased, and that he wrote just what he wanted to, and made just such impressions as he saw fit, and that was precisely the way the Lord wrote his laws in the heart of the sinner. He wrote when, where and as he pleased. The Savior said, "For as the Father raiseth up the dead and quickeneth them, even so the Son quickeneth whom he will." John v, 21.

I told them that I believed and preached the sovereignty of God, that I professed liberality, and that I would live religiously and doctrinally with any man that would just accept one text that I would quote and let all he preaches and practices be agreed with the naked reading of the text, without any comment. I would unite with any man on that text. Isa. lv. 10, 11. "For as the rain cometh down, and the snow from heaven, and returneth not thither, but watereth the earth, and maketh it bring forth and bud, that it may give seed to the sower and bread to the eater: So shall my word be that goeth forth out of my mouth: it shall not return unto me void, but it shall accomplish that which I please, and it shall prosper in the thing whereto I sent it." Just admit the truth of this text, without comment, and let all you believe and practice agree with that text, and we are together. I told them that we were often called "anti-mission" by people of other religious orders, because we stood aloof from everything of that sort, and that on that account we were often called selfish. I told them that I would join them on their own terms if they would have me. On their own terms, now they could have me, if they would. I had often made this offer to the Missionaries and they rejected me every time. I did not think it was fair for them to call me selfish if they would not have me in their societies, on their own platform; but they do. I told them that I would join them now, on their terms, and would now make the proposition. But, I told them that I wanted us all to understand those terms and that I would test the matter by asking a few questions. I would agree that if any man could convert a sinner that I could, and I believed that if I could I ought to, for I believed that I ought to do all the good that I could for myself, and for my fellow man and for the glory of God. Now, as it will be our business to convert sinners, I want to know first what you Missionaries think of the sinner prior to his conversion. As we have in our congregation a Methodist, two Missionary Baptist and one or two Campbellite preachers, this will certainly be a good time for me to make my application. Then I ask, is the sinner's heart right with God prior to his conversion? They all agreed that it is not. On that point, then, there was no difference between them and me, for we were agreed as to the condition of the sinner's heart. I ask again, will the sinner's works be accepted of God unless his heart is right? They all agreed that they would not. To this point then we were altogether agreed. Now, I have only one more question to ask, and a Scriptural answer to the question is all that is wanted, and I am ready to join to-night. I told them that I did not mean any foolishness about it, for I was in earnest. Then I ask, what is the first thing for us to do to the sinner? Tell me in the language of the Bible, and I will go immediately to work. Tell me! Tell me!! What will we do to that sinner first in order to convert him.? It will not do to tell the sinner to do something, for we all agree that his heart is not right with God, and that his works will not be accepted of God, unless his heart is right. If all this be true, his heart must, of necessity, be changed before the sinner works. Then if it is our business to do anything to convert him, we must do that something before he works any. After his heart is changed it will be too late for us to get our work in, for he will then be converted. Then whatever we do we must do before he is converted. In what book, chapter and verse will I find an answer to that question? I want no man's opinion, I ask for one text of Scripture, and that I must have, and you Missionaries must give it, or else I can not afford to join you. While I knock at your door for admission on your own terms, and you shut your doors against me, you should never call me illiberal and selfish. If your course is Scriptural, just give me one text, and if you do not, I shall take it for granted that I and my brethren have never done you any injustice by calling your new practices, with all their train of means and methods, and all your so-called benevolence, anti-scriptural. That is just what it is, and the Missionary people in this country would not be called on to confront such appeals as this if they had the Bible with them. They did not answer the question, and they never will. No man has ever said that it was not a fair question, that I have ever heard. I claim that it is pertinent, and that they are under obligations to answer it, but they will never do it. When I was through, Mr. Baker arose, and began a begging lecture for missions, without referring to me, or anything that I had said. He seemed to want to think, and to want all others to think that I was not there and had not been there. But they knew I was there, and when he began to draw almost to the point of lifting a collection for missionary purposes, the people arose and left the house without giving him time to pass the hat. There was a little too much contempt manifested on his part toward me, and what I had said, for thinking people not to notice it. I was told that he tried it again. In fact he made the announcement for another time, the evening I was there, but financially, it was a failure, so I was told.

I felt, after it was all over, that if those preachers could have answered my questions they would have done so. I am satisfied the practice of those people in those things is unscriptural. I am glad I am not in those unscriptural practices. But because I am not, I have had many frowns and epithets cast at me. Wry faces and ugly frowns have often met me because I could not sanction everything that the people attached the name of my Savior to, but it is all right. I feel that even among the most pious and influential religionists, when Jesus was here they despised Him and His doctrine. It is not likely that His doctrine should be any more popular now than it was then. If He refused to submit to the notions of others simply because they were popular, and was willing to bear the jeers and frowns of a respectable religious world, and bear it all for the good of His people, I, who am one of the beneficiaries of His grace, I hope, should be willing to follow His example.

CHAPTER L.

During the time of my ministry, I have had the care of churches almost all the time. I have been told many times by the brethren that they did not think I was suitable for a pastor, but that I should be foot-loose to go about among the churches, generally, and that others should remain at home and attend the churches. When I was younger, I thought that perhaps that might be the case, but I noticed, finally, that if a brother wanted me to visit his church once in a while, and I was so confined to churches that I could not, he was more apt to tell me that I ought not to be a pastor than if I was the pastor of his church. I have feared, many times, that I was not a good pastor, but I have enjoyed the care of churches as much as any work I have ever done as a minister. I think I have had as clear evidence of my call to preach, when laboring as a pastor, as when engaged in any sort of work in the ministry. It is true that I have traveled over a great deal of country and tried to preach, but whether it has been as profitable to the cause, as if I had spent my time differently, is a question that I have doubted. I have thought that perhaps, if I had gone to a church, and had given it my full time, instead of trying to visit many churches, I might have done more good. I have, as a rule, I think, been more successful in my labors when I have spent more time at one church. Sometimes it is necessary to stay several days in one place, if the people are to be taught in the fundamental doctrine and practice of the church, for no man can teach much in one or two discourses; and if the church needs the labors of a man to gather the little children of God, into the fold, he should not be obliged to leave his work just at a time that he is badly needed. While I am writing I can call to mind a number of churches that I have visited with the most satisfactory results. I have also attended churches as pastor, and have had the very best evidence of divine approbation. Perhaps about one dozen churches embrace all that I have ever served as pastor, long enough to do any good. I have spent the best part of my life, so far, in White County, Illinois, and Posey County, Indiana, as pastor of churches. I have, in all my labors, baptized about four hundred people, and married, perhaps, one hundred and twenty-five couples, and preached at least two hundred and fifty funerals. I have not kept an accurate account, but do not think these numbers are exaggerated. I have been requested to baptize some few that I could not, for they were away from my home, and I could not go on account of other engagements. I have also been called on many times to marry people; also to preach funerals, when I could not go. I have taken the care of churches as pastor a few times, simply because they could get no one else, and I have taken them when everything looked very gloomy, so far as the prospects of the churches were concerned, and I have been surprised at the good results of my little efforts to labor for them. I have tried to show as little partiality between members of the church in case of trouble among them, as I could, but I have not always been able to escape the accusation of partiality. I have sometimes felt partial, and I have sometimes been accused of it when I had no preference; but I would advise all pastors to show no partiality in case of difference between two members, if it is possible to avoid it.

On account of some local unpleasantness among some of the churches of Salem Association, the one I now live in, which affected the surrounding Associations to some extent, not in doctrine, nor practice, but I may say in personal feelings, a number of the corresponding Associations dropped correspondence with Salem, a few years ago, and some others withdrew correspondence from each other. The Bethel Association of Illinois, Highland, of Kentucky, Skillet Fork, of Illinois, and Blue River and Little Zion, of Indiana, all severed correspondence with Salem. The only reason assigned by Bethel for discontinuing the correspondence, was that it was not kept up profitably, and not that any unpleasant feeling existed between them. During those unpleasant times many hard things were said, and brethren of different Associations would denounce each other as disorderly, or unsound. These things, of course, are to be expected under circumstances of this kind. This was the dreadful state of affairs when I moved into this Association. All the original correspondence with Salem had been dropped, except Muddy River and Little Wabash Associations, in Illinois. In the meantime correspondence with White River and Danville Associations, in Indiana, had been taken up. But I feel happy to say, that amid all the jargon and severing of correspondence, there were no serious troubles in the Associations that amounted to much of a rent in any one of them. Each Association seemed to be at peace within itself. Finally, a better feeling began to grow among the ministry, the tide seemed to turn its course, the old breaches began to close up, correspondence began to be renewed, and one gap after another was closed, until all correspondence was restored except that of Highland, Kentucky.

Salem Association to-day corresponds with nine Associations, altogether numbering about six thousand five hundred members, including her own membership.

I will further state that she never divided on missionism, two-seedism, means, instrumentalities, eternal vital union, nor any other ism, and that there is not a Missionary Baptist Church in her bounds; neither are there any factions of two or three different sorts of Old Baptists. I do not know whether I have been profitable or not as a pastor, but I am happy to know that I have never sought to be the leader of a party, and I also know that under my ministry no church has ever divided into factions, each one claiming to be the church. I have heard of many ites, but I have never had any desire to hear of Potterites, for I have never thought such a thing would be any credit to me. I hope that if I have done no good for the cause, I have done no harm.

CHAPTER LI.

When I was a very young man in the ministry, I was forced into one or two little engagements called debates. The first one of the sort was when I had only been exercising in public about two years. I was living in the vicinity of my nativity, and teaching a winter school, and could not get very far from home to meetings, and there was a meeting house about four miles from where I lived, that was owned by the Campbellites, but was built with the understanding that all denominations might preach in it when they did not want it. I made an appointment or two at this place and filled them and on one occasion when I got there, I found their pastor was there, who lived several miles away. I thought that perhaps he had an appointment, and that I had better find out before I went too far, as it was his house, so I asked one of his brethren if he had an appointment, and I was told that he would not preach until in the afternoon, at two o'clock, and for me to make free and fill my appointment.

From that I went into the pulpit, and introduced my services, and began my little talk, when I noticed the preacher taking notes after me. His name was Sumner, and he had been preaching twenty years or more, and was thought to be very able. When he began to note I felt like giving him the best I could do, for this was the first time that any man had ever taken notes after me. When I was through I announced his appointment and dismissed, and as I came out of the stand he met me with a Bible in his hand, and said that I had quoted a text that was not in the Bible. I thought perhaps I had, for I lacked a great deal of being perfect in quoting Scripture. But I asked him what it was, and he said that I had quoted a text that "All that dwell on the face of the earth shall worship him, whose names are not written in the Book of Life of the Lamb slain from the foundation of the world." Rev. xiii, 8. He said that text was not in the Bible. As soon as he told me what text he had allusion to, I knew he was mistaken. He was very positive, and turned the lids of the Bible from one side to the other, saying that it was not between those lids. I told him that I knew it was there, and that I thought I could soon find it for him. He told me to find it then by two o'clock, and show it to him. I told him I could soon find it, and that I would not be there at two o'clock. He said I must, for he intended to reply to me at his meeting. I told him to reply to his satisfaction, but I should not be present. I had not the least idea of having any controversy with him, for I was really afraid of him. Besides I did not think it would be prudent for me to undertake such a thing, for I was young and inexperienced and he was old and experienced. As I would not agree to stay, the crowd seemed to hang around, as if they understood it, and finally one man made the suggestion that he preach now, and not go away until afterwards. He said that he would rather do without his dinner that much longer than to go home and back through the bad weather. This suggestion was agreed to, and the people were called in. By this time I had found the disputed text. I asked him if he could read, and he seemed almost indignant at that question, and said he could. I told him to read that verse, pointing it out to him, and then I turned the lids of the Bible as he had done, and told him that it looked to me like it was precisely between the lids. He said he did not know, before, that there was such a text as that. I suggested to him that perhaps he had better read his Bible before he replied to me. I told him I thought as he was going to reply he ought to tell what the text meant. He invited me into the stand with him, and I went up, and after he looked over his books a while, he turned to me and said that he was going to read the strongest Baptist chapter in the Bible. I told him I wished he would so I would know which one it was. He said he wished that all Baptist preachers could say that. He then arose and read I Pet. ii. That was an easy thing to do, for he did not offer a single comment on it. After he commenced his review of my discourse, only a few minutes, I concluded to reply. So, I took notes, and at the close of his harangue, I announced that I would reply at four o'clock that afternoon.

As I went away with some of my friends, they told me that they thought the whole thing was a put-up job, and that his brethren had notified him of my meeting, and requested him to be there. I answered him the best I could, and I felt satisfied with my effort, for it was no trouble to refute his arguments with the Bible. At the close of my remarks, I told him what I had heard, that it was all a preconceived arrangement, and that he was prepared for it, and had come down on purpose to whip me out of that day, and now, if he thought he had whipped me, not to boast about it, for I was the least Old Baptist preacher out, and if he could not whip me, what would he do in case one of our ordinary men, and especially, if one of our "big guns" should come along? Not being satisfied, he insisted that we debate during the following week, at night, and I finally consented to meet him on Thursday night. So, accordingly we met, and continued until Saturday night. This was my introduction to debates. I have had, now, thirty public discussions, and I doubt the propriety of such things except under very rare circumstances. If my brethren would let me alone, I would seldom ever accept any man's challenge for a debate. I think, many times that debates are gotten up more on the principle of a prize fight, or something of that sort, than a desire to know the truth of God's word. If a man comes along that we think is able, and seems to be the premium preacher we have heard for some time, the brethren frequently suggest the idea of hearing him in a debate, and from that on, if our brethren do not challenge, they provoke a challenge from the other side, which is no better, but more cowardly. If we wish to have a debate with others, why not walk up like men and make the challenge? To challenge is one thing necessary to debates, and if we want them, let us ask for them.

I have been called on many times to debate, but have managed to keep out of every one that I possibly could. The brethren have misjudged me, in thinking that I was never better pleased than when I was engaged in a debate. I will debate when my brethren think, in their sober judgment that the cause of our people needs defending. That is the only way.

CHAPTER LII.

Some years ago I visited Union City, Tennessee, where I held a meeting about a week, and had a pleasant time, baptizing one or two. After I closed my meeting, I took the train for home, about six o'clock in the evening, and ran up to Columbus, Kentucky, on the Mobile and Ohio Railroad, and from there across the Mississippi river, over to Charleston, Missouri. I had to change cars at ten o'clock, and had to wait until two, making a four hours' layover. I waited at the depot, as I was anxious to get home on the first train, and did not wish to wait until the next day for another train. When I landed off the train at Charleston, I found that there was a family getting off the same train, who were emigrating from some place in Tennessee, to Arkansas. The family consisted of a man and his wife and a large family of children. The children were of all sizes and ages it seemed from an infant in the mother's arms, to girls about grown. The first attractions this family of movers had for me, were the plaintive cries of one of the little boys, who, I suppose had been asleep in the car, and on being waked up and brought out into the cold, was very much displeased, and the first I heard from him was, "I want to go home." I noticed that the good mother had a child in her arms, and seemed to be very much cast down. The father was a large robust looking man, and seemed to be very calm and quiet, taking matters patiently, and in good spirits. I heard them say that the train they wanted would not go until three o'clock the next evening. A hotel man stepped up to the lady and asked her if she wished a hotel. She said she did not, for they had no money to go to a hotel; that the railroad agents had misrepresented matters to them about the connections, and they had spent so much time laying over, that they had almost gone through with what money they had. She said she was afraid they would suffer for something to eat before they got there, and that they had shipped all their clothing and bedding, so they could not get to them, and they would simply have to do the best they could without them. I found out also, that the poor woman had the sick headache until she was very miserable, but her babe would not allow anyone to touch it but her. The weather was cool, it being in the month of January, and the waiting room was not very comfortable, and none of the family had any extra wraps, only the clothing they had on. The man brought in a load of wood and made a good warm fire, and in a short time the children took their shawls and what wraps they had, and spread them on the cold floor, and laid down on them and went to sleep. The poor woman looked as if she could hardly hold her head up, but she had to sit up and hold her child, for it was cross, and would not allow anyone else to touch it. I had nothing to do but to sit by and see and hear, and I was, indeed, sorry for the poor woman.

About twelve o'clock the man laid down, and seemed soon to forget that he was moving to Arkansas, for he very soon began to snore, and I suppose he was sound asleep. Sometime after he went to sleep the child went to sleep, and the poor woman seemed to think that if he would get up and hold it, she might get a little rest, and she really looked like she needed it. So she undertook to wake her husband, whom she called 'Jim," but she failed. She spoke in a low tone to him, I suppose, for fear she would wake the child, and she would say, "Jim, Jim," and he would give a grunt, or a sort of groan, and she would say, "Get up and hold the baby, and let me sleep a while." After several efforts of this kind, and as many failures to get him up, I went to him, and put my hand on his shoulder. I said, "Jim! Jim!! Jim!!!" He answered me, and I told him to get up and hold the baby, and let his wife rest a while. He got up and took the child, and his wife laid down, and neither of them said a word to me, and I was glad he did not, for it was a wonder to me what he might have said. However, I suppose he thought it was all right, but neither he nor his wife said "I thank you," nor anything else. It was all right with me, and I am confident that I did her a favor, even if it was no accommodation to him. At two o'clock in the morning my train came, going to Cairo, and when I boarded it, I took a seat near the stove, for the weather was cool. I noticed a man on the seat just behind me, who from his dress, and outfit, and general appearance, I thought might be an Old Baptist minister. I did not know him, but I finally asked him where he got on the train, and he told me the name of the station down in Arkansas somewhere, and that he was going to Mayfield, Kentucky to see his father. During the conversation he found out who I was, and he told me that he had heard of me, and that his father was a member of the Primitive Baptist Church. So I found out that I had missed my guess. He said he did not belong to the church, but he was a Baptist in belief.

When we reached the Mississippi river, at Bird's Point, the passengers left the car and went into a transfer boat, to get over to Cairo. It was about three o'clock in the morning, and the moon was shining, and I was looking around to learn all I could, and as I passed the stove, I noticed my man in conversation with a stranger, and I heard him say, "That is a preacher." The other man asked him who it was, and he told him that it was Potter. On hearing this the gentleman arose and followed me up, and reached out to me his hand, and said "How-d'ye Lem?" I told him I would not do it. I said to him, "I do not know you." He told me that I used to know him when I was a little boy. He asked me if I did not remember a man that used to be at my father's when I was a boy, by the name of Benjamin Dame. I said, "Surely this is not Ben Dame!" He said it was, and I told him I could hardly believe it. But I told him that if I could hear him laugh, I thought I could tell then if it was Ben. At this he began to laugh and I said, "Yes, it is Ben, give me your hand." I remembered that Ben Dame was a great laugher.

I think it had been thirty years or more, since he used to be at father's, when I was but a boy. He had been down in Texas, and was on his return to his home, in Kentucky. After landing in Cairo I boarded another train, about five o'clock, and arrived at my home in Grayville, about ten that morning, having been in four states, and crossed the Mississippi river twice, since six o'clock the evening before, and being up all night without sleep, and exposed to the weather, and to all other dangers incident to such a trip, and making the acquaintances that I had made.

CHAPTER LIII.

Our Savior said, "Woe unto the world because of offenses." It has been my observation during my little career, that offenses and disturbances come, and that there is no knowing just when or how they will come. They get into the family, and into society, and especially do they get into the church. I have seen churches whose members seemed to be of one mind and one heart, and it seemed that, if any minister ought to be happy with his flock, that certainly he would be with a membership all in peace and love, and full of zeal for the cause of religion. What a pity that the great enemy of souls should ever be able to mar the peace and fellowship of so happy a community as this! Yet it is often done, and brethren and sisters who loved one another, become the most bitter enemies, and then, instead of trying to make each other happy, they take special pains to provoke and torment each other. I have seen a few cases in my life, where a member of the church seemed to think so much of his standing in the church, that he thought that he was in no danger of being disciplined by the church. I have noticed that when a man comes to such a conclusion as that about himself, as a rule, the more you indulge him the more trouble he will give you. If all church members were humble, and thought that they were hardly worthy to be in the church, and could always feel that way, it would not be such a hard matter to get them to do right. It is not to be expected that a man can live among the churches for thirty years, as a minister, and see no unpleasantness among his members. I believe that I will give an account of a little trouble that our church got into, at Grayville, Illinois, while I lived there. One time we were holding a meeting at that place, and the church was in a lively state, and there was, occasionally, one to join the church. There was an old sister, living out of town, about a mile, who for convenience I will call Aunt Polly. She was sick, and on that occasion she could not attend the meetings. One night a young lady, who for convenience, I will call Eliza, joined the church. After our meeting was dismissed that night, my wife and I went out to sit up with Aunt Polly, and as soon as we got in she began to inquire about the meeting, and I sat back and let my wife do the talking, and as we had received two or three members that night, it was an easy matter for her to tell Aunt Polly all about it. But when she told her that Eliza had joined, Aunt Polly seemed to get worse, and to feel very badly very suddenly. She soon let us know that she had no use for Eliza, and she said that there was hardness between them, and that during their unpleasantness, Eliza had cursed the Old Baptist Church to Aunt Polly, and told her that she intended to join it some day just to spite her. I saw that we were in trouble, and I began to study what would be the easiest way to get out of it. Aunt Polly said she would not live in the church with her, for she believed that Eliza had joined the church to spite her, and that if she had been there she would not have tried to join the church. My plan, at first, was to consider Aunt Polly's objection to her reception the same as if she had been at the meeting and voted against receiving her. The rules of the church required us to receive members only by unanimous vote. As Aunt Polly was sick, and not able to be there, I thought it would be no more than fair to count her vote, and consider Eliza not received. But when I mentioned the matter to some of the brethren, I found that they were not willing that the matter should end that way. They claimed, some of them, that Eliza had as much right in the church as any one else, and that Aunt Polly ought not to say that she would not live in the church with her. Others, again, plead that Aunt Polly had been a life-long member, and that Eliza should have gone to see her before she joined the church, and tried to adjust matters with her as she knew that there was not the right sort of feelings between them, and that the church, to say the least of it, ought to consider Aunt Polly's objection. In all this I had my preference; but I managed to keep it to myself. The church finally sent a committee of five sisters, to see the two, and try to get them to be reconciled to each other. The committee were divided, some of them in favor of Aunt Polly and some of them in sympathy with Eliza; and their prejudices were so high that they could not keep them hidden when they got there, so they failed to get the trouble settled. When they made their report to the church that it was not settled, it was an easy matter to see that the church was almost equally divided. Matters began to look very gloomy for that church at that time. If the church had decided in favor of Aunt Polly, and against Eliza, about half of the members would have left the church; and if they had decided in favor of Eliza and against Aunt Polly the result would have been about the same with the other half. It seemed that every wheel was clogged, and we could not even dismiss without doing something and it was impossible for us to do anything. The matter was before the church, and had to be disposed of some way before we could dismiss. Finally there was a motion made to appoint another committee, and let them try again to get them to be reconciled. The only salvation for the church was for them to be reconciled. I was afraid that it could not be done, and it did seem that if it was not done, the church would divide. We, however, appointed the committee, requesting them to report at the next meeting. I being the Moderator of the church, they put it on me to appoint the committee, which I did, but with no hopes of them effecting a reconciliation. Feeling a great desire for peace to be restored to the church, and having no hope that this committee could possibly do any good on account of their biased feelings, some for one, and some for the other, I concluded to make an effort to get them together and see if I could get them to settle. I had told no one how I stood, and neither of them knew which side I was on. I tried to ask the Lord to bless my efforts in the matter, for I saw no hope for the church, unless it could be settled. After meeting was dismissed, I asked Aunt Polly if she would be willing to meet Eliza in my presence, and have no one else present, and try to settle the matter with her, provided she was willing. She said she would, so I told her I would see Eliza, and then I would let her know. I went to Eliza and asked her if she would be willing to meet Aunt Polly in my presence, and have no one else present, and try to settle it with her, if she was willing. She said she would. So I told Aunt Polly to come to my house on the next Monday morning, and I would be at home, and have Eliza there. On Monday morning she rode up, and I helped her off her horse, and conducted her into the house, and told her that I would go and bring Eliza. Before I started I told Aunt Polly that I wanted her to talk kindly to Eliza, for, said I, "Eliza is young, and you are old, and if you talk ugly to her

I will have to stop you." She said she would treat her kindly, and so I went over after Eliza, which was only a short distance in town. As we came back together, I said to her, "Now, Eliza, you must be kind to Aunt Polly, for you are young and strong, and she is old and afflicted and peevish, and if you talk unkind to her I shall have to tell you to stop." She said she would not talk rough to her, so when we got there, and my wife had left the room, I told them to begin, and for Aunt Polly to begin first, and tell Eliza what she had against her, and what it would take to satisfy her, and then for Eliza to do the same. Aunt Polly turned to her and said, "Eliza, I want to hear you tell your experience." Eliza told her experience to the old sister, and when she was through Aunt Polly asked her a few questions, and then she said, "Now, Eliza, if I have ever done you any harm in the world, I want you to forgive me." Eliza said, "You never did me any harm in the world, and I want you to forgive me all the wrongs I have ever done you." Aunt Polly said, "You have never done me any wrong, and I have done wrong, and I ask your forgiveness." Thus, the matter was settled, and the dark cloud that brooded over the church withdrew, and light sprung up, and the sun shone brightly, and I felt like praising the Lord for His mercy.

I have been confident ever since, that if when we become irreconciled to our brethren, we would tell our experiences to one another, instead of trying to magnify one another's faults, difficulties would be more easily settled.

I feel confident that if Aunt Polly had been present when Eliza joined the church, that she would have been willing to receive her.

CHAPTER LIV.

There have been so many remarks made about the Old Baptists, and so many people have heard so many things about them, that it is hard to tell what has, or has not been said about them. I remember that on one occasion, I was attending an Association in Perry County, Illinois, at old Nine Mile Church, not far from the City of DuQuoin, and there was living in the city a Brother Allen, who made a public invitation for company, as is common with our people on such occasions. He also arranged for preaching in town, and on Saturday afternoon quite a number of the brethren and sisters went to his house. He was keeping a hotel, and we spent most of the afternoon at his hotel. During the afternoon Sister Allen met one of her near neighbors, who inquired of her why so many people were at their hotel. Sister Allen told her that these were her brethren and sisters who had come home with them from the Association. That we were to preach in the city to-night, and that they had come to spend the afternoon and night with them. The lady seemed surprised beyond measure. She said, "Those are not all Old Baptists, are they?" Sister Allen told her they were, and she exclaimed, "Well! Well!! Well!!! Those are all Old Baptists, are they? And some of them right well dressed!" It seems that this poor batch of ignorance was under the impression that if the Old Baptists wore any clothes at all, they must be coarse, ragged and dirty.

I was traveling one time, going up the railroad towards Mount Carmel, from Grayville, and as the train was pulling out from Keensburg, I noticed a man whom I knew to be a minister, coming down the aisle looking for a seat, and as he was about to pass me, I gave him a touch and invited him to a seat. I had held a debate with him, and as he took his seat, he said, "I wonder where you are going." I told him that I was going up the creek a little ways. He said, "You are going to skin some Campbellite, I expect." He was a preacher of that order. I told him that I was, if any of them got in my way, that I was just the one that could do it, and he knew it. After jesting in that manner for awhile, he said to me, "Do the Hard Shells pay you pretty well for preaching?" He spoke out rather loud, for he wanted the people in the car to hear it, for he thought it would be a little sport to ask me such a question, and give the people an opportunity to laugh at my expense. I told him that they paid me all they promised, that they were up now, and did not owe me a cent. I asked him how his brethren were on that question, and he began to clear up his throat, when I told him to sing it out, I did, and it was as fair for him to answer it as it was for me. He told me that they were behind with him some. I told him that a people who would not pay their debts I would not preach to, if I were in his place. I thought that they certainly had not been converted right, or they would pay up as they had promised.

In this country, the most of our churches are in the country, and the customs and forms of country people are different from those of the city. I suppose, that is one reason that our people are so often referred to as they are, and so many remarks made about them. My judgment is, however, that they are about as capable of attending to their own affairs as others. Before I close this chapter, I will relate one or two instances more. I filled an appointment at Stonefort, Illinois, many years ago, and there was a young Missionary Baptist preacher present, who invited me home with him to dinner. Elder Richard Fulkerson was with me, and we accepted the invitation, and went with him. He appeared to be very zealous, and while we were there he asked us a great many questions. He seemed, however, to put the most of them to me. He was very much interested on the subject of the support of the ministry; and while conversing on that subject he asked me if I believed in a call to the work of the ministry, and when I told him I did, he wanted to know if the Lord called a man to preach if it was his duty to plow. I told him that I thought it was his duty to preach; but if he did not preach all the time, I did not think it would hurt him to plow.

After talking for some time, on the subject of paying the minister a stipulated salary, I finally said that the Bible told every man just how much to pay the preacher, to the fraction of a cent, and that was what he had purposed in his heart, according as the Lord had prospered him. He said that was all right, but could not the man purpose at the beginning of the year, just as well as at the end of the year, then the minister would know just what to depend on. I told him that might all be true, but suppose I purpose in my heart to give you five dollars, and you will not preach unless I give you ten. I am under no obligation to give more, for the Bible has settled that question. I told him that while he claimed the right to set his price, he would not feel under obligations to take five dollars, so, it was very easy to see that his system and the Bible would conflict. I still view matters that way. Whenever a man invents a system of either doctrine or practice that will not work in harmony with the Bible, there could be no better evidence that his system is wrong. I have always been opposed to men hiring themselves out to preach the gospel.

In the year 1878, I held a debate in Benton, Illinois, with Elder Throgmorton, and in his first speech on the support of the ministry, he said that the "Hard Shells" treated their ministers as beggars. In my reply, I told him that we would test that matter now. I then called on Elder Fulkerson, one of our ministers, who was well known all over that country, and who had labored faithfully in the ministry for many years, and I said "Brother Fulkerson, did you ever ask any one for money, or anything else for preaching?" He said, "I never did in my life." I then called on Elder Elijah Webb, who had lived in the county all his life, and was well known to all the people of that country. He had been preaching for many years. I said, "Brother Webb, did you ever ask anybody for money or anything else for preaching?" He said, "Never." Well, said I, "Here is Elder Vance, a Missionary Baptist minister, and he told me this morning that he commenced preaching when he was a boy. Brother Vance has been familiarly known in this country for many years. Brother Vance, did you ever ask anybody for money for preaching?" He said, "Yes sir." I then appealed to Mr. Throgmorton, and he said he had asked for money for preaching. I told him that I had never done such a thing. Now, said I, "Who is the beggar?"

I still believe that too many preachers beg too much and preach the gospel too little.

CHAPTER LV.

When I first joined the church and began to preach, there was a great deal said about the Two Seed doctrine, and the most of our preachers of southern Illinois believed it. It was nothing uncommon to hear a minister speak out in favor of that doctrine in his sermons. It seemed that in our immediate connection, it had the ascendency. Some of the Associations in our correspondence passed resolutions that the belief or disbelief of that doctrine should not be a bar to fellowship. For several years after I commenced preaching, I rather favored it, enough to accept it at least, and without any investigation of the matter, I did not know but what it was the doctrine of our people generally. I finally began to study the matter for myself, and I soon became satisfied that if it was the Baptist doctrine I did not believe it. After trying to discourage the agitation of it for a few years, I studied the matter so much that I finally concluded to write on that subject, which I did, and put out a small work, giving my objections to it, in the year 1880.

After I had it printed, I sent quite a number of them to our brethren in the ministry, and to our Editors. Some of the brethren found some very serious objections to it, and it was subject to severe criticisms. Elder Coffee, of Saline County, Illinois, wrote me that he thought my positions were well taken, but that he did not look for perfection in any human production. Elder Fulkerson, of Pope

County, Illinois, wrote me that he did not endorse it all, or something to that amount, but that he did not think there was anything in it that was very dangerous, and if I would send him some he would try to sell them for me. I sent one to Elder Joe. Harris, of Perry County, Illinois, and if he ever told me whether he endorsed it or not, I do not remember it, but I was under the impression for a while that he did not; but he told me that he had heard it misrepresented, that he had heard men speak of what was in it when he knew they had not read it, for those things were not in it. He told me that he said to some of them that the man that could answer it would have to get up before day.

Elder Gilbert Beebe was the only editor that said anything about it through his paper, that I remember. He made quite a lengthy reply to one or two expressions that I made, which was published in the SIGNS OF THE TIMES, dated June 1, 1880. I wrote out a reply to his criticisms, in as kind a spirit as I was capable of, and sent it to him, and after he had kept it about three months, I sent him some stamps to pay postage on it, and requested him to return it if he did not wish to publish it, and by return mail I received it, but he paid the postage himself, and sent my stamps back to me. I have read his criticisms carefully, but I have seen no cause to retract any sentiment in what I had said. I have received quite a number of letters from brethren criticising me pretty severely; but so far I still stand by it, and the probabilities are that I shall continue to do so. The work denied two points, "Two Seeds in the Flesh," and "the pre-existence of the children of God."

I sent one to W. H. Smith, of Crawford County, Illinois, and he wrote to me that he could not harmonize it with his Bible. He invited me to visit his Association, stating in his letter to me, that his Association had a rule that to believe, or not believe the the Two Seed doctrine should not be a bar to fellowship among them.

During the fall I saw Elder Benjamin Coats, of Clay County, Illinois, and while in his company, I asked him if he had seen my pamphlet, and he said he had not, but that he had heard the brethren make remarks about it. He said that some of the brethren had told him that I had undertaken to meddle with matters that I knew nothing about. I sent him a book shortly afterwards, but in a short time he was called away from this world, and I never learned what he thought of it.

I accepted Elder Smith's invitation, and visited his Association, and when I got there I met a man whose name was Tabor. He seemed to be very noisy on the Two Seed doctrine. He and I were appointed to preach together at the meeting-house, at five o'clock in the afternoon, on Friday. In our arrangements he agreed to preach first. During his discourse he had a great deal to say about me. He did not seem to be very composed, and he finally turned to me and said, "Brother Potter, if I had you out here in front of me instead of at my back, I think I could manage you better." He seemed to be very much excited, and once in a while he would say, "Brother Potter will get up here and skin me all over directly." After he had pursued that course for a while, he said, "There never had been, and there never would be a sinner saved after the death of Christ." He turned to me and said, "Brother Potter, if your throat is too little to swallow that you had better go back to Skillet Fork." That was the name of my Association. He finally went off in a tangent, and when he stopped he remarked that he did not think that he had ever preached the Two Seed doctrine stronger than he was doing now. When he was through, I arose and told the people that this was my first meeting with Brother Tabor, and that I would not say that he was not a Christian, nor that he was not a gospel minister, for he had said some good things in his discourse. I told them that I did not see the Two Seed doctrine as he did, but that would not trouble me. I am not here to make a fight on that question. I then turned to Brother Smith, the Moderator of the Association, and said, "Your Moderator wrote me that you had a rule here, that the belief or disbelief of that doctrine was not a bar to fellowship here." So I took my text, and preached my sermon, without referring to him, or anyone else on that subject. After the services were over, I saw some of the brethren standing around in groups, and they seemed to have something very important among them. On that night there was preaching at the church house again, and every speaker from that on, referred to me in some way during his discourse. Also, on Saturday, it was the same thing over, and they seemed to think that our Savior did not die as a substitute, but that he, being the head, was responsible for the sins of his body (the church), the same as a man's head would be responsible for what his hand did.

After hearing so much of their noise, I made up my mind to come out plainly on all those points, if I should have an opportunity. After the Association was through with her business, on Saturday, and all the brethren had preached at the stand that had been appointed, I was invited to preach, by the Moderator, which invitation I accepted, and I occupied about an hour. I tried to be very plain, for I had become convinced that some of them thought I was afraid of them.

While I was at this Association, I met a brother James, who seemed to be a warm advocate of the Two Seed doctrine. He was not a minister, but he used his influence in favor of the doctrine. He came to me at one time; and told me that he wanted my company on our way home as far as we went the same road, which was about fifteen miles. He had another brother in the buggy with him, but he said we could exchange seats that far. I readily consented to his proposal, and told him that I would ride with him. He said he wanted to take my book and convince me by it that I was wrong. I told him that if I was wrong I wished to be right, and that I should consider him my friend, who would show me my wrongs. Of course, I expected to ride with him, but I was disappointed, for that was the last he said to me on that subject. When we got ready to start, I looked around for him, and saw that he had his partner in with him, so I said nothing more. I was told afterwards that he had never read my book, and that he did not know what was in it. I have suspicioned him as the man who told Elder Coats that I had meddled with things that I knew nothing about.

There has never been anything very serious between me and others on this question. As a rule all the brethren and I have gotten along pleasantly together, for if we differed, we did not say much about it, and the subject of Two Seeds is not very often referred to among us of late years. I still believe as I wrote in 1880, on that subject.

CHAPTER LVI.

Ever since the division with the Missionaries and Campbellites, it has been a question of controversy as to the use of the preaching of the gospel. Some fifteen years ago, I gave my views on the subject, which I will give now, a little revised. We will define the gospel first, and then proceed, in a brief manner to give our views of it, which we have had for fifteen years or more.

The gospel is good news, glad tidings,—the joyful intelligence of salvation through a crucified and risen Savior. It is called the gospel of God. "Paul, a servant of Jesus Christ, called to be an apostle, separated unto the gospel of God." Rom. i, 1. It is also called the Gospel of Christ, for I am not ashamed of the gospel of Christ; for it is the power of God unto salvation to every one that believeth: to the Jew first, and also to the Greek." Rom. i, 16. It is called the gospel of salvation. "In whom ye also trusted, after that ye heard the word of truth. the gospel of your salvation, in whom also, after that ye believed, ye were sealed with the Holy Spirit of promise." Eph. i, 13. In another place it is called the gospel of peace. "And your feet shod with the preparation of the gospel of peace." Eph. vi, 15 Paul, in speaking of what had been committed to his trust, called it a glorious gospel. 1 Tim. i, 11. Thus we have the Bible definition of the gospel that we are to preach in all the world to every creature. It was this gospel that our Lord commanded his disciples to go into all the world and preach to every creature. We understand from the commission that we are required to preach the gospel to all, both saint and sinner. We are aware of the fact that we are often accused of not preaching to any but believers. The apostle says, "For the Jews require a sign, and the Greeks seek after wisdom. But we preach Christ crucified, unto the Jews a stumbling block, and unto the Greeks foolishness; but unto them which are called, both Jews and Greeks, Christ the power of God, and the wisdom of God." 1 Cor. i, 22, 23, 24. Here is a plain, positive declaration of the apostle, that they preached the same gospel to the Jews and to the Greeks, to whom it was a stumbling block, and foolishness, that they preached to them that are called. The effect was different but the preaching was the same.

The gospel does contain invitations; but, as a rule, the majority of ministers fail to discern that it discriminates between the character of men in every invitation it makes. It never gives an invitation without describing the character it invites. In the invitation, "Ho, every one that thirsteth, come ye to the waters, and he that hath no money; come ye, buy, and eat, yea, come, buy wine and milk without money and without price." Isaiah lv, 1. The thirsty are the ones invited. If none are thirsty, none are invited; if all are thirsty, all are invited; and the invitation extends just so far, and no farther than to the thirsty. The same invitation is made in John, vii, 37, Rev. xxii, 17. In Matt. xi, 28, we have another invitation to all that labor, and are heavy laden. Hence it would be wrong in any of us to conclude that the gospel had no invitations in it, and just as great a wrong for any to claim that those invitations are general. There is not one gospel invitation in the Bible, that does not describe the character it invites. But the Arminian world seem to think they have a work to do that we have failed so far to find a Bible warrant for, and that is, they think it is the business of the minister to make people thirsty, and then invite them to come to the Lord. We deem it the business of God's ministers to invite those who are thirsty. But the gospel is not made up merely by invitations, and, as some would be proud to lug into it, propositions, that is it is not merely an offer of salvation to the world, for it is not an offer of salvation at all. It is a proclamation of salvation through Christ. One grand reason why men make so many mistakes as to the object of preaching the gospel, is because they fail to arrive at a proper conclusion of what it is. The primary object of the gospel is to encourage and comfort the children of God; and they derive their comfort from what it proclaims to them,—not what it proposes to them on conditions. The Lord says, "Comfort ye, comfort ye my people, saith your God. Speak ye comfortably to Jerusalem, and cry unto her, that her warfare is accomplished, that her iniquity is pardoned: for she hath received of the Lord's hand double for all her sins." Isaiah xl, i, 2. Here is a proclamation, and not a proposition, to the children of God. The object is to comfort. When Our Lord ascended he led captivity captive, and gave gifts unto men. "And He gave some, apostles; and some, prophets; and some, evangelists; and some, pastors and teachers; For the perfecting of the saints, for the work of the ministry, for the edifying of the body of Christ: Till we all come in the unity of the faith, and of the knowledge of the Son of God, unto a perfect man, unto the measure of the stature of the fullness of Christ." We are often asked the question, what is the use of preaching, if your doctrine be true?

There are four different objects for preaching the gospel in the above quotation, and not one of them for the making of saints. One is for the perfecting of the saints. The perfecting of the saints is to give them all the instruction in righteousness, that they may be thoroughly furnished unto all good works. It always directs their minds to a crucified Savior, as suitably adapted to their case, and that freely supplies all their wants. It reminds them of all his ordinances, and their obligations to observe them; it teaches them to deny ungodliness and worldly lusts, and live soberly, righteously and godly in this present world. When they see that there is no worthiness in themselves, and that Jesus has bestowed all His worthiness on them, freely, without any consideration on their part, and they are made to view Him as altogether lovely, and that His ways are perfectly just and right, and that there is a beauty in holiness, as well as joys that the world is utterly incapable of giving, and they are led to an implicit confidence in Him and His word, they are then willing and able to conform to His will, in obeying all the injunctions of His gospel. The ministry is to point all these out to the saints, and present to them all the blessed promises of the gospel, with a description of the evidences of Christianity, and how they are to be tested. In this, it is for the perfecting of the saints. It is for the edifying of the body of Christ. To edify is to build up in knowledge and piety. In this edification the saints mutually hold sweet communion with one another, their company becomes pleasant, and their fellowship is strengthened. "Let us therefore follow after the things which make for peace, and things wherewith one may edify another. Rom. xiv, 19. "Let every one of us please his neighbor for his good to edification." Rom. xv, 2. "Even so ye, for as much as ye are zealous of spiritual gifts, seek that ye may excel to the edifying of the church." 1 Cor. xiv, 12. Read 26th verse same chapter: "How is it then, brethren, when ye come together, every one of you hath a psalm, hath a doctrine, hath a tongue, hath a revelation, hath an interpretation? Let all things be done to edifying." Again: "Wherefore comfort yourselves together, and edify one another, even as also ye do." 1 Thess. v, 11. Again: "And let us consider one another to provoke unto love and to good works." Heb. x, 24. Here is the edification of the body of Christ, and this is one of the objects of the ministry. This noble work is to be performed by the Lord's ministers, till we all come in the unity of the faith, and of the knowledge of the Son of God, unto a perfect man, unto the measure of the stature of the fullness of Christ. What a glorious gift has the minister of Christ! He has news to tell the children of God that in its very nature is calculated to draw them together as one man. Built up in the most holy faith of God's elect, they willingly and zealously contend for "the faith once delivered to the saints." And the ultimatum of the matter is, "That we be no more children, tossed to and fro, and carried about with every wind of doctrine, by the sleight of men, and cunning craftiness, whereby they lie in wait to deceive." The Savior, when he was here with his disciples charged them, saying, "Take heed and beware of the leaven of the Pharisees and of the Sadducees." Matt. xvi, 6. He had allusion to their doctrine. The apostle considered it a matter of great importance that the saints be saved from false doctrine. He says, "But though we, or an angel from heaven, preach any other gospel unto you than that which we have preached unto you, let him be accursed." Gal. i, 8. The gospel discriminates between the doctrine of Christ, and the false doctrines. This is one of its grand objects. The apostle John makes an urgent appeal to the church, "Beloved, believe not every spirit, but try the spirits whether they are of God, because many false prophets are gone out into the world." 1 John, iv, 1.

Then, in view of the fact that the world is full of false teachers, and that the children of God cannot glorify God in the belief of false doctrines; and that, although they may rejoice in it for the present, it never looks farther ahead than this life; while the doctrine of Christ is repulsive to the world, yet in the enjoyment of the hearty belief of that doctrine, they can look far beyond all things that pertain to this life, and enjoy all the glorious promises of the gospel, what an important work is preaching the gospel! It is in this way that God by the foolishness of preaching saves them that believe. Hence it is that even according to the position occupied by us, there are abundant reasons for the preaching of the gospel to the saints. It seems to us that the man that would ask us the question, "What is the use of preaching?" with all these things before him, does not think it a matter of much importance what a man believes. Indeed, we often hear them say that they do not think it matters what a man believes, so he is honest in it. Then we ask in all candor and sincerity, why make such a noise about the heathen? They believe in idolatry, but they are honest in that faith. We think it a matter of considerable importance that the church of God hold tenaciously to the doctrine of God our Savior. The great apostle thought it a matter of so vast importance that he gave a very solemn charge to Timothy, "I charge therefore before God, and the Lord Jesus Christ, who shall judge the quick and dead, at his appearing and kingdom; Preach the word; be instant in season; out of season; reprove, rebuke, exhort with all long-suffering and doctrine. For the time will come when they will not endure sound doctrine; but after their own lusts shall they heap to themselves teachers, having itching ears; And they shall turn away their ears from the truth, and shall be turned unto fables." II Tim. iv, 1, 4. It sometimes occurs to us that the more unpopular the truth is, the farther some, even who profess to be Baptists, are from wanting to preach it. If there was ever a time when it was proper to oppose error, it is when that error is prevalent. One reason that Paul gave the charge as he did to Timothy, was because he knew the time was coming when it would not be endured. Brethren let us never be ashamed to preach the doctrine of Christ. But let us contend earnestly for the faith once delivered to the saints. By so doing, we save the church from false doctrine. Sound doctrine never has killed a church, but the want of it has. Sound practice never killed a church, but the want of it has. Sound preaching is more likely to produce sound practice than anything else.

The object of the gospel is a subject of no little controversy among men in the world. While the Arminian world hold that it is the medium through which God offers salvation to the race of mankind, they generally make the impression that it is the only means of giving life to the sinner. Or, in other words, that it is absolutely essential in the work of quickening the sinner into divine life. While they succeed in making their people believe this they have a good plea for their missionary organizations. They tell the people in their Bible lectures, that hundreds and thousands of souls are now writhing in hell, simply because they were not blessed with the Bible and preachers. In this they limit the salvation of God exclusively to those people whose lots have been cast in a land of Bibles. Their theory damns all those who have died in heathenism, and that without any chance of salvation. We are far from believing that God has wrapped Himself up in the Bible and minister, and has so limited his own operations that he can not and will not quicken sinners when and where and as He pleases; without the means of the Bible and preacher. He is limited in nothing. It is the Spirit that quickens the sinner into divine life, and to limit the work of the Spirit to the proclamation of the gospel, as the Campbellites and Missionary Baptists do, together with all others who hold that the gospel and Bible are essential to the conversion of sinners, is to deny the omnipresence of God. It is also to limit His power, and according to that position, He should not have made the promise that He did to Abraham; that in him, and his seed should all the nations of the earth be blessed. For if there is a nation of earth among whom there are no believers, the promise fails; for believers are the seed of Abraham. The literal Jews were the literal descendants, or literal seed of Abraham, but they were only one small nation. It could not have been that it was with those that all nations were to be blessed; but the apostle lets us know that believers are the seed of Abraham. Then believers are to bless all natious of the earth—not merely where the Bible and missionaries get to, but *all* nations. But where the gospel is preached, it is hid to some. The apostle says, "But if our gospel be hid, it is hid to them that are lost." II Cor. ii, 3. If they were so blinded that the gospel could not shine into them, and the Spirit of God could not operate in their hearts, unless it was through, or by means of the gospel, then they were beyond the reach of ever being converted. Who are they that the Gospel is hid to? Them that are lost.

CHAPTER LVII.

During the time of my ministry, I have heard and read a great deal about the humanity of Christ. Some have claimed that His body existed in heaven from all eternity. Others who have not claimed that His human body existed, have contended that His human nature existed. The following was written by me in the year 1874, and was published in the *Baptist Watchman:*

HUMANITY OF CHRIST.

"In his days Judah shall be saved, and Israel shall dwell safely; and this is his name whereby he shall be called: The Lord our Righteous," Jer. xxii, 6.

This is a portion of the prophecy of Jeremiah, concerning the coming of the Messiah, the Lord Jesus Christ, and is doubtless in perfect harmony with all that is written in the law and in the Psalms and prophets concerning Him. As there are some controversies in the present age about the humanity of Christ, and, we have often feared, many contentions by some without that strict and impartial investigation of the subject that every one should give before taking a permanent position, we have concluded not only to take a position, but to appeal to inspiration as the author of whatever position we may assume, as well as our warrant for opposing erroneous sentiments on this subject.

The first impression that we wish to make is, that

it is the humanity and not the divinity of Christ that this brief chapter will treat of; for while there may be a dissension between ourselves and others on the eternal humanity of Christ, we presume all will agree on His eternal divinity. If, therefore, the eternal existence of Christ should be denied in this investigation of the subject, it will be His humanity. The doctrine of the eternal humanity of Christ, we expect to disprove in this chapter, and to this question the chapter is devoted.

The verse preceding the one at the head of this chapter will doubtless prove advantageous to the cause in which we now engage. "Behold, the days come, saith the Lord, that I will raise unto David a righteous branch, and a king shall reign and prosper, and shall execute judgment in the earth." We do not apprehend for a moment that any would deny that the prophet in this language has direct allusion to Christ. Being confident that there will be no dispute on that point, we will examine closely what idea the language conveys. In the first place, allow us to say, that whatever of Christ might have existed before this, the branch here spoken of was something else. And while there are strong advocates for the doctrine that the body of Christ is eternal, and that at most he only received his blood from the Virgin Mary, His flesh and bone being eternal, we should notice very carefully what is said on the subject. Whatever it was that is so frequently called a branch of David, or seed of David, is what He took from His mother, whether it be blood exclusively, or flesh, bone and blood. We may also further consider that this branch came out of David, and not out of eternity. "And there shall come forth a root out of the stem of Jesse, and a branch shall grow out of his roots. Isa. xi, 1. Let us not forget that this is a prophecy, and that if it has ever been fulfilled, it has been since it was spoken by the prophets, and that the only existence this branch had at the time of the prophecy was in the loins of Jesse. If He did exist in eternity, in flesh and bone He could not be of the seed of David according to the flesh. Neither could it be true that He is in any way related to us in fleshly relation. But, in the Scriptural account of the succession of the kings of Isreal, we have the following: "And when He removed him (Saul) He raised up unto them David to be their king; to whom also he gave testimony, and said: I have found David the son of Jesse, a man after my own heart, which shall fulfill all my will. Of this man's seed hath God, according to His promise, raised unto Israel a Savior, Jesus." Acts xiii, 22, 23.

Let it be understood that in whatever sense Christ is related to David, is what is meant here. If he was not related to him at all, he is not of his seed; and more, to deny any relation is to deny the truth of the Scriptures quoted. Of this man's seed God had promised to raise up a Savior, Jesus. What are we to understand from the expression, "this man's seed?" Is it not plain to all that the manner in which it is used refers to his lineage, or posterity? Then Christ was of that particular lineage, and as he himself declares, he is the "root and the offspring of David, and the bright and morning star." Rev. xxii, 16. The seed of David is doubtless his offspring. It is in this sense that he is the Lion of the tribe of Judah. Revelations, v, 5.

It is He that is spoken of in this language: "The sceptre shall not depart from Judah, nor a law-giver from between his feet, until Shiloh come; and unto him shall the gathering of the people be." Gen. xlix, 10. Shiloh, in this text, simply means Christ, and Judah is one of the twelve sons of Jacob, the head of one of the twelve tribes of Israel; and by following the history of this tribe through to the coming of Christ, we are assured that no law-giver came out of it until Christ came. "For it is evident that our Lord sprang out of Judah; of which tribe Moses spake nothing concerning priesthood." Heb. vii, 14. If the Lord sprang out of Judah and was so carefully preserved through all generations from Judah down to the time of his birth of the Virgin Mary, was He not properly of the lineage of Judah? It is, surely in this sense that He is the seed of David according to the flesh. But the objector says that His flesh and bone and nature were in heaven, and were put forth in the womb of the Virgin Mary when she was overshadowed by the Holy Ghost, and then He took His blood. But a difficulty occurs in this. John, in his vision of the book sealed with seven seals, saw "A strong angel proclaiming with a loud voice, Who is worthy to open the book, and to loose the seals thereof? And no man in heaven, nor in earth, neither under the earth, was able to open the book, neither to look thereon."

After John had wept, doubtless under the true conviction of his heart of the dreadful state of affairs, looking at and meditating upon the justice of God's wrath kindled against a ruined and wretched world, " One of the elders said, weep not; behold, the Lion of the tribe of Judah, the root of David hath prevailed to take the book, and to open the seven seals thereof."

The difficulty is, where was the body of Christ, at that time? It could not have been in heaven, nor earth, nor under the earth; for none was found in either that was able to do the work of opening the sealed book. But the branch of David, the son of man, the high Priest from the tribe of Judah comes up, according to prophecy, fully authorized to do the work. He, by being a near kinsman, can assume our debts, and is adequate to the task of paying them off for us. Divinity and humanity unite and compose a complete Son of God, and just as complete a Son of man.

But let us proceed with the Scriptural testimony relative to His assuming humanity. The apostle gives the following admonition: "Let this mind be in you, which was also in Christ Jesus; who, being in the form of God, thought it not robbery to be equal with God; but made himself of no reputation, and took upon him the form of a servant, and was made in the likeness of men. And being found in fashion as a man, be humbled himself and became obedient unto death, even the death of the cross."

Phil. ii, 5, 8. What was it that was made in the likeness of men? It could not have been his body, if it existed in eternity in the form of a man; for that which already existed could not be made. It could not have been human nature if He always possessed that, and yet He was made in the likeness of men. In this it seems clear from the Scriptures already quoted, that he became like a man by taking on Him the nature and body of a man. Whatever the nature of a man is, is the human nature, and it is strictly in this sense that He was of the tribe of Judah. But I am asked, what was it that took this nature? I answer, Divinity. And when, Divinity took upon Himself the form and nature of a man, He possessed two natures—human and divine. When the angel explained to Joseph the condition of Mary, he did not say that an eternal human body or nature had been put forth in the womb of the blessed Virgin, but that something was conceived or begotten in her; he did not say it was of humanity, but of the Holy Ghost. Mat. i, 20. "Hence the truth that he is begotten of God, and is known in Scripture as the only begotten of the Father." John iii, 15, 18. Jesus being thus begotten of God and born of the Virgin Mary, comes into the world just what had been promised from the time man needed a Savior.

It is sometimes said that "necessity is the mother of invention," and the doctrine of the eternal humanity of Christ being an invention of some one, we have often wondered what was the necessity of it. For the Bible never mentions eternal humanity at all.

Then let us ask all who may read this, and at the same time believe the doctrine of eternal humanity, what advantage is it to you? Is the doctrine of the perfection of God in all attributes easier established by assuming that position? Is the doctrine of election and salvation by grace through Christ more easily established by holding the doctrine of eternal humanity than it would otherwise be? Is it any advantage to you in establishing any one or more of the doctrinal points in the Bible? If not, and you find nothing said about eternal humanity, why do you contend for it so earnestly to the great grief of those who wish to have, at least, one "Thus saith the Lord" for what they believe? But it is sometimes urged that God is immutable, yet "It repented him that he had made man on the earth, and it grieved him at his heart." Gen. iv, 6.

It is thought that as God never changes, the one who repented of making man was the humanity of God, or it was Christ. It is further urged that to say otherwise would involve us in a difficulty which we could not solve, for God never changes. But suppose we show that Christ as God is just as immutable as the Father, especially when spoken of as the Lord, as in this case, would not the same difficulty come up then? Would it be any easier solved then, by claiming the doctrine of eternal humanity? Let us see if the Son as well as the Father, is not unchangeable. "But unto the Son, he saith, Thy throne, O God, is forever and ever: a sceptre of righteousness is a sceptre of thy kingdom. Thou hast loved righteousness, and hated iniquity; therefore God, even thy God, hath anointed thee with oil of gladness above thy fellows. And thou, Lord, in the beginning hast laid the foundation of the earth; and the heavens are the work of thine hands. They shall perish, but thou remainest: and they shall all wax old as doth a garment. And as a vesture shalt thou fold them up, and they shall be changed; but thou art the same, and thy years shall not fail." Heb. i, 8, 12. In this quotation the Father addresses the Son. And it is certain the language of the text is as emphatic on the immutability of the Son, as it ever occurs relative to the Father; but this is not all, for when we read in the Scriptures of the "three that bear record in heaven, the Father, the Word and the Holy Ghost," he says emphatically, "and these three are one." I John v, 7. If the three are one, we would think that they were all three immutable alike. One is not contrary to the other, so that one can be unchangeable and the other not. So, without introducing any further testimony to prove the immutability of Christ, it is plain that to assume the doctrine of eternal humanity does not let us out of the difficulty introduced in the case above referred to. Hence, we now propose to notice Him in His original capacity. In His original nature He is God. His name—Son of God—imports divinity: "The same in substance, equal in power and glory," with the Father and the Holy Ghost. He is called God in the highest sense; God over all; the true, the great God, Jehovah; Jehovah of hosts.

"In the year that King Uzziah died I saw also the Lord sitting upon a throne high and lifted up, and his train filled the temple." Isa. vi, 1. The Son of God, or "The Word," is equally holy with the Father. "And one cried unto another and said, Holy, Holy, Holy, is the Lord of hosts; the whole earth is filled with His glory." Isa. vi, 3. The works of creation are ascribed to him. "I said, O my God, take me not away in the midst of my days: thy years are throughout all generations. Of old hast thou laid the foundation of the earth; the heavens are the work of thy hands." Ps. cii, 24, 25. How beautiful this language harmonizes with the first verses of St. John: "In the beginning was the Word, and the Word was with God, and the Word was God." We have known the position taken by those claiming eternal human nature, that there were two Words here; one that was God, which was divine nature, and the other that was with God, which was human nature. Such extremes are doubtless necessary in the work of advocating the doctrine of the eternal humanity of God. But in this text only one word is mentioned, and that one is both God and with God. It is one of the three that bear record in heaven; and these three being one God, it is impossible to speak of one and not the others. If we call upon God in our petitions at a throne of grace, we address the Three; and so, if we call on the Word or Holy Spirit. Either of these is properly God. One of the three, to-wit: the Word is the one mentioned in the verse quoted. The Word was in the beginning, and was truly God; and also was just as truly with God, being with the Father and the Holy Ghost. "The same was in the beginning with God. All things were made by him; and without him was not anything made."

Let us not forget that the subject here is the Word, one of the three that bear record in heaven; and that so far as His existence is concerned, He is co-eternal with the Father. We read on down to the 14th verse; it is said, "The Word was made flesh, and dwelt among us, full of grace and truth." Here is when he assumes humanity. He was not flesh in eternity; but the Word that was in eternity was made flesh and dwelt among us, (and we beheld his glory, the glory as of the only begotten of the Father,) full of grace and truth. But when we ask, how could that be made flesh that was always flesh? we are met with this answer: It does not say when it was made flesh. That indeed is masterly, as if it could be eternal at all, and yet be made. It does not matter when it was made flesh; but was it made flesh at all? If so, flesh is not eternal; for that which is made is not eternal. The Word was eternal, but flesh was not. Hence, when we speak of the Word that was in the beginning, we speak of the Son in His original capacity. We have already said that in His original nature He is God, and that the works of creation were ascribed to Him. "For thy Maker is thine husband. The Lord of Hosts is his name; and thy Redeemer, the Holy One of Israel; the God of the whole earth shall He be called." Isa. liv, 5.

This quotation tells what He is, the nearness that He sustains to His bride, and what He shall be called in the future. We see all this verified; for after He had taken upon Himself the form of a servant, and become obedient unto death, "God for that reason hath highly exalted Him, and given Him a name which is above every name; that at the name of Jesus every knee should bow, of things in heaven, and things in earth, and things under the earth. And that every tongue should confess that Jesus Christ is Lord, to the glory of God the Father." Phil. ii, 9, 10.

Although it was by Him the worlds were made, and He is truly said to have come down from heaven; yet His flesh and bone; or human nature, did not come down; for it was "Made of a woman, made under the law, (not made in heaven,) to redeem them that were under the law." Gal. iv, 4, 5.

Notwithstanding He was in the fulness of time, made of a woman, yet in His original state all the attributes of God did belong to Him. We have already shown that He was as unchangeable as the Father, so is He everlasting. "But thou, Bethlehem, Ephratah, though thou be little among the thousands of Judah, yet out of thee shall he come forth unto Me that is to be the Ruler in Israel; whose goings forth have been from of old, from everlasting." Micah, v, 2. Again, "I am Alpha and Omega, the beginning and the ending, saith the Lord, which is, and which was, and which is to come, the Almighty." Rev. i, 8. Also, "Thus saith the Lord the King of Israel, and his Redeemer the Lord of Hosts; I am the first and I am the last; and besides Me there is no God." Isa. xliv, 6. "Hearken unto Me, O Jacob and Israel, my called; I am He; I am the first; I also am the last." Isa. xlviii, 12.

The foregoing scriptures doubtless refer to the Word that was with God, and was God, by whom the worlds were framed. Not only does it prove to us conclusively that He possessed the attributes of God before He took our nature, but He still retains all the attributes while here in His humility. He is not only everlasting, but omniscient and omnipresent. "For where two or three are gathered together in my name, there am I in the midst of them." Mat. xviii, 20. "And no man hath ascended up to heaven, but he that come down from heaven, even the Son of man which is in heaven." John iii, 13.

From this we are clearly taught that even when He was in the flesh He filled immensity. He was here teaching the people, and yet was in heaven. If it was necessary for Him to have a body in eternity in order to exist as the Son of man it would now become necessary for Him to have two bodies; one on earth, and one in heaven. But this text is sometimes used to prove that He came down from heaven in a body, undertaking to show from it that whatever of Jesus ascends to heaven first came down from heaven. But it always seems to prove too much when it is all quoted, and according to the interpretation they give it, that nothing will go to heaven only what comes from there, the body of the Savior will be excluded from heaven; for He is here in the body, and says no man has ascended up to heaven but the Son of man which is in heaven. His body is not in heaven when He makes use of the expression. This is not all that we may learn from this text; for something has descended from heaven, and whatever is called the Son of man now without a human body, may also have existed in eternity as the Son of man without a human body. But it seems that this is as good an opportunity as is afforded in the Bible anywhere for us to ascertain whether the body of Christ did come down from heaven or not. Whatever was in heaven called the Son of man was that which had ascended; and that which had ascended, had come down from heaven. If the body had not ascended it had not come down from heaven, and yet something had come down from heaven, and that something had ascended while the body of Jesus was still on earth. Hence, it is easily understood from this that when the Bible gives any account of the Savior coming down from heaven, it has direct allusion to something besides his body. It must therefore be understood to be that which was in the beginning with God, which is the Word. He, in this capacity, as the Son of man, held the office of Redeemer before the creation; for, in view of His fulfilling this office, and as a part of his work, the creation of other worlds, as well as our own, and all that it contains, was assigned Him by the Father. He, therefore, existed before He appeared in the world; yea, He sat upon the mediatorial throne and executed His office from the beginning of time.

Divinity is essential to His office as Redeemer. His divinity lays the foundation and qualifies Him for the assumption of the duties of His office. As divine He owes no obedience to that violated law under which sinners are condemned; on Him, as the Son of God, that law has no claims whatever. As divine, He has a perfect right to undertake the office and work of the Redeemer if He shall so choose to do. As divine, He possesses every attribute of wisdom, power, holiness, justice, goodness and truth in an infinite degree to enable Him without the shadow of failure, to meet every demand, and perform every duty required of Him on behalf of God and man, and, finally, descends from heaven to earth, assumes human nature, takes upon Him a body of human flesh, bone and blood, to which body His divinity adds an infinite dignity and value, and all to His obedience, suffering and death. He is able to stand before the Eternal God, and bear all His just demands against His creatures, and He is also able to stand before men as "their Lord and their God," to deliver them from their emnity by His Holy Spirit, to raise up from corruption and misery, clothe them with His glorious righteousness, and reconcile them to God. Help is therefore laid upon one, not only willing, but able to save. In His assumed nature He is man. He came not to assist angels but men; therefore, was He "the seed of the woman," "partaker of flesh and blood" and one "made under the law," otherwise He could not have obeyed, suffered and died, nor been our example, and faithful sympathizing High Priest, "Wherefore in all things it behooved Him to be made like unto His brethren, that He might be a merciful and faithful High Priest in things pertaining to God, to make reconciliation for the sins of the people. Heb. ii, 15, 18. Two distinct natures, human and divine, are (in a manner incomprehensible to us) united, and form one person, Immanuel, God with us. Everything belonging to God is ascribed unto and belongs to Him; and everything belonging to man is ascribed unto and belongs to Him, sin excepted.

Such is the Scriptural account of our most glorious Redeemer.

CHAPTER LVIII.

I will now give, in this chapter, a discourse, the substance of which has been published in the *Church Advocate*. I now reproduce it and revise it, and by its study, the reader will find my views on several points of doctrine. I hope it may be beneficial to the reader, and also that it may be instructive.

"In whom also we have obtained an inheritance, being predestinated according to the purpose of him who worketh all things after the counsel of his own will. That we should be to the praise of his glory who first trusted in Christ." Ephesians, i–11, 12.

My object in introducing this text, is for the subject matter contained in it. It is the language of the inspired apostle, to the saints at Ephesus, and to the faithful in Christ Jesus. The text seems to be a description of what God has done for His people, with their future and eternal welfare in view. By noticing the few preceding verses we may come to a better understanding of the text. "Having made known unto us the mystery of his will, according to his good pleasure which he hath purposed in himself; that in the dispensation of the fulness of times, he might gather together in one all things in Christ, both which are in heaven, and which are on earth, even in him." Then comes the text: "In whom," that is, in Christ, "also we have obtained an inheritance," etc. It is very evident from the wording of this chapter, from its commencement to the text, inclusive, that all that the Lord has done for us, and every provision made for our eternal and spiritual welfare, has been done in Christ. All spiritual blessings are in Him; and the Apostle Peter has said: "Neither is there salvation in any other, for there is none other name under heaven, given among men whereby we must be saved," Acts iv, 12. Now, in order that we might have a proper understanding of the text, we will notice first, that it is according to God's will that we receive spiritual blessings in Christ. The text says "He worketh all things after the counsel of his own will." Let us then begin to read with the third verse, and comment. "Blessed be the God and Father of our Lord Jesus Christ, who hath blessed us, with all spiritual blessings, in heavenly places in Christ." Everything we need is in Christ; all spiritual blessings are there, and that is all that men need. "According as he hath chosen us in him before the foundation of the world, that we should be holy and without blame before him in love." I wish to notice some expressions that have been made concerning this passage of Scripture. One man of considerable ability, who believed in the doctrine of the pre-existence of God's children, referred to this text as showing that God had blessed His people with all spiritual blessings, in heavenly places in Christ before the foundation of the world. The text does not say so. Neither is there any other text that says so, and I am of the opinion that this able expositor of God's word would not have said so, had it not been that his creed required it. It is not only a mis-quotation of Scripture but it is a gross misrepresentation of the apostle's language. The text does say "who hath blessed us with all spiritual blessings in heavenly places in Christ, according as he hath chosen us in him, before the foundation of the world." Not that He hath blessed us with those blessings before the foundation of the world, but that He had chosen us in Christ before the foundation of the world, and according to that choice, or agreeable to that choice, or in harmony with that choice, or as a consequence of that choice, He has now, in time blessed the saints with spiritual blessings in heavenly places in Christ. I also wish to notice a criticism that an objector to the doctrine of unconditional election has frequently made upon the idea of being chosen in Christ before the foundation of the world. I have met several able men in discussion, in my life, and in order to evade the force of this text, as proof of unconditional election to eternal salvation, they have argued that the word "world" in this text referred to the Christian Era, and not to the universe; that the word was translated from the Greek "kosmos," and that it did not mean the universe, and that the persons chosen in this text were simply the apostles, chosen to the apostleship. I wish to reply to that criticism, and investigate it in the light of divine truth. That it was the apostles chosen to the apostleship, is without any foundation whatever, from the fact that the text does not say "chosen to the apostleship;" but it does say "chosen in Christ, that we should be holy,"—not that we should be apostles— "and without blame before him in love." But if it was the apostles simply, that were chosen, it must be an unconditional choice of twelve men, at least, to holiness, and unblameableness before the Lord.

But I wish to give one more reason why I cannot accept the idea that the choice in this connection means chosen to the office of apostles. The writer is the Apostle Paul, and when he uses the pronoun "we," and "us," he includes himself all along. He was not one of the twelve, neither was he chosen to apostleship prior to the beginning of the gospel dispensation. He was not called to be an apostle for several years after the commencement of the gospel day. This very fact presents a difficulty in the way of that theory that no man will ever touch. Unless the apostle Paul was one of the twelve, and was called on to be an apostle before the gospel dispensation was ushered in, neither of which is true, then the idea that the choice here means the election of the apostles to the apostleship, contradicts the very text in dispute. I simply believe that all the people of God are embraced in this text, and that they were chosen to eternal salvation.

But to undertake to argue that it does not mean the universe because the term world is translated from the Greek "kosmos," is a grand mistake, as we propose to show. We do not have to be Greek scholars in order to find out the true meaning of the word "kosmos." Webster gives it in his Unabridged Dictionary. In English it is spelled c-o-s-m-o-s; in Greek it is spelled k-o-s-m-o-s. Webster says: "COSMOS: (from the Greek kosmos. Order, harmony.) 1. The universe, or universality of created things, so called from its perfect arrangement. 2. The doctrine of the universe; the system of law, harmony and truth combined within the universe." It does not seem from Webster that "kosmos" simply means a dispensation of time, or a definite period or age, but that it means the universe; and I claim that the apostles, as well as all the elect of God, that will ever sing his praises in heaven, were chosen in Christ Jesus before the creation of the universe, and that this text proves it. I wish to notice a few texts now, in which that word is used, to see whether the word "kosmos" generally means "age" or not. I call attention to Matt. iv, 8. It reads: "Again the devil taketh him up into an exceeding high mountain, and showeth him all the kingdoms of the world (kosmos), and the glory of them." The kingdoms of the world, that the devil showed the Savior, were not the gospel dispensation, nor the Jewish dispensation, and there is no construction that we can put upon that text, to make it mean an age, or a period of time, but it alludes to the universe. Again, Romans iv, 13. It reads: "For the promise that he should be the heir of the world, was not to Abraham, or to his seed through the law, but through the righteousness of faith." The word "world" there is translated from "kosmos." Again, John i, 10. "He was in the world, and the world was made by him, and the world knew him not." Here we have the word "world" three times, and all of them from "kosmos," and neither of them means an age. Again, Matt. xxv, 34. "Then shall the King say unto them on his right hand, Come, ye blessed of my Father, inherit the kingdom prepared for you from the foundation of the world." (kosmos). That could not have been an age. 1 Tim. vi, 17, which reads, "Charge them that are rich in this world, (kosmos), that they be not high-minded, nor trust in uncertain riches, but in the living God who giveth us all things richly to enjoy." Again, 1 Tim. vi, 7. "For we brought nothing into this world, (kosmos), and it is certain we can carry nothing out." Again, 1 Tim. iii, 16. "And without controversy great is the mystery of godliness: God was manifest in the flesh, justified in the Spirit, seen of angels, preached unto the Gentiles, believed on in the world (kosmos) received up into glory." Hebrews ix, 26. "For then must he often have suffered since the foundation of the world (kosmos,) but now once in the end of the world (Aionon, age), hath he appeared to put away sin by the sacrifice of himself." I claim that the word "world" is the universe; that kosmos does mean the universe; let it mean whatever else it may, it sometimes means the universe, the created world, and I have no recollection of a single place where it is translated age. So I rely upon the arguments and Scriptures I have already introduced as positive proof that God chose His people in Christ Jesus, to eternal salvation, and arranged every provision, and every means necessary to bring about the consummation of His eternal purpose, in Christ Jesus, before He created this world in which we live. There is another position taken on this text by some that I wish to notice. One man who believed in the doctrine of the pre-existence of God's children, in reply to an article that I had written, some years ago, stated that he could not see how God chose His people in Christ, before the foundation of the world, if they did not exist then; that He did not choose them into Christ, but that He chose them in Christ, was his argument, and that they must have been there, in some sense or other, or He could not have done it. I claim that God foreknew His people, and that He was as well acquainted with them, before they had a being, as He is after they have a being, and that He did choose them in Christ to eternal salvation, before the foundation of the world, although they had no actual being at that time.

On the subject of the pre-existence of God's children, there has been a great deal said, and the legitimate result of that doctrine is a denial of the resurrection of the bodies of God's people. I was asked, in a debate on this question once, if the people of God did not exist through all eternity, where did He get them? My answer was, He made them, and I refer to Isaiah, liv, 5, as one text that proves that He did make them: "For thy Maker is thine husband; the Lord of hosts is his name; and thy Redeemer, the Holy One of Israel. The God of the whole earth shall he be called." From this it sounds like the church had a maker, and I never could conceive of a maker of something that had existed from eternity. God's people were made. He made them of the dust of the ground. They were the first people in existence. The apostle Paul said, "The first man is of the earth earthly." If the earthly man is the first man, I argue that there was no man before him, hence, the earthly man is the first man. Again the apostle says: "Howbeit that was not first which is spiritual, but that which is natural, and afterwards that which is spiritual." The natural man is the earthly man, and he was made of the dust of the earth, and there was no man before him, consequently it would be impossible for God's people to have existed before the first man existed. I published a work a few years ago, entitled, "Unconditional Election Stated and Defined; or a Denial of the Doctrine of Eternal Children, or Two Seeds in the Flesh." I sent a copy of it to all the editors of Old School Baptist periodicals in this country. One man wrote a lengthy editorial in reply to the position I took against the pre-existence of God's children. He said: "According to Bro. Potter's views, God has no people, only as he takes them out of Adam's family and adopts them into His own." That is just precisely what I believe, and I feel proud that I am understood, even if I am not endorsed, on that subject. I believe that the subject of salvation is the Adam sinner, and I do not believe that he had an eternal existence. The apostle speaks of God's people as being foreknown. "Whom He foreknew He did also predestinate, to be conformed to the image of His Son, that He might be the firstborn among many brethren." Again, whom He did predestinate, them He also called, and whom He called, them He also justified," etc. I take the position that if God's people were as old as Himself, that He did not foreknow them. To foreknow a thing is to know it beforehand, and He foreknew His people, and it was the people that He foreknew that He predestinated to be conformed to the image of Christ. I take the position that God purposed the salvation of His people, and that He saves the people according to His purpose. The text says that we are predestinated according to the purpose of Him who worketh all things after the counsel of His own will." This is the way we are predestinated. The apostle says, "We know that all things work together for good to them that love God"—to them who are the called according to His purpose.

There are two descriptions given of the children of God in that text; one is that they love God, and the other is that they are called according to God's purpose. I understand the call there to be that they are called to be saints. The apostle again, to Timothy, says: "Who hath saved us and called us with an holy calling, not according to our works, but according to his own purpose and grace which was given us in Christ Jesus before the world began." From this text we learn that it is according to His purpose and not according to our works. It cannot be according to our works and at the same time be according to His purpose, for His purpose is unalterable, but if the matter depended upon the condition of our works, His purpose might fluctuate as our works do; hence, it is not according to our works, but according to His own purpose and grace which was given us in Christ Jesus, before the world began. I see no good reason for objecting to the doctrine that God eternally purposed the salvation of His people, and that according to that purpose He saves them. To illustrate: Here is an old brother, who professes to be a Christian, and I presume that the neighbors, both saints and sinners, believe him to be just what he pretends to be—an honest, candid, upright Christian man. If he is a saint, as he professes to be, what does God intend to do with him finally? I ask every conditionalist for an answer to that question. What do you believe God intends to do with that man? that very individual man? Oh, you say, God intends to take him to heaven after awhile. That is just what I say; that is God's intention concerning this man. He intends that this man shall live in heaven by and by. If that is God's intention now concerning this man, how long has it been His intention concerning this same man? When did it begin to be His intention? Was it at some period in the history of this man's life? If it was God's intention one moment before he became a Christian, so far as the principle is concerned, He may as well have purposed it from all eternity, and I ask, if it is God's intention now to save him, was there ever a period either in time or eternity that it was not God's intention to save this man? God's intention and God's purpose are about the same thing, and if He intends to save a man now, it has been His intention from all eternity to save that man, and if that is true with one that He saves, so is it true with all that He will ever save. Hence, it is consistent with the text, to say that "He worketh all things after the counsel of his own will." It is not according to man's will that he is saved, but "He worketh all things after the counsel of his own will," and if so, it cannot be after the counsel of our will. I now wish to see if I can find out how far back God's purpose runs, and I call attention to Eph. iii, 11. "According to his eternal purpose which he purposed in Christ Jesus our Lord." His purpose is eternal, and we are predestinated according to that purpose. Now God's purpose to save us has been from all eternity, and that purpose embraces every soul that will ever be saved, and every means and every purpose necessary to bring about the end. Man is not saved according to his own will. The apostle says: "Having predestinated us unto the adoption of children by Jesus Christ himself according to the good pleasure of his will, that we should be to the praise of the glory of his grace, wherein he hath made us accepted in the beloved." Who made us accepted in the beloved? God has already made us accepted in the beloved. The beloved here is Jesus Christ, and God has made us accepted in Jesus Christ. "In whom—that is in Jesus Christ—we have redemption through his blood the forgiveness of sins according to the riches of his grace." It will be seen that everything here has been done for us, not according to any of our wills, or actions, but all according to God's will and purpose and grace. "Having made known unto us the mystery of his will according to his good pleasure—not our good pleasure—which he hath purposed in himself, that in the dispensation of the fulness of times, he might gather together in one, all things in Christ, both which are in heaven, and which are on earth, even in him;" then comes the text, "In whom also we have obtained an inheritance," etc. I wish to notice the strength of the word "obtained," for a moment. I was in a discussion with a gentleman once, who made an argument that if we obtained a thing, that we got that thing by our own effort; that obtain was the same as to get by an effort. I, being aware that he would undertake that argument, took pains to look the matter up, and I found out by reference to Webster's Dictionary, that we might obtain anything by the effort of another, as well as by our own effort. Hence, the reading of the text: "We have obtained this inheritance in Christ, not in ourselves;" thus it is by what He has done for us that we have obtained it, and not what we have done for Him. Hence, the argument, that because we have obtained it, it must have been by our own effort, must simply fall to the ground of its own weakness.

But there is another thing that I wish to notice, and that is the inheritance. We have obtained an inheritance. An inheritance is something that we cannot buy. We cannot buy it with money, nor with love, nor with works. If we were worth millions of dollars, we could not purchase an inheritance. We could buy property and possessions, but that would not be an inheritance. An inheritance is something that we receive on account of our relationship to some one; for instance, you see that little boy over there; he has a claim upon his father and mother for nourishment, cleanliness, plenty to eat and wear, protection from disease and danger, proper training and education, a doctor if he gets sick, patient, tender nursing during his sickness, and finally to his share of his father's estate, whatever that may be. This claim he now has upon his father and mother. How did he come by such a claim as that? It was not by his works. It was not because he loved his father and mother. There must be some other cause of his having such claims. The truth is, he came by those claims by his birth. He is an heir, and as an heir he is entitled to those things. There are only two ways of becoming heirs; one is by birth, the other by adoption. He is an heir by birth. Sometimes men adopt children into their families, but as a rule, they do it because there is something in the child to admire. This is not the case when God adopts a child, from the fact that His children in their natural depraved state are unworthy and have nothing in them to admire. But in adoption, in civil adoption, there is one thing true, if I wanted my son adopted into the family of some lord or noble, I could not have it done, just simply because I willed it, and if the son himself was ever so eager for such an adoption, he could not have it just because he wanted it; if all our friends were to intercede, we could not have it simply because it was our wish. But there is the will of one who must be consulted, and that is the will of Him who does the adopting. It must all be done according to His will. Again, the birth is not according to the will of man, but John says "who were born not of blood, nor of the will of the flesh, nor of the will of man, but of God." Hence, it is all according to the will of God. There is another point about inheritance that I wish to notice, and that is that we were not eternally heirs, but we have obtained the inheritance in Christ. The idea of the pre-existence of God's children involves the idea that we were eternally heirs. That is a mistake. Paul says that "Being justified by his grace we should be made heirs according to the hope of eternal life." If we were made heirs, then we were not eternally heirs, and we wish that point noted. One more feature in the text that I wish to notice is controverted sometimes. "Who worketh all things after the counsel of his own will." I believe that the "all things" in that text have allusion to the all things necessary to our spiritual welfare, but that it does not have allusion to everything that takes place in the world, but "God worketh all things, pertaining to our salvation, after the counsel of his own will." I think that is a poor text to prove the doctrine of the absolute predestination of all things whatsoever come to pass by. The text itself says, "Being predestinated according to the purpose of him who worketh all things after the counsel of his own will." So far as the doctrine of the absolute predestination of all things is concerned, I have thought that perhaps that question has been agitated among our brethren more than was profitable, and I have been opposed to its agitation. There have been brethren among us, who occupy a position on both sides of that issue, ever since I have been acquainted with the Baptists, and it has never been made a bar to fellowship in a great many places. Another reason I have for objecting to its agitation has been that I do not know what it is. I hear one man contend for it, and another man object to it, and I read their writings, and hear their arguments, and their objections pro and con, and both parties have claimed to be misunderstood, or misrepresented, almost universally. If a man makes a statement of what he believes, I can soon tell whether I endorse that statement or not, but to be certain as to what the doctrine of the absolute predestination of all things is, I do not know where to go to find out. I was talking with a brother not many weeks ago, who seemed eager to agitate the question, but I begged him to let it alone, as I did not enjoy controversy on that subject, but he seemed eager to talk about it, as if he thought I dreaded him. I asked him if he believed that the devil was doing God's will. He undertook to evade the answer, until I remarked to him that as he was a matter-of-fact sort of a man, and this was a doctrine of such importance to him, he must answer that question, and he finally admitted that he did believe the devil was doing God's will. I do not endorse that. If that is the doctrine of the absolute predestination of all things, I do not believe it. Another man once began the agitation of that question with me, and I begged him to let it alone, but finding that he was determined, I told him that if God had predestined all things and that was the cause of their coming to pass, that no man could evade the position that he was the author of all things, to which he replied that God's predestination of all things was not the cause of them coming to pass. I told him all right. I have no more to say. I have no fight to make against your doctrine of predestination. I always understood that God's predestination of the salvation of His people caused it to come to pass, and I would have applied the same rule to God's predestination of other things, but if it was not applicable I have no more to say. It will be seen, then, that I believe in the salvation of all the elect; and that they are men and women of Adam's family, such as compose my congregation, and the soul is born of the Spirit of God, in the work of regeneration, in time; but at the dissolution of the body, the soul goes to heaven. Soul and spirit, in Scripture means the same thing frequently. Stephen said, "Lord Jesus receive my spirit." He saw heaven opened, and Jesus sitting on the right hand of the throne of God, and I believe his spirit went immediately to heaven, at the death of the body. Again, I believe that the body will be raised at the last day; the very same body that we bury in the ground will be raised up from the dead, and fashioned like unto the glorious body of the Redeemer. It will not be another body, gotten up in the place of the one we bury, for that would not be resurrection. To put down one body, and take up another, would not be resurrection. Resurrection means to restore to life that that once had life, and to give vitality to that which never had it, would not be resurrection. But the bodies of the saints die, and they are to be made alive, and wafted home to glory, forever to bask in the ocean of God's unbounded love, to praise Him throughout the ceaseless ages of a never ending eternity. Amen.

CHAPTER LIX.

As there are many controverted points among Christian people, it will be impossible for me to give space to all of them in a limited work like this, but I will give one brief chapter on the subject "Born of Water." There are some people who, I think, are over-confident that this text proves that water baptism is essential to salvation. I give this chapter against that doctrine.

"Except a man be born of water and of the spirit, he cannot enter into the kingdom of God."

This text is relied on to prove that baptism is in order to remission of sins, and is referred to as confidently, as if there could be no question about it. Mr. Campbell argues that being "born again," and "being immersed," are, in the apostle's style, two names for the same act. Christianity Restored, page 270. This being their view of the matter, it would be very difficult for them to think of a man being born again, without thinking of water. For if he is right, no one has been born again in the absence of water; hence it is not particularly necessary to them that you prove water baptism to them, in case of a new birth. They see as much water in verse 3 as they do in verse 5, and as much water in verse 7, as in verse 5, only water is mentioned in verse 5, and it is not in the other two, but they think it is understood, so it answers their purpose all the same.

The nearest reference to baptism in this text is that water is in the text, and while many able commentators, who believe in baptismal regeneration, and some who do not. give it as their opinion that the Savior meant water baptism, it is mere opinion, and as it suits their theory very well, they have accepted that opinion, and are building upon it. We have read the opinion of quite a number of very able men on the text who hold that it is water baptism, and none of them, that we have ever read, give that opinion as the result of their studies as scholars. Mr. Campbell undertakes to prove that it is water baptism by other commentators, instead of giving his own scholarly reasons for it. Why should such a man as he call on Wesley, Whitfield, or any one else to prove it, if it could be proven by scholastic investigation? It is not common for him to call on others for the proper rendering of a text. Why did he not, at least, give us the benefit of his own rendering of this text?

We simply have the opinion of a great many who think the Savior meant water baptism, in the text, while we have the opinion of quite a number who differ. We do not see fit to begin to build a theory on the opinion of men, without some investigation at least. In the 3d verse, no doubt, the Savior meant the same birth that he did in verse 5, and in verse 3, He says, "Except a man be born again, he cannot see the kingdom of God." All scholars are aware of the fact that the words "born again," verse 3, and also, in verse 7, in the original are "born from above," *gennethe anothen*, born from above. Hence the Savior told Nicodemus "Except a man be born from above, he cannot see the kingdom of God." The apostle tells us, "But Jerusalem which is above is free, which is the mother of us all." Gal. iv, 26.

All God's children are born of their mother, and, instead of our mother being below, she is above. It will not be hard for us to see what Paul meant by Jerusalem which is above, if we will only refer to Rev. iii, 12, where John says, "Him that overcometh will I make a pillar in the temple of my God, and he shall go no more out, and I will write upon him the name of my God, and the name of the city of my God, which is New Jerusalem, which cometh down out of heaven from my God: and I will write upon him my new name."

Mr. Burgess accuses Elder Thompson of "presenting before the people, the inconceivable monstrosity of a man born in the world with only one parent—a man born with a father, but without any mother." Thompson and Burgess debate, page 219. This accusation was made because Elder Thompson did not recognize water baptism in the text. We can hardly tell which would be the greatest monstrosity, for a child to be born of two mothers at the same birth, or to have no mother at all. If the water is the mother of which the children of God are born, then they have two mothers, the water is one, and Jerusalem which is above is the other. But lest some one should think we are not representing them correctly, we will give another extract from Mr. Burgess, in the same book. He says, "It is monstrous to suppose that but a single parent is requisite to the new birth; and there can be no such thing as the sinner's becoming a new creature in Christ Jesus, until he comes forth out of the womb of the waters, and having been made dead to sin, is made alive to God." Page 204. We need not take much pains here to make any one see that he recognizes the water as the mother of the children of God; and Paul says Jerusalem is our mother; so we have two mothers.

As the children of God are born from above, and Jerusalem is their mother, we doubt very seriously, that water in the text has any allusion to baptism at all. Before we accept it as meaning baptism, we shall demand the proof by better witnesses than the opinion of men, even if they are able. If there is no other method of proving it, it cannot be proven, and it is strange that there is some way of proving it, and yet it has never been done. The burden of proof rests on those who affirm that water, in the text, means baptism, and we shall take the privilege of denying it until the evidence is produced.

There are only two births known to the universe; and one of them is the fleshly, and the other the spiritual birth. They are both mentioned in John iii, 6, and John i, 12, 13, and in 1 Pet. i, 23. The birth of the flesh is the birth by which we are born into this world, and the birth of the Spirit is that birth which brings us into spiritual relationship to God. When we are born of the Spirit, or into the spiritual family, we are born from above. We are of the opinion that the water in the text means the water of life, that is so frequently mentioned in the Scriptures. But we do deny that it means water baptism, for reasons already assigned, and that we will now give.

If the believer in Christ is born of God, (as the Apostle John says he is, "Whosoever believeth that Jesus is the Christ is born of God," I John v, 1,) and none are to be baptized but believers, then it necessarily follows that the believer does not have to be baptized in order to be born. The only way to baptize a man before he is born of God, is to baptize him before he believes. This the Campbellites will not do. Then to be born of water and of the Spirit cannot mean the water of baptism, because the believer is born of God before he comes to baptism.

But the Campbellites get matters fearfully mixed up, trying to make this text answer their purpose. We have already noticed that Mr. Brents said, "The church of God is entered by a birth of water and Spirit," and that Mr. Campbell's Living Oracles say, "And the Lord daily added the saved to the congregation," and that the whole fraternity of them teach that born of water means baptism. Let us put these three positions of Campbellism together, and look at them.

First—The sinner must be saved before he enters the church.

Second—The sinner must be baptized before he is saved.

Third—The sinner must be added to the church by baptism.

The Campbellites alone are responsible for these contradictions; the Bible does not teach them, and they are not misrepresentations by the opponents of Campbellism; but each one of the three positions is a prominent and distinguishing feature of their doctrine.

But another difficulty arises, that we think worthy of attention. According to Campbellism, there has been a wonderful change of affairs since the conversation of the Savior with Nicodemus. The church had not been set up at Jerusalem yet, they say, and there was no church for Nicodemus to have been born into. They teach that when a man is born again, he is born into the church.

Mr. Brents says, "Having seen that a man must be born again, in order to enter the kingdom, and that it is the office of the new birth to introduce the party born into the kingdom, it follows that a more important subject never engaged the attention of man." pp. 189 and 190. Mr. Campbell says, "This second, or new birth, which inducts the party born into the kingdom of God, is always subsequent to a death and burial, as it will be into the everlasting kingdom of glory." Chris. Res. p. 163.

If it is the office of the new birth to introduce the party born into the kingdom, and there was no kingdom till the day of Pentecost, as they teach, could Nicodemus have been born again, if he had wished to, at the time of his conversation with the Savior? If the church was not set up till the day of Pentecost, it is certain that he could not have been born into the church. Was it true or not, at the time the Savior made use of this language, that a man must be born again to be saved? Could Nicodemus have been saved at that time without being born again?

We think, to put the most liberal construction on the subject, the Campbellites should fix this matter up, so they will have it themselves. It is very evidet that "born of water and of the Spirit," does not mean water baptism; for there is no mention of baptism as a birth in all that is said on that subject. The text itself says nothing about baptism.

Dr. Doddridge says, "When our Lord says, except a man be born of water and of the Spirit, he cannot enter into the kingdom of of God; it is (after all the contempt with which that interpretation has been treated) very possible he may mean, by a well known figure, to express one idea by two clauses, that is, the purifying influence of the Spirit cleansing the mind, as water does the body; as elsewhere to be baptized by the Spirit operating like fire. But if there is indeed a reference to baptism in these words (which I own I am much inclined to believe) it will by no means follow that baptism is regeneration." It will be easily seen that while the Doctor is inclined to believe reference is had to baptism, that he recognizes the fact that it is merely an opinion without any proof, but if it is baptism, yet baptism is not regeneration.

The argument by this learned divine was not gotten up to oppose Mr. Campbell's views, for it was written in the year 1745, nearly one hundred years before Campbellism was known.

CHAPTER LX.

On the subject of work of the Holy Spirit, in the regeneration of the sinner, the following gives the position, as held by me in the year 1884, when I debated with Elder Treat, on that subject. It is taken from the notes of a speech that I made in that discussion, and was written out directly after the discussion was over.

" In the conversion of the sinner, the Spirit of God operates directly and immediately upon the heart."

Definition:—By "the conversion of the sinner," I mean his regeneration; or his being born of God. By the term "Spirit of God," I mean that Spirit which Jesus said gives life; or by which the love of God is shed abroad in our hearts. By the term "immediately" and "directly," I mean that the Spirit of God comes into immediate contact with the heart. There is no medium between the Spirit and the heart.

We can judge better by what agency or means the sinner is converted, and how that agency or means operated in his conversion, by first finding what has been done for the sinner in his conversion. Natural agencies, operating on natural substances, will always be productive of natural results; so that in order to elevate that which is of itself natural to be spiritual, it becomes necessary that the agency of the Holy Spirit be employed.

The Holy Spirit, in its operations upon that which is natural, never becomes natural itself, but in every case of which we have any Scriptural account, it makes that upon which it operates, spiritual. By the immediate operation of the Holy Spirit, in the miraculous conception and birth of the Son of God, although the mother of Jesus was natural, yet the result of this immediate operation was the birth of a spiritual man into the world.

In consequence of this great work of the Holy Spirit, bringing a man into the world that was not natural, but spiritual, as the apostle says: "Howbeit, that was not first which is spiritual, but that which is natural; and afterwards that which is spiritual," I Cor. xv, 46, He is said to have come from heaven. So when Jesus said to Nicodemus, "Except a man be born again," John iii, 3, the marginal reading says, "Born from above."

It is, also, in consequence of the immediate operation of the Spirit of God upon the natural body, in the resurrection, that it is changed from a natural to a spiritual body.

You may claim that since the days of the apostles, miracles have ceased; and that there are no such things as miracles now; but if you mean by that, that the conversion of a sinner is the result of natural agencies, and that it takes place agreeable to the established laws of nature, I deny it. If you mean that there are no invisible workings of the Spirit in the heart of a sinner in his conversion, I deny it. It is natural for men who are born of natural parents to be natural men, but it would be very unnatural for a man who is born of natural parents to be spiritual.

Let it be borne in mind, that the man that is born of natural parents, and is, therefore, natural, is the same man that must be born again, and thereby be made spiritual. We can readily conceive how men come into possession of human nature,—it is by being born of human parents. It is natural for them to possess human nature; but is it also natural for the same man to be made partaker of the divine nature?

We might learn something about the work of the Holy Spirit, in the conversion of the sinner, by an investigation of his condition after his conversion. The man that is born of God is in possession of what no man can have by a natural birth, and what can not be brought about by natural agencies or exertions, and he is in possession of those things from the moment of his conversion. He is not converted until he has them. This being true, he must of necessity receive them in his conversion. Rom. viii, 18: "And if Christ be in you, the body is dead because of sin; but the Spirit is life because of righteousness." From this text we learn that the believer has Christ in him. I Cor. ii, 16: "But we have the mind of Christ." This is a clear statement that the man that is born of God has the mind of Christ."

Rom. v, 5: "And hope maketh not ashamed; because the love of God is shed abroad in our hearts by the Holy Ghost which is given unto us." Then the child of God has the love of God in his heart. He has been delivered from the power of darkness and translated into the kingdom of God's dear Son.

Col. i, 13. Created in Christ Jesus unto good works. Eph. ii, 10. He has been quickened together with Christ. Eph. ii, 5. The eyes of their understanding have been enlightened. Eph. i, 18. They were sometime darkness, but are now light in the Lord. Eph. v, 8. They have passed from death unto life. I John iii, 14. God dwelleth in them. I John iv, 16.

The man that is born of God has all this, and cannot be truly said to be born of God unless he does have them. In his unconverted state, he has none of them; so it necessarily follows that he receives them in his conversion. He must receive them by an immediate or direct operation of the Spirit of God. It is certainly a heart work, or a work in the heart, that gives the sinner all these things.

I argue that in the conversion, or regeneration, of the sinner, there is something more done for him than merely going out from one government to another. A man might come from England to this country, and take the oath of allegiance to the government, and not undergo a change of heart, or character, or any other essential change in himself. But a man cannot pass from the power and dominion of sin to the service of God, and still possess the same heart, character, will and affections.

A man may come from England to this country, without being born again; but he cannot pass into the kingdom of God, and become a loyal citizen of His government unless he is born of God. He cannot know the things of God without he first has His Spirit. Paul says, "Now we have received, not the spirit of the world, but the Spirit which is of God; that we might know the things that are freely given to us of God." I Cor. ii, 12. If we knew as well the things that are freely given to us of God, while we were yet without the Spirit, then we need not receive the Spirit for that purpose. But we have received the Spirit of God for a special purpose; and that is that we might know the things that are given to us of God. Is the gospel one of the things that are freely given to us of God? If so, then the Spirit we must have to know the gospel.

"Which things also we speak, not in the words which man's wisdom teacheth, but which the Holy Ghost teacheth, comparing spiritual things with spiritual," verse 13. The apostle argues here, that he and the other apostles speak the things that are freely given to us of God, and that in order to know them when they do speak them, we must first receive the Spirit of God. I argue that this is the burden of the apostle's argument here, and I call your especial attention to it, and request that, if I am mistaken, you tell me wherein I am wrong. Do not pass this without giving it some notice, for I think I have a point here in my favor, and if you do not think so, please tell me why. The apostle continues: "But the natural man receiveth not the things of the Spirit of God; for they are foolishness unto him, neither can he know them, because they are spiritually discerned," verse 14. I claim that this text, and its connection teaches that it is absolutely necessary, that before a sinner can know the things of the Spirit of God, he must have an immediate operation of the Spirit upon his heart.

ARGUMENT I.—I argue that the apostle teaches the same thing, in II Cor. iv, 3, 4. "But if our gospel be hid, it is hid to them that are lost; in whom the god of this world hath blinded the minds of them that believe not, lest the light of the glorious gospel of Christ, who is the image of God, should shine unto them." In this text the god of this world, the prince of the power of the air, that worketh in the children of disobedience, is represented as blinding the minds of unbelievers, so that the light of the gospel does not shine unto them. If you blind every avenue of light into your room, you will have a dark room, even at noon day, when the sun shines with his greatest splendor. Until those blinds are removed, the sun will not shine into that room. Neither is it the office of the light of the sun to remove blindness, but simply to give light to those who can see. A man can not see when he is blind, no matter how brightly the sun may shine. Now, the gospel shines, or gives light, but it is no more the office of the light of the gospel to remove blindness than it is the office of the light of the sun to open your window blinds so that it can shine into your room. If you were shut up in a dark room where no light could come, the sun would be hid to you. So, the gospel is hid to the unbeliever, because his mind is blinded by the god of this world; if then, the preaching of the gospel to him, or the reading of the Bible to him is God's only medium of enlightening him, He will never reach him. The blindness of his mind must be removed some way or other before the light of the gospel will shine unto him. I argue in such a case, the absolute necessity of the direct and immediate operation of the Spirit of God, to remove the blindness of the mind, so that the light of the gospel can shine unto them. All unbelievers are thus blinded, so that in every case of conversion, a direct influence of the Spirit is necessary. I call especial attention to this text, and the argument I make from it.

Matt. xiii, 3, 11, "And he spake many things unto them in parables, saying, Behold a sower went forth to sow; and when he sowed, some seeds fell by the way side, and the fowls came and devoured them up; some fell upon stony places where they had not much earth; and forthwith they sprung up, because they had no deepness of earth; and when the sun was up, they were scorched, and because they had no root, they withered away. And some fell among thorns, and the thorns sprung up, and choked them; but others fell into good ground, and brought forth fruit, some a hundred fold, some sixty fold, some thirty fold. Who hath ears to hear, let him hear. And the disciples came and said unto him, Why speakest thou unto them parables? He answered and said unto them, Because it is given unto you to know the mysteries of the kingdom of heaven, but to them it is not given." Doubtless this parable is intended to teach the effect of the preached gospel, dependent on the state or condition of the heart. The unconverted heart is represented by the way side, and the gospel fails to reach such a heart effectually. The fruit of the gospel in such a heart is as certain to be a failure as the natural seed sown by the way side, which fowls devour up. The same is also true in the case of the stony ground, and the thorny ground. In the parable, the reason all the seed sown on these three different grounds was a failure, is because the ground had not been previously prepared for the reception of the seed. As that is true, literally, so it is true that the human heart must, of necessity, have a previous preparation for the reception of the gospel, in order that the gospel bring forth fruit to perfection. The seed that fell into the ground, that had been prepared for the reception of seed, was the only ground that was productive of fruit, as the result of sowing seed in it. Just as that is true, literally, so, in order that the gospel preached to a person bring forth fruit, it is absolutely necessary that the heart have previous preparation. Seed could not fall in good ground, if there was no good ground for it to fall into, and the fact that some seed fell into good ground is the most conclusive evidence that the ground was good before the seed fell into it. So the heart must be good before the gospel is preached, if it brings forth any fruit. Then, as we have found from this parable, the necessity of a previous preparation of heart in order to the reception of the gospel, we will see next where this preparation comes from. Prov. xvi, 1, "The preparations of the heart in man, and the answer of the tongue, is from the Lord." I hope you will give this your special attention, for I am anxious that my argument be answered, if it can be; and it certainly can, if I am wrong. Do not tell us that man prepares his own heart, for you know that would contradict God's word.

"And the disciples came, and said unto him, Why speakest thou unto them in parables? He answered and said unto them, Because it is given to you to know the mysteries of the kingdom of heaven but to them it is not given." The disciples knew the mysteries of the kingdom of heaven, and the Savior speaks of that knowledge as something that had been given to the disciples; but it had not been given to the multitude. The word "mysteries" in Scripture is not used in its classical sense—of religious secrets, nor yet of things incomprehensible, or in their own nature difficult to be understood, but in the sense of things of purely divine revelation. The things of the kingdom of heaven then, to a man that has not been born again, are mysteries. "Except a man be born again, he can not see the kingdom of God." John iii, 3. So the multitude, to whom He spake this parable, did not know the mysteries of the kingdom, because they had not been born again. The disciples had been born again and therefore they knew the mysteries of the kingdom of heaven. To those who are born again, those mysteries are fully published in the gospel. Jesus said, "No man knoweth the Son, but the Father; neither knoweth any man the Father, save the Son, and he to whomsoever the Son will reveal him." Matt. xi, 27. So a revelation is necessary in order to know Jesus. That revelation is something more than merely presenting Him to them in person, and having Him testify to them that He is the Christ, as He did when on earth; for that failed to teach them to know Him then. It means more than to simply read the four evangelists, now, for what we read in them is what the people in that day witnessed with their own eyes and ears, and after they saw and heard all that we read of in the evangelists, they did not know Him. He said Himself that a revelation was necessary to a knowledge of Him; hence He meant more than simply seeing and hearing. I have never yet seen any account of but one revealing agent in the Bible, and that is God's Spirit. I Cor. ii, 10. In this revelation a direct and immediate operation of the Spirit is necessary. No man can understand the gospel without it.

I now quote Heb. iv, 1, 2: "Let us therefore fear, lest, a promise being left us of entering into his rest, any of you should seem to come short of it. For unto us was the gospel preached, as well as unto them; but the word preached did not profit them, not being mixed with faith in them that heard it." The gospel preached presents Jesus with all the fulness of His grace and mercy, and His suitable adaptability to the needs of lost sinners, and as the only way of life and salvation, and directs the attention of its hearers to that heavenly rest for which all the saints hope, and to which faith is the avenue, and from which unbelief excludes. So then, in order to a profitable hearing of the gospel, faith is a prerequisite. It did not profit them, because they did not have faith. The gospel preached is the food of the soul of the saint, and as our natural food must pass into flesh and blood when it is taken into a healthy stomach, so the preached word is good and profitable to our souls when we appropriate it to ourselves in faith. It is not the office of the natural food that we eat to prepare the stomach for its reception and digestion. So the gospel does not prepare the heart for the reception of itself by faith. Neither do we prepare our own hearts, as I have already proved. Hearing the gospel, alone, is of as little profit to us as undigested food in a bad stomach. Those who hear the gospel profitably must first have faith. If the gospel must necessarily be preached to them before they have faith, then it follows that they must of necessity hear the gospel unprofitably before they can have faith. If this preaching must be done in order that a man have faith, then we have it that a man must hear the gospel unprofitably in order that he may have faith, after which he will hear the gospel profitably. Now the truth taught in this text is that a man must have faith to enable him to hear the gospel in a profitable manner. This faith is the fruit of the Spirit of God. Gal. v, 22: "But the fruit of the Spirit is love, joy, peace, long-suffering, gentleness, goodness, faith." If faith is the fruit of the Spirit, and a man must have faith in order to hear the gospel profitably, then a direct or immediate operation of the Spirit upon the heart is necessary; for man believes with the heart, and the Spirit is not likely to bear fruit where it is not. If it produces faith in the sinner's heart it must be in his heart. This must take place before he receives the gospel. If this is not so, tell us what is, and how you know.

ARGUMENT II.—I argue that in the conversion and regeneration of the sinner there is an internal work done, that external ideas or evidences will never accomplish. The first proof text I will give, in support of this argument, is Ezek. xxxvi, 25, 26, 27, "Then will I sprinkle clean water upon you, and you shall be clean: from all your filthiness, and from all your idols, will I cleanse you. A new heart also will I give you, and a new spirit will I put within you; and I will take away the stony heart out of your flesh, and I will give you a heart of flesh. And I will put my Spirit within you, and cause you to walk in my statutes, and ye shall keep my judgments, and do them."

From this passage, we are taught that the external restoration must be preceded by an internal restoration. The change in their condition must not be superficial, but must be based on a radical renewal of the heart. Then the heathen, understanding from the regenerated lives of God's people how holy God is, would perceive Israel's past troubles to have been only the necessary vindications of His righteousness. Thus God's name would be sanctified before the heathen, and God's people be prepared for outward blessings. "Sprinkle clean water" is a phraseology of the law; the water mixed with the ashes of an heifer sprinkling the unclean, which the apostle says, "sanctifieth to the purifying of the flesh;" but the thing signified by this sprinkling, is the cleansing blood of Christ sprinkled on the heart and conscience. "From all your idols," means covetousness, and prejudices against Jesus Christ; as literal idolatry had ceased among the Jews, since the captivity. "I will give you a new heart," must be that He will give them a new mind, or will; as Paul tells in Phillipians, "For it is God that worketh in you both to will and to do of his good pleasure." "And a new spirit will I put within you," means that He will give them a proper motive or principle of action. "I will take away the stony heart." The stony heart is certainly the stony ground mentioned in the parable, in Mat. xii, that I have already quoted. A stony heart represents something unimpressible in serious things It is unfit to receive the good seed so as to bring forth fruit. So the Lord says He will take it away. I believe this work is done in the conversion of the sinner, and it is an internal work that no other agency can do but the Spirit of God.

If He takes it away, and gives a heart of flesh, which He says He will do, then He gives a heart that is impressible; and one into which the gospel will find access, and bring forth fruit. Such is the good and honest heart that the Lord speaks of in the parable. But do not forget that God gives this new heart, and that before the gospel is preached to him profitably. Man cannot make himself a new heart, but God can give him one, and He says in this text that He will. "And I will put my Spirit within you."

This is the work of the Lord, and He does all this before they walk in obedience to His law. Thus the ability to obey is given in conversion, or in the change of heart. I argue that all this is the effect of the immediate operation of the Spirit of God upon the heart, and I further claim that there is no one regenerated for whom this work has never been done. This work of the Spirit is productive of spiritual mindedness, which is life and peace, and all who are carnally minded are dead; for to be carnally minded is death.

All men in an unconverted state are carnally minded. All who are regenerated are spiritually minded, which is life and peace. This work is an internal work, and the mind is changed, which cannot be the voluntary act of the man himself, for if it could be there would be no necessity of God doing it for him. But God says He will do it, and He would not say it if He did not intend to do it. When it is done it is productive of good works. Thus, good works are the products of a new heart, and not the cause of it. A new heart is the product of God's work, and not the cause of it.

Life is given, in the conversion of a sinner, and Jesus plainly says, "It is the Spirit that quickeneth." John vi, 63. To quicken is to give life, and I know of nothing that quickens but the Spirit. Eph. ii, 4, 5, "But God, who is rich in mercy, for his great love, wherewith he loved us, even when we were dead in sins, hath quickened us together with Christ." The work of quickening is done in the conversion of the sinner; and as it is the work of the Spirit to quicken, then the Spirit does a work in the conversion of the sinner. This work is distinct from, and in addition to, the preaching of the gospel, or else man would never be able to believe the gospel. It is not an external work, it is not outwardly on the body, the apostle did not teach the brethren that their bodies had been made alive, but he had allusion to the work of His Grace in their hearts. How such a work is done without a direct and immediate operation of the Spirit of God in the heart I cannot tell. God says He will put His Spirit within them, and He must either put His Spirit in them to make them alive, or else He makes them alive without His Spirit, and then afterwards gives them His Spirit because they are alive. If He makes them alive before He gives them His Spirit, then it is not the Spirit that makes them alive. I claim that I have proven that it is the Spirit that makes alive, and I have also proven that it is an internal work from the text I have quoted in Ezekiel. Not only is it an internal work, but it is a work in the heart. How much plainer could anything be made? If I have misunderstood these passages, do tell me what they mean, for I am very anxious to know. Give me something better than merely your word.

ARGUMENT III.—My third argument is based on the fact that in the conversion of the sinner, there is a work of creation, which precedes any good works, and imparts a divine nature to the sinner. To prove this, I quote Eph. ii, 10, "For we are his workmanship, created in Christ Jesus unto good works, which God hath before ordained that we should walk in them." His workmanship means a thing of His making, and this is what the apostle says Christians are. He speaks of this matter as if we were passive in His hands in this work, like anything made is passive in the hands of its maker. He is not talking about their physical creation, or the creation of their bodies, but he is talking about our creation in Christ, not by our good works, nor on account of our good work, but unto good works. Good works can not be performed until we have been created unto them. As Paul never calls the works of the law good works, so he must necessarily have allusion to gospel obedience. Then this work of creation is unto gospel obedience, and is unconditional. It is the work of God, so the apostle says, and as it is entirely His work, I am forced to believe that it is His work by the operation of the Spirit, directly upon the heart. The same thing is taught in II Cor. v, 17, 18. " Therefore if any be in Christ, he is a new creature; old things have passed away; behold, all things are become new. And all things are of God, who hath reconciled us to himself by Jesus Christ, and hath given to us the ministry of reconciliation." All things are of God. All what things? The apostle is on the subject of a man being a new creature in Christ. He says God hath reconciled us to Himself by Jesus Christ. This work of reconciliation is God's work, and there can be no question as to the subject, for he is on the subject of being new creatures in

Christ. This is the subject of our conversion, and after He reconciles us to Christ, He then gives us the ministry of reconciliation. God was in Christ reconciling the world unto Himself. This whole work is of God. Then the sinner, in his conversion, is created in Christ Jesus unto good works. This creation is necessarily the work of the Spirit of God upon the heart.

CHAPTER LXI.

ALL GUILTY.

"Now we know that whatsoever the law saith, it saith to them who are under the law: that every mouth may be stopped, and all the world become guilty before God." Rom. iii, 19.

It seems from this text that none need plead not guilty of a violation of God's law, for the expression that every mouth may be stopped," seems to signify that no one should, for a moment plead self-justification. "And all the world become guilty before God." This expression seems to signify that all should confess guilt, or plead guilty of sin, and a consequent forfeiture, on their part, of all claims on the Lord for any of the benefits of grace. It is impossible to preach salvation by grace, and at the same time preach that the sinner has any claim on the Lord for that grace; or, as many in this age say, an offer of grace. If the sinner is saved by grace, it must be that he might have been justly lost without grace. If he could not have been justly lost without grace, then he could have been justly saved without it. It is only the man that is guilty and undeserving, and unable to make satisfaction for his wrongs, or pay his debts or meet his obligations, and that might justly be required to do all those things at any moment, and sent to torment if he did not, that can be saved by grace and mercy. No sinner is saved without grace, for no sinner has any other way of being saved. The doctrine of grace, as has always been held by those who hold the doctrine of a conditional salvation, is about as well expressed in the following as in any language we could use to express it as we understand it: "As all men have sinned in Adam, and have become exposed to the curse and eternal death, God would have done no injustice to anyone, if he had determined to leave the whole human race under sin and the curse, and to condemn them on account of sin; according to the language of the text, all the world is become guilty before God." It does seem to us very reasonable, that if the law of God is just—and we presume that no Christian will deny the justice of the law—that the sinner in the violation of that law is justly condemned by it. If he is justly condemned, he has no right to claim even a chance to be justified. The doctrine that the sinner has rights in this respect contradicts the doctrine that his mouth should be stopped, for as long as he has any claim for leniency, or a way to escape the punishment of the law, he has a right to open his mouth and claim his rights in the face of justice. We heard a man say at one time, that if he was lost he would always claim that it was unjust. Such men have no idea of their need of grace and mercy, for they seem to think that they could, of right, sue for heaven on the plea of their just title to it. They have no idea that their mouths should be stopped, and that they should become, or plead guilty before God. We heard another man say that under a deep-felt sense of his guilt and just condemnation, he felt like saying that if he was sent to hell, he would have no complaints to enter, for he felt so guilty that he could plead nothing but his own guilt, and that was sufficient to cut him off from all hope of heaven. These two men are certainly fairly represented in the Pharisee and the Publican. If the condition of man is so deplorable as to deny him the right to present any claim for the opportunity to be saved; then the Arminian ought to stop telling us that God must give the sinner a chance, or fail to maintain His justice. Parson Brownlow, who was on a sick bed, (he and some of his friends thought his death bed,) when asked about his prospects for the future, said: "I think that if the books in the other world have been correctly kept, there is a small balance in my favor." This sounds a great deal as if the Lord were keeping a balance sheet, and that He was measuring men by it. If they do more good than evil, then the balance will be in their favor. If this is the correct way of viewing this matter, then it would seem that when a man does wrong, all that is necessary for him to do to expiate the wrong, is to simply turn about and do some good thing, and the whole matter is adjusted. If it were possible for man to do more good deeds, than evil ones, he would be saved, from the fact that no sin would be alleged to him. Where is the need of Jesus Christ as a Savior in that theory? He need not atone for the sins of men, for they can atone for their own sins by doing good works.

But any person that has any idea of a law of justice and equity, knows that when he breaks the law in one point, he is guilty of the whole law, and all the good deeds he can do in a long life-time can never release him from the claims of the law for its violation. The murderer might obey the law to perfection for a thousand years, and it would not remove the guilt from him. He is just as guilty of murder after a long season of strict obedience as he was the moment he first committed the crime. If a man lives in wickedness and disobedience until he is twenty, thirty or forty years old, and then comes to the Lord and begins to say: "Lord, I have been a sinner all my life, and I have abhorred the church and the gospel, and denied the blessed Savior and His mercy, and have even mistreated those who exhorted and persuaded me to do better. Now, Lord, if thou wilt forgive all the past, and let it all go, and save me at last, I will love thee all the remainder of my life, and obey thy law perpetually and to perfection while I stay upon the earth, for, O Lord, thou knowest I do not want to die and go to hell," it seems that the Lord might justly, according to every conception of justice and equity, tell him, that, of course, he must keep the law the remainder of his life. The law requires it, and its demands are just, and must be honored. When you keep the law from now until your death, you have done no more than the law required you to do all your life. Your obedience to the law from this time forward will not be considered as atonement for the past; therefore you must at last, suffer its penalty for the wickedness of your former life. Now, if all the world is guilty before God, then no man has any right to expect anything but the infliction of the severe penalty of the violated law. We can conceive of nothing that man can do, nor any course he can pursue, that would entitle him to open his mouth and claim heaven, or a chance to obtain it upon any system of works or merit of his own. In all he can do, or in all his friends can tell him to do, he is still a sinner when he is done, and his mouth is closed, and he is still guilty. He may rummage the whole realm of nature for some good work that would commend him to God, and he finds nothing behind which he can shelter from the just demands of the law, for it cries out for satisfaction for all the sins of his life. He may explore the whole country, and overhaul all the family records for some good trait in some relative that might assist him in some way or other to come to God and be accepted, but the Scriptures say, "born, not of blood," so the character of his father or mother will not help him, but if they would he has no relative that is not in the same predicament that he himself is in. Their mouths are stopped, and they are guilty before God. This is the moral condition of the whole world of mankind, in this state they have no claim upon God for anything that would better their condition. Is God under obligation to those who are so guilty, and justly condemned by his righteous and holy law? If this is the true condition of man, how can the Arminian say that if the Lord does not give him a chance to be saved, He is unjust? He certainly is not unjust for punishing the guilty. Man in this state is perfectly satisfied with himself, and thinks himself good and worthy. He has no desire to turn and be godly, because his heart is set in him to do evil. He will never be saved if he does not turn, or unless the Lord turns him. The Lord is under no obligation to turn him, and the Arminian says if the Lord turns him that he coerces him. The Arminian does not believe in coersion, but thinks the sinner must come to God of his own free will, and that God will save him on the condition that he comes that way. That might meet his case if he had the will, but Jesus said "Ye will not come to me that you might have life." John v, 40. Is God under obligation to give him a will? It seems to us that He might as well turn him and be done with it, as to give him a will to turn himself. But it does seem that the only hope for him is for the Lord to turn him, and He is under no obligation to do so. If He does turn the sinner when He is under no obligation to, what shall we call such a work? The only name we can give it is the Bible name, and that is grace. As long as the Lord is under any obligation whatever, to turn him, it is not grace, and if He must turn him, and is under no obligation to, then it is of grace, and unconditional. But if the Lord turns one sinner, must He turn all sinners, or be unjust? According to the text, the whole world stands convicted before God, and as they do, and He is the judge before whose tribunal they are convicted, He certainly has the unquestionable right to dispose of them as He sees fit. If He should see fit to have mercy on one and forgive him all his sins, he certainly does no more than to exercise his own sovereign right, and no one has any right to object to or interfere in the affair. It does not follow, that because He extends mercy to one, that he is under obligations to extend it to another. This is the very question that Paul the apostle was on when he said: "Therefore hath he mercy on whom he will have mercy, and whom he will he hardeneth." Rom. ix, 18. If he has a just right to make such a discrimination as this between guilty men, then the most objectionable feature of the doctrine of unconditional election on the part of Arminians is sustained. By "hardening" in this text is meant that he will judicially abandon them to the hardening influences of sin. David says: "But my people would not hearken to my voice; and Israel would none of me. So I gave them up into their own heart's lust; and they walked in their own counsels." Ps. lxxxi, 11, 12. It seems from this text that they have already been tried, and adjudged guilty, and as a punishment for their guilt, the judge gives them up to hardness, and to simply follow the evil natures of their own hearts. In this way he hardens them. This is the righteous judgment of the great judge of all things, and when the people are thus judged, they only receive justice at the hands of the Holy One, whose law they have wickedly broken. This is the manner in which all punishment is inflicted, and in it the true character of the Divine Lawgiver is made known. This doctrine is in harmony with human responsibility, for the man that is not responsible to law for what he does, cannot be punished, justly, by that law for violating it. So when the Lord reckons with man, and finds him guilty, He punishes him by just simply giving him up to hardness of heart. It is not necessary that the Lord decree that such a man shall do wickedly, for that is just what every man will do unless restrained by grace. The rich man was thus given up to work out the evil nature of his own wicked heart, and finally be tormented in the flame for his own wickedness. Just so is every case of those who are finally lost. They will not turn from their sins, and we feel sure that no one will claim that the Lord is under any obligation to turn them. It is thus, then that He hardens some.

But He does not harden all, for the text says He will have mercy on some. But the great apostle anticipates an objection. "Why doth he yet find fault? for who hath resisted his will?" This objection seems to say that if God chooses and leaves out, pardons and punishes, whom He pleases, why are those blamed who, if left out of His choice, cannot help sinning and perishing? This is an objection to some doctrine or other that was held and taught by the apostle in this text; and we think this would be a good place to determine whether this supposed objection was raised against the doctrine of Arminianism, as held in this age of the world, that pardon is offered to all alike, on gospel terms, and that men are fully able to comply with the terms, and thereby be saved and escape torment, and enjoy all the benefits of pardon, and that none need to be lost, or is it an objection to the doctrine of God's discriminating and electing grace that saves some, and leaves the others out? Our experience in the world has taught us that when we teach the doctrine of election, and that God is the elector, all Arminians contend that it destroys the responsibility of man, and that if the doctrine is true, man is a mere machine. But we have never heard such an objection to the doctrine of Arminianism; so we conclude that it was not the Arminian doctrine Paul was advocating here, for such an objection is never urged against that doctrine. Hence, this objection shows conclusively that it is the election of some to eternal salvation, and the leaving out of others, prior to any difference of personal character. There is no other doctrine that could suggest the objection here stated, and to this doctrine the objection seems reasonable to many. Then what are we left to conclude, only that, in this Scripture the doctrine of unconditional election is taught? If it is taught here it must be the doctrine of the Bible, though all the world should object to it. The objection itself is founded on a misunderstanding of the relation between God and His sinful creatures, supposing that He is under obligation to extend His grace to all, whereas He is under obligation to none. If He is under any such obligation, then every mouth is not stopped, for they have a right to call on the Lord, not as penitents, but as they who have just and legal claims have a right to plead for such claims, they have the right to simply ask God—not for mercy, but to fulfill His obligation to them. But our text denies man any such right. His mouth is stopped and he can plead nothing. Men of this standing are dealt with according Rom. ix, 18: The Lord has mercy on one and hardens another.

But we have already shown that none will turn from sin and seek God unless the Lord turns them. Jesus said: "And ye will not come unto me that ye might have life." John v, 40. This text clearly shows their unwillingness to come to the Lord for life. Just let them alone to do as their evil natures would lead them, and they never would come. Offer them salvation on the condition that they, of their own free will, come to the Savior, and they would not be saved on that plan. But Jesus again says: "No man can come to me, except the Father which hath sent me draw him: and I will raise him up at the last day." John vi, 44. From this text it is seen that man cannot come to Christ. The Father must draw him, or he cannot come. If the Father draws a sinner to Christ, that sinner is certain to get there, but, if the Father does not draw him, he will not get there, for he cannot come except the Father draw him. On what does the sinner coming to Christ depend? Does it depend on his own will and ability? We say no. It depends altogether on the Father drawing him. Do men come to Christ? Yes, many of them do; then the Father draws them. Does the Father draw all the race of men to Christ? If not, then he must draw some and leave others out. We understand this to be the apostle's meaning when he said: "Therefore hath he mercy on whom he will, and whom he will he hardeneth." In this no man is shut away from Christ by a decree of the Lord, for they will not come, and it is not necessary to decree that they shall not come. None will come unless the Lord brings them, therefore he has decreed to bring some, and in harmony with that decree He draws them to Him and saves them. In this way He has mercy on those he brings. In this way the language of Jesus is fulfilled that says: "All that the Father giveth me shall come to me, and him that cometh to me, I will in no wise cast out." John vi, 37.

CHAPTER LXII.

THE ELDER SHALL SERVE THE YOUNGER.

The author of this wonderful expression, about which there has been as much confusion and as many theological speculations as any other one text in the Bible, is the God of heaven. It does not matter what poor puny, and ignorant mortals like we are, may think of the language, nor that from our way of looking at it we may think His arrangements in the matter are unfair, and far from being just, yet God said, "The elder shall serve the younger," and we must concede that it is perfectly just and right or He would not have said it. This familiar portion of God's word refers, literally, to Jacob and Esau. "For the children being not yet born, neither having done any good or evil, that the purpose of God according to election might stand, not of works, but of him that calleth. It was said unto her, the elder shall serve the younger." Why the Lord would reverse the law that governed all such cases, by giving the inheritance to the younger, instead of giving it to the elder, of course, cannot be accounted for, merely by any literal construction of the text. The law gave the first born the preference, and by virtue of his birth he was entitled to the blessing, and the younger could, under no circumstances, interfere with it. It must be, and the text intimates clearly that there is a very important lesson, concerning the principles of sovereign and discriminating grace to be learned from the manner of God's dealings with

Jacob and Esau. It is not merely to deprive Esau of his literal birth right with nothing more in view, but the apostle says, "that the purpose of God according to election might stand, not of works but of him that calleth." It is very clearly shown from the Scriptural account of these two brothers that the service was not of a personal nature, for if Esau ever did serve Jacob in the capacity of a servant personally, we have no special account of it. We know that he sold his birth right to Jacob for a mess of pottage, after coming in from his hunt, faint, and, as he thought, ready to die, and that gave Jacob the right to the place of the first born, for he had purchased it, and when we examine the matter carefully, there are some points in it which go to show that God will carry out His purpose over every opposition, no matter from what source it may come. The idea that the elder should serve the younger did not hinge on the will or actions of men, for if it had God's purpose would not have been carried out. Isaac, notwithstanding the Lord had told Rebecca that the elder should serve the younger, was very desirous to confer the blessing on Esau his first born. The apostle says, "So then, it is not of him that willeth, nor of him that runneth, but of God that sheweth mercy." The truth of this declaration is exhibited clearly in the salvation of every sinner that is saved. But it is never more clearly shown than in the cases of Isaac and Ishmael, and Jacob and Esau. Abraham and Sarah willed, and if their will could have been respected in the affair, Isaac would never have been born, and God's purpose would not have stood. God's purpose was that Abraham should be the father of a great nation, and that for that purpose Sarah, although she had been barren, and was, at the time of God's promise to Abraham, past the flower of her age, was to have a son, and from a human standpoint it seemed impossible that God's promise ever could be verified. After Ishmael was born, Abraham was perfectly willing he should be the heir of promise, saying, "O that Ishmael might live before thee. Gen. xxvii, 18. But instead of the Lord respecting the will of Abraham in the matter, he said, "Sarah thy wife shall bear thee a son indeed; and thou shalt call his name Isaac; and I will establish my covenant with him for an everlasting covenant, and with his seed after him. And as for Ishmael, I have heard thee: Behold I have blessed him, and will make him fruitful, and will multiply him exceedingly; twelve princes shall he beget, and I will make him a great nation. But my covenant will I establish with Isaac, which Sarah shall bear unto thee at this set time in the next year." Gen. xxvii, 19, 20, 21. It is very clearly seen here that it is not of him that willeth nor of him that runneth, but of God that sheweth mercy. While Abraham was the literal father of the Jews, yet his seed were not all Jews, and more; while the Jews were the literal seed of Abraham, yet they were not all children. The apostle says, "Neither, because they are the seed of Abraham, are they all children; but in Isaac shall thy seed be called. That is, they which are the children of the flesh, these are not the children of God: but the children of the promise are counted for the seed." Rom. ix, 7, 8. If because they were the seed of Abraham they were all children, then Ishmael and all his descendants, and Esau and all his progeny would have been included in the covenant with Isaac. Or, if the children of the flesh were the children of God, then Esau and all his offspring, and all others of the descendants of Abraham and Isaac would have been included. But from what we have already observed Ishmael and his posterity do not stand upon an equality with Isaac. "Nevertheless what saith the Scripture? Cast out the bond woman and her son; for the son of the bond woman shall not be heir with the son of the free woman." Gal. iv, 30. As to Esau we know what the Lord has said concerning him. He was called Edom from the time he sold his birth right. Gen. xxv, 30, and he lived in the land of Sier, the country of Edom, and the Lord by the prophet Malachi, said, "I have loved you saith the Lord. Yet ye say, Wherein hast thou loved us? Was not Esau Jacob's brother? Saith the Lord; yet I loved Jacob, and I hated Esau, and laid his mountains and his heritage waste for the dragons of the wilderness. Whereas Edom saith, We are impoverished, but we will return and build the desolate places; thus saith the Lord of hosts, They shall build, but I will throw down; and they shall call them the border of wickedness, and the people against whom the Lord hath indignation forever." Mal. i, 2, 3, 4.

We do not believe that the Lord saves any man because of his flesh and blood relation to Abraham, neither do we believe that he damns any because they are related to Ishmael or Esau according to the flesh; but it is quite certain that there were discriminations made between Jacob and Esau, and that it was not on account of works. Before they were born, neither having done any good or evil, the Lord said, "The elder shall serve the younger." There shall be some sense in which this is true, and that upon the principle mentioned in this text. It could not have been that the descendants of Esau were to serve Jacob or his descendants as slaves, for this was never the case literally. Jacob did flee from Esau, after he had obtained the blessing, for he knew Esau was angry with him, and on his return with his wives and children he feared Esau, and when he met him he bowed himself to the ground seven times, until he came near to him. This looks more like he was the servant than the ruler. But we know that Jacob did get the blessing from his father that Esau ran for. Isaac willed, and Esau ran, and Jacob obtained the blessing. In this case the elder served the younger. The promised seed was not propagated through Ishmael nor Esau, but Isaac and Jacob. It is very certain that there is a sense in which Jacob and Esau represent God's election of some men to salvation, and His non-election of others, and this election is not suspended on creature conditions. If the will of man has anything to do in governing God in the choice of men to salvation, how is it that He set aside every effort on the part of man, and disregarded his will in the affair, as he did Abraham in the case of Ishmael, and Isaac in the case of Esau? Man was not counselled in the whole arrangement. We are often told by work mongers that it is dangerous to wait for the Lord to work. Abraham and Sarah thought the same thing, and in harmony with the doctrine they put forth both will and effort, and, as a result instead of favoring the purpose of God, there was one born who persecuted the heir of promise when he was born. We have always been accused of waiting the Lord's good time, and have often been blamed because we would not put forth an effort to bring about the good results that God had promised. But God did promise Abraham that, "At this time will I come, and Sarah shall have a son." Rom. ix, 9. All the willingness manifested by Abraham and Sarah did not facilitate the work a particle, nor cause it to to come to pass any sooner. The Lord had set the time, and man could not hurry it up. It was wicked, and showed great distrust on their part to undertake it. By the efforts of men the Lord's purpose may be, and have been opposed, but by the efforts of men the Lord's work has never been hurried, nor hindered. At His appointed time, and in His appointed way, and by His appointed means He does His work. If it was His purpose that Sarah should have a son in whom His seed should be called, even if Sarah does not believe it, and if she and Abraham laugh at the thought of a thing so unreasonable, it is still as true as if they believed it, for it is God's work to bring it about, and if they undertake to assist the Lord in the accomplishment of His purpose, by some expediency of their own, He will not accept their labor. Ishmael, the child of the human free-will effort was not only not permitted to be the heir, but he was not allowed any part in the matter. Are there any Ishmaelites to-day? Ishmael was born after the flesh, and persecuted Him that was born after the Spirit, which was Isaac, and the apostle says: "But as then he that was born after the flesh persecuted him that was born after the Spirit, even so it is now." Gal. iv, 29. As an evidence that Ishmael represented him that is born after the flesh, see verses 22, 23, of the same chapter. "For it is written that Abraham had two sons, the one by a bondmaid, and the other by a free woman. But he who was of the bondwoman was born after the flesh; but he of the free woman was by promise."

The fulfillment of the promise to Abraham that, (although he was childless, and thought that his property would descend to Eliezer, the stranger who held the next rank in his tribe, on which account he complained to the Lord,) he should have a son, and that his seed should be as countless as the stars of heaven, was delayed until God's own time. Why wait till the Lord's own time rolls round? We are often told that His time is now; and that if we wait we run a very dangerous risk. This is what Sarah thought no doubt, as she knew that Abraham was old. She had despaired of the promise ever being fulfilled, in her person, so she gave her handmaid to Abraham, that the promise might not fail. It is wonderful to see man stretch forth his mighty arm to assist in the accomplishment of the mighty works of the Lord. Why would it not do as well in the Lord's plan to let Ishmael be the heir? Hagar, according to the custom of those times, had become the secondary wife ot Abraham, and children born in this manner had the privileges of legitimacy, and then they need not wait longer for the fulfillment of the promise. But it would not do, no matter how plausible it may appear to others, it was not God's purpose. That God that by His own hand stretched out the heavens, that sitteth upon the circle of the earth, that weighs the hills in the balance, and the mountains in scales, and picks up the isles as a small thing,—that God who wields His holy sceptre over the whole universe, who commanded the light to shine out of darkness, and who commands and it stands fast, and who Himself is immutable and His purposes unfrustrable, is able to make good His promise to Abraham without condescending to accept Ishmael as the promised heir, no matter how sincere and honest Sarah might have been in her effort to hinder the Lord's promise from being a failure. Wait until His time and all things will work out right and His plans will be executed. It is very common, in this day of means and human expediencies, for people to ridicule the idea of awaiting the Lord's good time. The zeal of the people will not allow them to wait, but they must put forth their efforts to hurry up matters by the use of some expediency or other. But we have always been of the opinion that the Lord will not do His work until His own time, and while we may think His time is slow to roll around, we must wait. Isaac was promised at least ten years before Ishmael was born, and simply because Sarah feared the purpose of God might never be accomplished, if they waited, she evidently being very eager for the certainty of the matter, concluded that it would be best not to run the risk of waiting. Hence, human effort was put forth, in order to make all things sure, so that there could be no failure. But the Lord did not accept this grand outcome of human will and works, but they must wait until His time rolled around.

It was about twenty-five years from the time Isaac was promised until he was born. But we would be asked now, why wait so long? O, how impatient poor frail human nature is! But there is, perhaps, as much grace required to prepare us to wait until the Lord is ready, as to prepare us for any other service. The God of heaven had a purpose, and that purpose must stand. Abraham was to be the natural progenitor of a great nation, and he was to be the great representative of all the Lord's elect people. "In thee and in thy seed shall all the families of the earth be blest," means more than a promise hinged upon human conditions and efforts, but it means that the Lord will save his people from among all the families of the world. It is just as impossible for this promise to fail as it was to frustrate the Lord's promise that Isaac should be born. In Isaac was the promised seed, and the promised seed here embraces all of God's elect, all over the earth, and of every age of the world. There will never be one saved that was not embraced in this promise. Have we good reasons for so saying? Let us see. There will be none saved that are not Christ's; and none are Christ's only the seed of Abraham; and those who are the seed of Abraham; are heirs according to the promise. The apostle says, "And if ye be Christ's then are ye Abraham's seed, and heirs according to the promise. Gal. iii, 29. It may seem to many that the Lord will never fulfill this promise, but He is just as certain to make it good as He has made it. The history of the world to the present time demonstrates the fact most conclusively that if the Lord depends on human effort, and human liberality, and human goodness to make his promise sure, it will be a signal failure. The most zealous men the world has are too fond of earthly ease and comfort, and the honors and distinctions that this world gives, to lavish a sufficient amount of means for missionary purposes to do much towards evangelizing the world. If the Lord waits for such avaricious creatures to put forth a sufficient amount of means and labor in the interest of the heathen, to save them, then we think we may begin to doubt the words of the Savior, when He says, "All that the Father giveth me shall come to me." John, vi, 37. But, if He undertakes to save sinners by and through Christ, then we presume He will be able to meet the most stubborn oppositions, and overcome them, and subdue and conquer the most formidable enemies, no matter how numerous nor how strong. The most perplexing difficulties will give way in the presence of conquering and reigning grace, like the morning dew before the sun. Sinners will be saved! O, what a mighty work to conquer, subdue and save sinners who are entirely unworthy that God should notice them! It will be done, and God's purpose according to election shall stand, not of works, but of him that calleth. "The elder shall serve the younger." Nothing can hinder it. It can never be made to turn out some other way, no matter who may will nor who may run. It may not be pleasant to the elder to submit to such service, but it must be that way, and just as certain as it is, just that certain the doctrine of unconditional election is true. God chooses some men to salvation and leaves others out just on the same principle that he loved Jacob and hated Esau. There may be an effort to have the younger serve the elder, but it will not change God's arrangement any. All the efforts that are, have been, or will be, will never change the Lord's purpose in the least. Election looks as hard and unjust to many people, as the distinction the Lord made between Jacob and Esau. If man, by any stratagem that he could invent were to change the purpose of God in a single instance, there is no way of knowing what the result would be. But "God declared the end from the beginning, and from ancient times the things that are not yet done, saying, "My counsel shall stand, and I will do all my pleasure." We cannot believe that men, with all the efforts they put forth, have ever, or will ever cause one single soul to be saved that would not be saved without them. God purposed the salvation of all that will be saved.

CHAPTER LXIII.

THE LONG-SUFFERING OF GOD.

On this I subject, feel disposed to offer a few thoughts, for the careful consideration of my readers, hoping that our minds may be drawn to the magnitude and importance of the fact, that God is the moral ruler and governor of all things. Although men of wicked tempers and passions may commit crime of the most aggravated nature, and with great impunity, without suffering any immediate penalty of law, yet it is abundantly taught in God's word, that there will be a reckoning, in which men will have to account for their wicked actions, of this life. It is hardly necessary for us to undertake now, to argue that there will be in the future, a judgment, and that wicked men will suffer the consequences of their wickedness, and impenitence hereafter. In proof of our position that men will suffer hereafter for what they do in this life, we call your attention to the Savior's language: Matt. xxv, 46. "And these shall go away into everlasting punishment." We base an argument upon the word PUNISHMENT. If people are to be punished hereafter, it must be for something they have done, as the word punishment, itself, signifies a just retribution for crime. Hence, the wicked shall go away, and suffer the just retribution for their crimes; and there is no escape from the just penalty of an offended law, outside of the grace of our Lord Jesus Christ, and upon this very hypothesis the inspired apostle preaches to his Roman brethren in the following language: "Therefore, thou art inexcusable, O, man, whoever thou art that judgest, for wherein thou judgest another, thou condemnest thyself; for thou that judgest doest the same things. But we are sure that the judgment of God is according to truth against them which commit such things. And thinkest thou this, O man, that judgest them which do such things, and doest the same, that thou shalt escape the judgment of God?" Rom. ii, 1, 2, 3. The apostle, in this language, refers, doubtless, to the wickedness alluded to in the preceding chapter; and while a man is guilty of the things mentioned and does not suffer immediate punishment for his sins, the apostle's reasoning seems to be, that he is under a terrible delusion, if he thinks that he shall escape, finally, the judgments of God. It is but an exhibition of God's long-suffering that men can go on with great impunity, and commit crime without being immediately punished. We can only account for why the Lord does not smite wicked men, immediately, as he did Gehaza, of old, and King Herod, when he suffered himself deified by the people, and the Lord smote him to death, or Uzza, who stretched forth his hand to steady the ark, when the oxen shook it, or the two Hebrews who kindled a fire on the Sabbath day, contrary to law, and were smitten down for their crime. We say we can only account for why the Lord does not still execute His judgments on men for their wickedness now; only that He bears with them for the present time, and men sometimes come to the conclusion, that because we do not see His judgments executed now, that in all probability there never will be a judgment. But the Apostle Peter says: "For if God spared not the angels that sinned, but cast them down to hell, and delivered them into chains of darkness, to be reserved unto judgment; and spared not the old world, but saved Noah the eighth person, a preacher of righteousness, bringing in the flood upon the world of the ungodly, etc." II Peter ii, 4, 5, 6. We learn from the Apostle Peter here, that wicked men are reserved unto judgment; and not only are they reserved unto judgment, but when we read the ninth verse of the same chapter, we have the following unmistakable language: "The Lord knoweth how to deliver the godly out of temptation, and to reserve the unjust unto the day of judgment to be punished." Notice here the apostle intimates that the Lord reserves the unjust unto the day of judgment to be punished.

We never could see any comfort to a Christian, in denying that there will be, in the futute, a general reckoning, and that men will be judged. This seems to be so abundantly set forth in the Scriptures, that to question it, is, almost to betray infidelity, it seems to us. In the language of the apostle, in his noted sermon, at Marrs Hill, he says: "Because he hath appointed a day, in the which he will judge the world, in righteousness by that man whom he hath ordained; whereof he hath given assurance unto all men, in that he hath raised him from the dead." Acts xvii, 31. There is a day coming when the wicked shall be judged, but God bears with the wickedness of the world now. He does not intend to bring the wickedness of the world into judgment to-day. As the Great Judge and Moral Disposer of all things, He has a right to preserve the people, and to bear with all manner of wickedness and abominations, that they are guilty of, but He has given us His word that the fact that He does not punish them to-day, is no evidence whatever that He will never punish them, at all; hence the language that we have already quoted from the Apostle Paul, to the Romans seems to be to the point. "Thinkest thou this, O man, that judgest them which do such things, and doest the same, that thou shalt escape the judgment of God?" One man judging another man for doing wickedly, and he doing the very same things himself, and yet thinks that he will escape God's judgment! This seems to be the argument of the great apostle on this occasion. "Or," he continues, "despiset thou the riches of his goodness and forbearance, and longsuffering; not knowing that the goodness of God, leadeth thee to repentance?" It seems that the apostle would infer, that to think that we can be guilty of crime, and yet escape the judgment of God, simply, because we are not punished at once, is an evidence that we despise His goodness and forbearance and longsuffering. Our judgment is that God has a use for the world, and that he will bear with the wickedness of men until the great work of the salvation of His people is accomplished. Forbearance means to withhold punishment that might be inflicted now, and longsuffering means to continue to forbear; hence God bears with the world of wicked men; that is, He withholds the penalty that might be justly inflicted now, upon men for their wickedness, and He continues to forbear, which amounts to longsuffering. The Apostle Peter speaks of this matter when he says: "The Lord is not slack concerning his promise, as some men count slackness; but is longsuffering to us-ward, not willing that any should perish, but that all should come to repentance." 2 Peter iii, 9. The promise in this text is evidently the second coming of Christ, for, the apostle informs us, "That there shall come in the last days scoffers walking after their own lusts, and saying, Where is the promise of his coming? for since the fathers fell asleep, all things continue as they were from the beginning of the creation." Some of the apostles and early Christians expected to live to see the day of the second coming of Christ into the world, and there were others who doubted that He would ever come, even as there are some to-day, professing Christianity, that are denying, absolutely, that Christ will ever make another personal visit to this world. In these things, the Apostle Peter was certainly a true prophet. But Peter goes on to say:

"For this they willingly are ignorant of, that by the word of God the heavens were of old, and the earth standing out of the water and in the water: Whereby the world that then was, being overflowed with water, perished; but the heavens and the earth, which are now, by the same word are kept in store, reserved unto fire against the day of judgment and perdition of ungodly men. But, beloved, be not ignorant of this one thing, that one day is with the Lord as a thousand years, and a thousand years as one day." Then comes the text: "The Lord is not slack concerning his promise, as some men count slackness; but is longsuffering to us-ward, etc."

He promised that Christ would come into the world again, and He is certain to come, and the fact that we do not see any sign of His coming now, and that, as those false teachers say, all things continue as they were from the creation, is not an evidence that He shall never come. He will come. "God is not slack concerning His promise, as some men count slackness, but is longsuffering to us-ward, not willing that any should perish, but that all should come to repentance." We have heard different men give an interpretation of this text, but we will give our interpretation of it. Some have interpreted it that the Lord is longsuffering to us-ward—us Christians, saints, not willing that any of the saints should perish, but that they should all come to repentance. We are under the impression that this is not what the apostle means by the language. He intended to convey the idea that God is longsuffering to the world—the whole world of the ungodly—that is, He bears long with them, and continues to forbear, and the reason He does it, the Apostle Peter says, He is not willing that any should perish, but that all should come to repentance. Our version of this text would be that there are hundreds and thousands and multiplied thousands of God's elect, who were embraced in the covenant of grace from the very ancients of eternity, chosen in Christ before the foundation of the world to salvation, predestinated unto the adoption of the children of God, that are yet in a state of unregeneracy, and multiplied thousands of them, perhaps, yet unborn. If the world was to be brought to a close to-day all such would perish. God is not willing that any of them should perish; that is, any of the elect, but that all should come to repentance. And, in order to bring this all about, He bears with the wickedness of men, and continues to forbear, and is longsuffering toward them, until all the great work of His salvation has been consummated, and His people saved. But, while we wait, let us not consider that He will never come, for the apostle says: "But the day of the Lord will come as a thief in the night; in the which the heavens shall pass away with a great noise, and the elements shall melt with fervent heat, the earth also, and the works that are therein shall be burned up. Seeing then that all these things shall be dissolved, what manner of persons ought ye to be in all holy conversation and godliness? Looking for and hasting unto the coming of the day of God, wherein the heavens being on fire shall be dissolved, and the elements shall melt with fervent heat? Nevertheless, we, according to His promise, look for new heavens and a new earth, wherein dwelleth righteousness. Wherefore beloved, seeing that ye look for such things, be diligent that ye may be found of Him in peace without spot, and blameless. And account that the longsuffering of our Lord is salvation." The reader will observe here that Christians are to look for and hasten to the coming of the day of God. Looking according to His promise for a new heaven and a new earth, and seeing that we look for such things that we should be diligent; that is, that we should live up to our duties, and show our confidence in the coming of those things. But that of most importance in this subject is, that we should count that the longsuffering of God is salvation,—not that it is an opportunity to be saved, or that it is an offer of salvation to an ungodly world, but that it is absolutely salvation. We firmly believe that it will be the salvation of all God's elect, and while the work is going on, it is necessary that the world stand, and while the world stands and wickedness pervades the earth among all nations and ranks of men—God bears with it reserving them until the day of judgment, and this is His forbearance.

While we maintain that the wicked will be punished for what they do in this world, and that God is just as certain to bring the world into judgment as His word is true, we want to be distinctly understood that we do not believe that salvation is conditional, and depends upon the work of the creature. We have been accused by some of preaching the doctrine of a conditional salvation, on the ground that we claim that men will be punished hereafter for what they do in this life. We believe that men are condemned and punished for what they do, and we believe that all men on account of their own evil works are justly under a sentence of condemnation, but while we believe that, we hold that Jesus Christ came into the world full of grace and truth, for the purpose of suffering for the sins of His people, for which they must have suffered, had He not, and that His sufferings were an equivalent to the demands of the law against them, on which account sinners are redeemed from the curse of the law, lifted up to a state of holiness, and happiness, and to the dignified position of being the children of God, and that they, so far as themselves are concerned, are wholly unworthy of any of the benefits of the atoning sacrifice of Christ. They are unworthy to receive any of the benefits of His salvation and grace. Yet they feel a desire to give glory and honor and praise to the name of the Savior that brought salvation to such unworthy, ungodly sinners, as they know themselves to be, and while wicked men trample upon the mercies of God, and despise His judgments, it should be considered the highest privilege of the saint to be desiring to know what God's will is, and then doing that will when he knows it. For him to knowingly refuse to obey the Lord, or try to do His will, is for him to despise the goodness and long-forbearance, and long-suffering of God. But for him to take up the cross, deny himself and follow the Savior in humility, love and godly fear, is to reflect to the world the glories and excellencies of the character of the true Savior who gave Himself for poor sinners such as we are.

And now may we all be able to come unto mount Zion, and unto the city of the living God, the heavenly Jerusalem, and to an innumerable company of angels, to the general assembly and church of the firstborn, which are written in heaven, and to God the Judge of all, and to the spirits of just men made perfect, and to Jesus the mediator of the new covenant, and to the blood of sprinkling, that speaketh better things than that of Abel.

www.ingramcontent.com/pod-product-compliance
Lightning Source LLC
Chambersburg PA
CBHW020232240426
43672CB00006B/501